Trapped in Apartheid

A Socio-Theological History
of the English-Speaking Churches

Charles Villa-Vicencio

ORBIS ✸ BOOKS

Maryknoll, New York 10545

David Philip (dp) Publisher
Cape Town   South Africa

Copyright © 1988 by Charles Villa-Vicencio
Published by Orbis Books, Maryknoll, NY 10545

Published 1988 in Southern Africa by David Philip, Publisher (Pty) Ltd, 217
Werdmuller Centre, Claremont, South Africa

Manufactured in the United States of America

LIBRARY OF CONGRESS
Library of Congress Cataloging-in-Publication Data

Villa-Vicencio, Charles.
    Trapped in apartheid : a socio-theological history of the English-
speaking churches / Charles Villa-Vicencio.
        p.   cm.
    Bibliography: p.
    Includes index.
    ISBN 0-88344-519-0 (pbk.)
    1. South Africa—Church history   2. Christian sects—South
Africa.   3. Apartheid—South Africa.   4. Sociology, Christian.
5. Liberation theology.   I. Title.
BR1450.V5   1988
276.8—dc19   88-5348
                                                            CIP

ORBIS/ISBN 0-88344-519-0
DAVID PHILIP (PTY)/ISBN 0-86486-098-6

Trapped in Apartheid

Dedicated to those who strive
for the renewal of Christ's Church

". . . the church within the church,
as the true ecclesia and hope of the world."
Martin Luther King, Jr.
in "Letter from Birmingham City Jail," 1963

Contents

Foreword

Over the past forty years the word "apartheid" has moved out of South Africa and into the world. It is now quite difficult to imagine a time when people had no conception of what it means. It has been the task of many individuals and many organizations to arouse the conscience of the world to an issue that is in every way comparable with that of the struggle for the abolition of slavery in the last century. Nevertheless it is also true that great moral and ethical issues create not only a conflict but also a highly complex situation in which the antagonists are constantly challenged to clarify their positions.

Although a great deal of literature on the subject of apartheid has seen the light of day in recent years, there are areas that have not been given the detailed analysis that is needed by anyone who is serious in approaching the subject of such a struggle. Charles Villa-Vicencio has already written a great deal of well-researched study on apartheid, but here for the first time is an assessment of the history of the English-speaking churches in South Africa in their attitudes to events as they have developed over the years. The book gives detailed evidence to support its own title *Trapped in Apartheid*. Part One is specific and highly documented. Part Two enlarges on the meaning of the sociological and theological background to all that has been written.

In my own experience a constant difficulty in trying to communicate the reality of apartheid as a moral challenge to the conscience of humanity is always to give accurate evidence of the changing attitudes of the Christian churches. There are so few people who really understand the history of the conflict in the past half century, yet without that history we are in great danger of simply using rhetoric without the essential and actual evidence. There is a great danger in taking up a cause enthusiastically but not really knowing what one is enthusiastic about. It is a book like this with the careful research upon which it is based that can become one of the most effective instruments in our hands.

I can only say personally how privileged I am to have the opportunity of writing this foreword and even more to have been given the opportunity of reading this book. Although I was personally involved quite deeply in the events of the 1940s and 1950s, it was a great encouragement to me to read an objective assessment, such as the section on the Bantu Education Act, and to realize that my judgment at the time was not false and has been justified by subsequent events.

I hope this book will have the wide readership that it so eminently deserves.

The Right Reverend Trevor Huddleston, C.R.
London, January 1988

Churches, Political Movements, and Church Documents

SOUTH AFRICAN CHURCHES AND POLITICAL MOVEMENTS REFERRED TO IN THE TEXT

African Indigenous Churches

African National Congress, ANC

Afrikaanse Protestantse Kerk, breakaway church from the NGK formed in 1986 in protest against the NGK document *Church and Society*

All African Conference of Churches, AACC

Alliance of Black Reformed Churches of Southern Africa, Abrecsa

American Methodist Episcopal Church, AME

Belydendekring, the confessing movement of the Nederduitse Gereformeerde family of churches

Church of England in South Africa

Church of the Province of Southern Africa (Anglican), CPSA

Conservative Evangelical Churches, comprising Baptist, Pentecostal and Apostolic Churches

Evangelical Lutheran Church in Southern Africa, ELCSA

Federation of Evangelical Lutheran Churches in Southern Africa, FELCSA

Gereformeerde Kerk, GK

London Missionary Society, LMS

Lutheran World Federation, LWF

Methodist Church of Southern Africa, MCSA

Nederduitse Gereformeerde Kerk, NGK

Nederduitse Gereformeerde Kerk in Afrika (NGK black mission church), NGKA

Nederduitse Gereformeerde Sendingkerk (NGK "colored" mission church), NGSK

Nederduitsch Hervormde Kerk, NHK

Ossewabrandwag, militant Afrikaner movement formed in opposition to the decision of the Smuts government to enter World War II in 1939

Pan-Africanist Congress, PAC

Presbyterian Church of Southern Africa, PCSA

Program to Combat Racism (program of the WCC), PCR

Reformed Church (NGK Indian mission church), formerly Indian Reformed Church

Roman Catholic Church

South African Council of Churches, SACC

South African Native National Congress (later to become ANC), SANNC

Southern African Catholic Bishops' Conference, SACBC

Umkhonto we Sizwe, armed wing of the African National Congress

United Congregational Church of Southern Africa, UCCSA

World Alliance of Reformed Churches, WARC

World Council of Churches, WCC

CHURCH DOCUMENTS REFERRED
TO IN THE TEXT

Belhar Confession (1982), a confessional statement of the NGSK

Theological Rationale and a Call to Prayer for an End to Unjust Rule (June 1985), a statement of the SACC

Church and Society (Kerk en Samelewing) (1986), a document of the NGK

Harare Declaration (1986), a declaration of church leaders meeting in Harare at the invitation of the WCC

Human Relations and the South African Scene in the Light of Scripture (1974), a document of the NGK

Kairos Document (1986), a document published as a challenge to the churches by a group of "concerned Christians"

Lusaka Statement (May 1987), a statement emerging from a meeting in Lusaka of representatives of South African churches and members of South African liberation movements at the invitation of the WCC

Introduction

The "church of faith" and the "church of history" have never been identical. The former relates to the latter as an ideal intended to draw it forward to what in its better moments it knows it ought to have become. To take refuge, however, in the notion of this ideal church while evading the historical reality of the existing church is a dangerous and irresponsible exercise in religious subterfuge. To give attention to what the church is intended to be rather than to face the harsh reality of what it *is* can, in turn, lead to a variety of ecclesial maladies. These range from naive optimism to spiritual arrogance, theological hypocrisy and ecclesial triumphalism.

All social structures are, to a greater or lesser extent, captive to their history. Yet when we cling to self-affirming and legitimating myths concerning structures, refusing to become self-critical in our historical consciousness, it is unlikely that we will be able to control our present or creatively shape our future. The most critical reassessment of historical identity in the light of emerging new evidence concerning our past is therefore a prerequisite for social renewal. In theological terms it acquires a soteriological function. The analysis of the English-speaking churches which follows is undertaken with this intent, as a basis for ecclesial renewal.

A HISTORICAL COMMENT

In order to understand the character of the church in South Africa and to identify its social function in the socio-economic and political development of the country, it is necessary to remember the essential developments of this history. In the few paragraphs that follow only the broadest contours of this history are identified, essentially for those who are unfamiliar with events that have during the past three and a quarter centuries contributed to the

1

ideology of apartheid—within which the English-speaking churches are trapped.

The first church erected on South African soil was built by Portuguese Catholics in Mossel Bay in 1501, but it soon fell into disrepair, leaving only the scantest memory of a Christian presence. The origins of the church in South Africa must rather be traced to the first serious encounter between blacks and whites in 1652 when the Dutch East India Company established a refueling station at the Cape of Good Hope. Here ships en route to India called to take on fresh water, vegetables and meat.

The 1652 settlers were mainly Dutch Calvinists. They were joined by French Huguenot refugees in 1688 and German Protestants a while later. Together they brought with them a spirit of dissent and a legacy of resentment against the dominant classes of Europe. They evolved a common language, found themselves bound together by common ideals and called themselves Afrikaners, people of Africa.

Long before their arrival, however, Bantu-speaking Africans had already settled in the territory that today is known as South Africa. Archaeological research shows that people were already settled in the Transvaal as early as 270 CE and by 600 CE early Iron Age settlements could be found in the northern and eastern Transvaal, extending as far south as the coastal regions of Zululand and Natal. From the fourteenth century onward black settlements extended to the eastern Cape, into central Natal and into the Highveld. The Khoikhoi had, in turn, already roamed the southern parts of the country from the beginning of the common era.

The encounter between white settlers and the black inhabitants of the land initiated an enduring struggle for domination. It was, however, with the replacement of the Dutch by the British as the occupying force in the Cape that the conflict between black and white spread beyond the existing borders of the colony. It was a process within which the church soon became integrally involved, a conflict which still remains to be resolved with the church continuing to play an ambiguous role.

The British first occupied the Cape in 1795 but after a few years withdrew, returning the territory to the Dutch. However, the second British occupation of 1806 during the Napoleonic Wars had extensive implications. Colonialism was at its height and the missionary endeavor of the churches soon became part and parcel of the imperialist dream. British settlers began to farm along the eastern frontier of the colony throughout the 1820s and British interests were firmly entrenched. The eastern frontier was consistently pushed back and the Xhosa people subjugated.

Between 1835 and 1837 approximately five thousand Afrikaner *Voortrekkers* (and as many black servants) crossed the Orange and Vaal rivers to escape British domination and established independent Boer republics in Natal, the Transvaal and Orange Free State. In so doing they fought, defeated and dominated black tribes in much the same way that the British subdued the Xhosa on the eastern frontier and, in time, the Zulu in Natal.

When diamonds were discovered in 1870 in Kimberley, and gold on the Witwatersrand in 1886, British colonial and mercantile interests were extended northwards. Fired by imperial and material greed the British defeated the Boer republics and hoisted the Union Jack in Pretoria and Bloemfontein. The Union of the British territories followed in 1910 and less than forty years later (in 1948) the Afrikaners won a "whites only" victory at the polls, placing the National Party in power. Apartheid was entrenched and in 1960 Hendrik Verwoerd led South Africa out of the British Commonwealth to become an independent republic.

Black inhabitants fought frontier wars but failed to repel the invading white colonizers. Their land was expropriated, they were deprived of their political identity, and their religious and cultural identity was suppressed. They clung to tracts of land designated "reserves," squatted on white-owned farms and were compelled by the imposition of taxes and labor recruitment for the mines to migrate to the cities. With some exceptions the black population was reduced to impoverished peasants and unskilled industrial workers clinging to the margins of industrialized cities. It was the beginning of a form of oppression which characterizes the social structure of South Africa today. Protest and resistance has marked every phase of this oppression, but to date this has proved insufficient to arrest the entrenchment of white economic and racial domination.

The role of the church in South Africa, and more especially the history of the English-speaking churches in this process is considered in the chapters that follow. This is undertaken not as an end in itself. The past is rather studied with a view to understanding the present—and this as a basis for providing a critical assessment of the options facing the church as the present crisis intensifies within church and society in South Africa. In so doing the writer makes no claim to be a historian, although he finds it necessary to draw on history to understand the essential character of the contemporary church. Indeed, a theological assessment of this church which does not address itself to the recalcitrant reality of the past, or which contents itself with reflection on what this church *says* rather than what it *is*, needs to be dismissed as idealistic reverie. We need to be acutely aware of the burden of the past. Karl Marx observed that "men make their own history but they do not make it under circumstances chosen by themselves but under circumstances directly encountered, given and transmitted from the past. The tradition of all dead generations weighs like a nightmare on the brain of the living."[1] Common sense tells us that we need to acknowledge the nature of our given reality in order to seriously entertain the possibility of transforming it. The crucial question whether the church can ever become other than what it already is must begin with a hard-nosed analysis of the nature of the existing church. And the gospel teaches that it is out of concrete reality, even if that reality is a cross of repression and death, that the resurrected Christ emerges.

Born within a particular historical context and shaped by the dominant socio-economic and political forces which have characterized the history of South Africa since the beginning of the last century, the English-speaking churches cannot be understood apart from the forces of racial and economic domination today summed up in apartheid. The theological imperative, on the other hand, that inspires all that is written in the pages that follow addresses the need for a church redeemed by the power of the gospel in order that it may become an instrument of liberation in a country that is being sucked into a whirlwind of death.

A THEOLOGICAL OBSERVATION

From a theological perspective: To deny that Christ can still appear among his people and renew those who follow him with the creativity that accompanied his first appearances to his first disciples would be to deny that Christ is still alive. It would be to deny that his spirit still breathes life into frightened and defeated people. From a historical analysis: To fail to account for a restless presence that has disturbed the church throughout its long and checkered history is to fail to do justice to the reality of that history itself. It is to fail to recognize the presence of an alternative church, a church in resistance which has throughout history existed adjacent to the dominant church—suppressed but neither silenced nor defeated. It is this church that offers new life to both the dominant church and society itself. Fired by the memory of a community of people gathered around the poor man of Nazareth who was crucified on the cross of an occupying power, it occupies the margins of the institutional churches. It is a church which seeks to make concrete what Johan-Baptist Metz has called the "dangerous memory" of the Christian tradition in a history-making community.[2] It is a church which in South Africa hears the cries of the oppressed and is disturbed by a residual theological memory which contradicts the social location of the institutional churches. Confronted with the collapse of the socio-economic order of which it is a part and faced with a crisis that threatens the identity of both society and church, it seeks to reaffirm that gospel which promises life and hope amid death and despair.

THE BOOK IN OUTLINE

The study that follows is divided into two sections. Section One consists of a socio-theological analysis of the English-speaking churches from their historical origins to the present. Chapter 1 locates the English-speaking churches theologically and historically in relation to the other major churches in the South African context. Entitled "Nothing Harsh or Rigorous," it is there suggested that while these churches are different essentially because of the different constituencies of which they are a part, they find common ground in providing a moderate and cautious reflection of their social contexts rather than a spirited challenge to the existing order. Chapter 2 addresses the early mission history of the English-speaking churches within nineteenth-century British colonialism. Chapter 3 gives attention to the impact on the churches of the discovery of gold and the industrialization process. In chapter 4 consideration is given to the response of the English-speaking churches to the Bantu Education Act (1953), the decision of the World Council of Churches to provide humanitarian aid to the southern Africa liberation movements (1970), and the present call for economic disinvestment. The response of the churches is characterized by the title of the chapter, "Protest Without Resistance." In chapter 5 the existence of an alternative church of resistance within the dominant English-speaking churches is theologically identified. Chapter 6 addresses the character of English-speaking churches in relation to the white Nederduitse Gereformeerde Kerk (NGK). It is argued that the *Kairos Document* has become to the English-speaking churches what the 1986 *Kerk en Samelewing* (*Church and Society*) document is to the NGK. Both produce deep divisions within these churches showing them to be moderating and restraining influences within their respective communities. Shaped by their respective contexts, they are trapped within the ethos which the gospel challenges them to transform.

Section Two differs in style and content from Section One in that it provides a sociological and theological reflection on the social function of religion. Chapter 7 takes the form of a sociological excursus concerning the social function of religion, providing theoretical reflection on the question as to whether it is possible for a church trapped within the iron cage of the past to be renewed. Chapter 8 addresses the theological need for this renewal and the necessity for a liberating ecclesiology, which is here developed in relation to the ministry of Jesus and the parable of the sheep and the goats. Such an ecclesiology, it is argued, is a theological imperative.

WAS THERE ANOTHER WAY?

Concerned to preserve its place and influence in society, the dominant church has rationalized the demands of the gospel, heeding the demands of the rich and powerful rather than the cries of the poor and oppressed. Theologically compelled to show charity and given to dealing kindly with those who suffer most, the English-speaking churches have nevertheless refused to contradict the dominant social order or reject the legitimacy of the state; thus they find themselves *trapped in apartheid*. In seeking to preserve their social status, one needs to ask at what cost.

In her remarkable book *The March of Folly* Barbara Tuchman discerns "a phenomenon noticeable throughout history, regardless of place and period." It has to do with institutions and governments pursuing policies contrary to their own interests. To qualify for such folly, suggests Tuchman, the policy adopted must meet three criteria: It must have been perceived as counter-productive in its own time, not merely by hindsight. Second, a feasible alternative course of action must have been available. Third, the policy in question should be that of a group and should persist beyond any one generation.[3] It is for readers to judge the extent to which the English-speaking churches have been guilty of this historical malady. There consistently have been those within the ranks of these churches who have pointed to the theologically deviant behavior of these churches. Whether the alternative responses to the crises described in the pages that follow were "feasible" will, no doubt, be judged differently by different social groups in accordance with their basic socio-economic and political values. Christians are required, however, to answer this question theologically and to consider the theological nature of folly. More than that, such matters need to be tried and tested in relation to the New Testament ethic of Jesus. What *is* suggested in this study on the English-speaking churches is that their present moderate and cautious character has been forged over many years.

ACKNOWLEDGMENTS

During recent decades several histories of the church in South Africa have appeared. Many of these provide important information and have become useful tools not only for people seeking to understand the nature of church-state relations in South Africa, but also for those engaged in the struggle for a qualitatively different and just South Africa. Among these is my colleague John de Gruchy's *The Church Struggle in South Africa*, first published almost a decade ago. The present study provides a more detailed and critical assessment of the English-speaking churches than that found in de Gruchy's book. It also persistently considers the socio-economic and political function of these churches in relation to the structures of domination in South Africa in a way that de Gruchy does not, although he acknowledges the need for this kind of analysis in the second edition of *The Church Struggle in South Africa,* published in 1987. The church, however, can only remain indebted to him for the important historical narrative provided in his book.

A more recent publication is James Cochrane's *Servants of Power: The Role of the English-speaking Churches 1903-1930.* This is a detailed and important analysis of the Anglican and Methodist churches during a critical phase of South African history, which deserves serious study. Based on careful and serious archival research and theoretical interpretation, Cochrane tests and tries the policy, practice and theology of these churches in the light of the history of socio-economic oppression in South Africa. The present study, especially chapters 2 and 3, presupposes much of what Cochrane's research substantiates.

In writing a book of this nature I could not help but be acutely aware of my own identity as a member of the English-speaking churches. In some ways it has been a cathartic experience, requiring me to understand my own heritage as a basis for sharing in a small way in the renewal of church and society. I am indebted to the alternative church, located on the margins (and at times outside) of the institutional churches. There I have experienced a vitality akin to that which one reads about in the New Testament. Within this church of the poor and oppressed I began to read the Bible and understand the Christian tradition in a new way. I experientially realized in a demanding way what I had hitherto known at the level of theory and witnessed only with a measure of indifference, namely, that the institutional church has deviated far from the New Testament community of Jesus.

What does it mean to seek to show solidarity with the oppressed? What does it mean to be part of the church of the poor? These are questions with which every Christian is obliged to wrestle. Some feel it means one must oneself become poor, while others suggest this is not realistic or even authentic. One who has acquired social, educational and material wealth can never know what it is to be trapped in poverty. I am neither poor nor oppressed, and I write this book from a comfortable study. When I visit Crossroads, Khayelitsha or a resettlement camp, I recognize a gulf that I can voluntarily cross only as an empathetic *visitor*. Can a rich person enter the kingdom of God? This problem is reflected on in the final chapter.

I am grateful to many colleagues and students in the Department of Religious Studies at the University of Cape Town as well as co-workers in the Institute of Contextual Theology in Johannesburg who have read sections of this study or the manuscript in its entirety. These include John de Gruchy, Itumeleng Mosala, Malusi Mpumlwana and Albert Nolan. They have all contributed significantly to the final text. Yet none, it is customary and necessary to say, can be held responsible for errors of fact or judgment which may be found in the pages that follow. Postgraduate students in the Department of Religious Studies at the University of Cape Town who registered for the seminar on Christianity in Southern Africa during the second semester of 1987 worked through sections of this book while still in manuscript form. I am grateful for their insightful comments. Alan Brews was a teaching assistant on the course at the time and Mary Armour proofread and facilitated the preparation of the manuscript in a most helpful manner. Pat Lawrence, in turn, assisted with secretarial work. I acknowledge with gratitude their contribution. I am also grateful to Charles Martin of Orbis Books who steered the book through its production phase with a sense of purpose and diligence. My wife, Eileen, and our daughters, Heidi and Tanya, tolerated and shared in the birthpangs of the book. This I value and appreciate.

Bishop Trevor Huddleston has suffered but never faltered in his opposition to apartheid or in his challenge to the church. He helped shape a period of resistance thirty years ago which continues to haunt the English-speaking churches. He also provided a vision of an alternative church. I thank him for writing the foreword to this book.

Charles Villa-Vicencio
Cape Town, October 1987

PART ONE

A SOCIAL HISTORY
OF THE CHURCHES

Chapter One

Nothing Harsh or Rigorous

Edward Knapp-Fisher, Bishop of Pretoria and a leading ecumenical voice in the 1950s, prefaces his book *The Churchman's Heritage* with an intriguing prayer written by Bishop Thomas Ken in 1718:

> Glory be to thee, O Lord God, who hast made me a member of a particular Church of England whose faith and government and worship are holy, and catholic, and apostolic, and free from the extremes of irreverence and superstition which I firmly believe to be part of the Church Universal; and which teaches me charity to them who dissent from me.[1]

The *via media* of the eighteenth-century Anglican Church steered itself between what many within that church regarded as the excesses of both Nonconformist anti-papal rowdyism given to political rather than religious ends, and the perceived redundancies of Catholic lore and hegemony. One is tempted to root such moderation in what Stephen Neill called the "fresh and remarkable" missionary initiative of the Benedictine order that contrasted so sharply with the earlier rough-hewn forms of Celtic Christianity as established in the British Isles.[2] The extremes of earlier ascetics gave way to Benedictine spirituality designed, suggests Edmund Bishop, to manifest "at the same time both realistic and practical qualities

13

which would not scare away the faint-hearted." In the words of Benedict, "There shall be nothing harsh or rigorous."[3]

This moderate and "realistic" ecclesial character, it is argued in the pages that follow, has come to characterize not only the Anglican Church but all English-speaking churches in South Africa. With the political situation being torn apart by a clash between Afrikaner and black nationalisms, the South African English have found themselves becoming increasingly marginalized in matters political. The English-speaking churches have, in turn, manifested a laissez-faire outlook in such matters, often seen by those outside their ranks to border on powerlessness and stoic resignation. Able to depend on the theological and cultural resources of their denominational links in Britain and elsewhere, their identity has never really been hammered out in relation to the hard realities of the South African context. It is this, perhaps more than anything else, that has caused other churches, and especially the Afrikaner and black churches, not to take the English-speaking churches too seriously. And unless the emerging black leadership within the English-speaking churches succeeds in steering them into the eye of the brewing storm, forcing them to forge a contextual theology relevant to the South African crisis, the contribution of these churches to the resolution of conflict can only be minimal.

What has dogged the English-speaking churches most has been their inability to translate their noblest theological declarations and ethical ideals into practice. This reality, not uncommon to the character of churches elsewhere in the world, is in this country solidly grounded in an obligation to minister to both black and white members in a society which separates these two groups by law and social practice. Refusing to take sides in the inevitable conflict generated by this division, these churches find themselves locked into moderation and caution. They are given to "nothing harsh or rigorous" in either their theological identity or in their social allegiance. From this has come a broad tolerance of diversity within these churches, the calculated use of ambiguity to ensure maximum unity in matters of theology and church policy, compromise in areas of political difference, and the shepherding of all along the *via media*, suitably backed by socio-political expediency and theological incentive. Yet, it needs to be added, ultimately the other ecclesial groups within the country, while different from the

English-speaking churches and in most instances finding their social identity elsewhere, have themselves shown a similar tendency toward moderation within their own contexts.

A major turning point for the churches in South Africa came when the Afrikaner nationalists were elected to power in 1948. In the wake of this the Christian Council, consisting largely of the English-speaking churches and excluding the Afrikaans churches, convened in 1949 to reassess their common mission. It had to do, they argued, with the essential belief that "beyond all differences there remains an essential unity" and that "the real need of South Africa is not *apartheid* but *eendrag* [unity through teamwork]." The demarcation between the Afrikaans Reformed churches, influential in the Afrikaner election victory, and the English-speaking churches was clearly stated. This demarcation, however, has become increasingly blurred in the past few years (see chapter 5).

WHERE THE CHURCHES DIVIDE

In order to discern the character of the English-speaking churches in relation to this demarcation, it is necessary to identify the different ecclesial groupings in South Africa. In so doing it will be shown that in spite of important theological differences between the churches, the social character of the different churches is shaped by the different social contexts of which they are a part. It is this which suggests that the church is essentially a social respondent in society rather than a vanguard for change. At the same time the church is haunted and disturbed by a theology which contradicts its social location and causes some within its ranks to question its social identity. Under certain socio-political conditions this enables the church to initiate change in the society to which it belongs. It is this factor that takes on increasing significance as the clamor intensifies for political change in South Africa.

The identification of the historical divisions between churches offered here is cursory and intended to provide no more than a background against which to discuss the nature and identity of the English-speaking churches in subsequent chapters. Briefly stated, if the Afrikaans Reformed churches have for various historical reasons come to symbolize the legitimation of the white status quo, and the black churches the legitimation of the black quest for liberation, the English-speaking churches must find their identity between the two. The remaining churches, in turn, find their respective identities in relation to these dominant groups.

The English-Speaking Churches

The phrase *English-speaking churches* is a misnomer, having acquired a rather specific connotation in South Africa. It refers to those churches which originated in Great Britain, and use English as an official language, although the majority of their members (who are black) would regard one of the African languages as a first language. While the language factor also applies to the Roman Catholic Church, this church i not regarded as part of the group of churches under consideration, being neither of British origin nor sharing the characteristics of the Protestant milieu. The English-speaking churches are the Anglican Church or Church of the Province of South Africa, the Methodist Church of Southern Africa, the Presbyterian Church of Southern Africa, and the United Congregational Church of Southern Africa.

There are other churches which use English as their official language and can trace their origins either directly or indirectly back to Britain, which are not normally considered part of this family of churches. The Church of England of South Africa is a small church whose roots go back to the heresy charge laid by the bishop of Cape Town, Robert Gray, against Bishop Colenso of Natal in the middle of the last century. The consequence was schism between the larger Church of the Province of South Africa (the Anglican church) and Colenso's Church of England in South Africa. Today this church still regards itself to be in continuity with the Church of England and holds resolutely to the 1662 Book of Common Prayer; however, it is not recognized as part of the Anglican communion by Canterbury. It has also turned away from what Peter Hinchliff identifies as Colenso's "revolutionary and unpopular missionary policies" which involved the proclamation of a gospel with "definite social implications" and a brand of critical biblical scholarship which in the nineteenth century was enough to get Gray's heresy charge to stick.[4]

The Baptist Union of South Africa has tended to isolate itself from the issues that bind the Anglicans, Methodists, Presbyterians and Congregationalists together. Like the Church of England in South Africa, the Baptist Union is not included in that alliance of churches designated as the English-speaking churches. It does not belong to the South African Council of Churches (SACC), of which the Anglicans, Methodists, Presbyterians and United Congregationalists are among the most significant member churches. Neither does it belong to the Church Unity Commission whose membership is constituted by these four churches, and it tends to shun the broader ecumenical movement. In this study English-speaking churches refers specifically to those churches already identified.

The *social* factors which contribute to the quest for unity by the Anglicans, Methodists, Presbyterians and United Congregationalists are as important (and perhaps more interesting) than the theological factors which both unite and divide them. Their historical origins, cultural and political loyalties, and the marginalization of these churches by the political victory of the Afrikaner nationalists in 1948 are all decisive factors in this regard.

The social differences among these churches, however, have militated against any attempt on their part to adopt an entirely common front against apartheid. The Anglicans and Methodists are large denominations. Their respective memberships are essentially black, although representing a fair cross-section of the entire population—black and white, workers and management, rich and poor, dominant and oppressed. If any churches are torn between loyalty to both rulers and ruled it is these churches. The Presbyterian Church of Southern Africa is predominantly white and generally speaking (although not consistently so) more conservative than the other English-speaking churches. For various historical, social and cultural reasons it finds itself closer to the Afrikaans Reformed churches than to the other three English-speaking churches. The United Congregational Church is overwhelmingly black, a factor which together with a strong non-conformist tradition makes it the most progressive of the English-speaking churches. Its roots reach back to the London Missionary Society (LMS) and the American Board of Missions in the early nineteenth century. When the Congregational Union (a union of black and white settler and LMS congregations), the Bantu Congregational Church and the LMS in

Botswana united in 1967, the white component of this church was reduced to less than 10 percent of the total membership. The differences between the English-speaking churches are clearly manifest in the responses of these churches to the issues discussed in the chapters that follow.

The birth of the English-speaking churches goes back to nineteenth-century colonial expansionism. The missionaries who arrived with the traders, the settlers, the explorers and the military were soon thrust into both confrontation and cooperation with the colonial rulers. On occasions they intervened on behalf of the indigenous population and often found themselves in confrontation with the white settler churches as well as the colonial government, and yet they never doubted the superiority of English cultural values over those of the African people whom they sought to proselytize. The kind of Christianity which they brought to this country had a formative influence on the identity of the English-speaking churches.

The English-speaking churches take pride in their non-racial membership. Critics of these churches, however, regard this self-accolade as a deception and form of dangerous idealism, which deludes these churches into assuming a level of achievement which denies the extent of division within their ranks. Of such pretensions, it is said, comes political complacency. "There can be no church unity in a divided land!" is the cry. The fact remains that what semblance of unity exists within these churches has been hard won and is not easily surrendered. Two incidents in particular have taken on major symbolic and emotional importance in this regard.

The first is the response of the churches to the "church clause" of the Native Laws Amendment Bill, introduced in 1957 by Hendrik Verwoerd, Minister of Native Affairs at the time. The church clause made it virtually impossible for black people to worship in churches located in white areas. The Anglican Archbishop of Cape Town, Geoffrey Clayton, with support from the leaders of the other English-speaking churches protested against this bill, rejecting the right of a secular agency to determine where a church member may worship. The outcome was a modified bill allowing the minister to prevent black Christians from worshipping with their fellow white Christians should anyone complain that they were a "nuisance" or worshipping in "excessive numbers"! A pastoral letter read in Anglican churches, calling on all clergy and laity to ignore the new legislation, stated:

> Before God and with you as my witnesses, I solemnly state that not only shall I not obey any direction of the Minister of Native Affairs in this regard, but I solemnly counsel you, both clergy and people, to do the same.[5]

This response is cherished and cited by Anglicans and others alike as a moment of theological integrity which celebrates the unity of the church. It is a response not to be compromised or deprecated, and yet when viewed in relation to the refusal by the English-speaking churches to show similar resistance to other violations of the ministry of the church, this particular stand witnesses to a rather limited perception by these churches of the socio-political implications of the gospel they preached.

The other incident highlights the trauma affecting Methodism in this regard. The apartheid mindset had penetrated deep into this church, and its 1958 conference debated, behind closed doors, the feasibility of establishing four separate churches (white, black, "colored" and Indian) in compliance with apartheid ideology. The outcome was a vote for unity, expressed in the following resolution:

> The conference declares its conviction that it should be *one and undivided*, trusting to the lead of God to bring this ideal to ultimate fruition, and that this be the general basis of our missionary policy.[6]

Methodists, both black and white, have clung to this in the face of forces threatening to destroy their confessed oneness. There is, however, no easy route to unity in churches where the daily existence of their members is shaped and manipulated by the divisions of apartheid. The English-speaking churches have inevitably failed in this context to realize in praxis what they affirm in principle. The inevitable compromise entailed in ministering to both whites who benefit from the apartheid system and blacks who are exploited by it cannot be underestimated. The consequences of the alternative, namely the affirmation of exclusive diversity is, however, even more frightening. One consequence would be a religious legitimation of the resulting conflict, pride and antagonism—and a denial in principle of the ideals of gospel. Does the affirmation of unity, even as practiced in the English-speaking churches, have any more significant contribution to make in terms of praxis to the body politic in South Africa?

The political appeal of a homogeneous church is obvious; it provides the social cohesion necessary to attain a specific ideological goal. And in a polarized society such as South Africa, the possibility of mutually exclusive churches which provide legitimation for the opposing forces is a near inevitability. To quote a revered Afrikaner theologian, Andrew Murray, "the danger always exists that the voice of blood, the voice of passion, of partisanship, of group interest will overpower the voice of the gospel."[7] History is cluttered with instances of the abusive use of the gospel as a vehicle to convey what is so often an alien message of domination and oppression rather than one of hope and liberation. It is then, states Dietrich Bonhoeffer, that "the message is trimmed and cropped until it fits the frame which has been decided, and the result is that the eagle [with clipped wings] can no longer rise and fly away to its true element but can be pointed out as a special showpiece among the animals."[8] As a result, that eschatological hope which always demands more than any particular political ideology can give is abandoned and the unique contribution of the gospel to political ethics is destroyed.

There is no easy answer to this dilemma. The sociology-of-knowledge debate convinces us that all ideas, including religious ideas, are shaped by the society within which they emerge. The most that can be hoped for is a situation in which our respective ideas and experiences are tested in relation to the ideas and experience of others. In so doing conflicting parties, each locked into their own group-determined perception of the gospel, are afforded the possibility of confronting one another's gospel. It is this possibility which the English-speaking churches (together with the Roman Catholic Church) with their diverse memberships should be better equipped to provide than any of the other churches under consideration. They afford their members—of different racial groups, different classes, and different political allegiances—the opportunity of being part of a single structure. Herein lies the potential strength and the weakness of these churches. It is a strength because it affords the opportunity for something radically new in the South African context to emerge as blacks and whites are required to negotiate a common ecclesial and social identity in a land given to division and conflict. It is a weakness because it can degenerate into little more than a sterile deception, with the noblest theological notions of unity being separated from the social reality of division and conflict. The pity is that too often this common meeting place is simply too limited, failing to expose ordinary church members to a common pew or the hospitality of one another's homes. It is this that leaves grass-roots members unexposed to one another's experience, and church hierarchies remaining fearful of the repercussions that may result from imposing common structures on their members. This is the trap, historically imposed and socially conditioned, in which the English-speaking churches find themselves.

The possibilities which can, however, emerge from the dialectic of creative conflict is a component which a society facing the threat of violent destruction cannot afford to ignore either in a pre- or post-revolutionary era. From such conflict can come the basis of political renewal, creative restitution and genuine reconciliation. Reinhold Niebuhr's social and ethical vision of "a body of citizens . . . who see the issues between their own nations (or groups) more clearly than the ignorant patriot and more disinterestedly than the dominant classes" has a certain elitist ring about it.[9] But when this community of people emerges from within the dialectic of conflict and commits itself through participation to be part of the resolution of social conflict, it provides an eschatological or utopian vision that no society can afford to ignore. It is this possibility which the heterogeneous composition of the English-speaking churches can symbolize better than any other church. It is this which ought to be the goal of all churches, and it is this possibility which the greatest daughters and sons of all the churches in South Africa have sought to celebrate and advance.

The tragedy is that the English-speaking churches have failed to be the kind of institutions within which the possibility of moving society from polarized conflict to a higher level of community is possible. In a subtle and therefore complex and menacing way these churches have themselves become trapped within their particular social context no less than any other church. Purporting to provide a context within which their diverse membership can find a common purpose and identity (being what Christians usually call the Body of Christ), the wider political divisions weigh heavily on these structures forcing them to the breaking point.

Trapped between their respective black and white constituencies, the English-speaking churches find themselves in a different captivity from either the Afrikaner or the black churches which in the case of the former minister exclusively to whites and in the case of the latter exclusively to blacks. Yet these churches have shown a political moderation not vastly different from the moderation of the English-speaking churches when viewed in relation to the less temperate voices in their own communities.

The Afrikaans Reformed Churches

Also known as the Dutch Reformed Churches, this group consists of the powerful Nederduitse Gereformeerde Kerk to which the majority of white South Africans belong and two smaller churches, the Nederduitsch Hervormde Kerk (NHK) and the Gereformeerde Kerk.

The Nederduitse Gereformeerde Kerk (NGK) was established in the Cape by the Dutch East India Company in 1652 and provided the religious center of the Dutch settler community. When the Dutch settlers trekked north to escape the consequences of British rule in 1836, however, they went without the blessing of their church.[10] An inevitable schism followed. The Nederduitsch Hervormde Kerk (NHK) was born as the *Volkskerk* of the Boer Republic in the Transvaal, and for theological rather than political reasons the ultra-Calvinist Gereformeerde Kerk was established several years later.[11]

In spite of significant involvement in the rise of Afrikanerdom and overt support for the apartheid ideology, historical evidence indicates a reluctance on the part of these churches to support the most zealous and militant acts of the Afrikaner struggle. Different in so many ways from their English-speaking counterparts these churches, like the English-speaking churches, have allowed themselves to be formed by the dominant society of which they are a part rather than shaping and directing that society from within. Thus at several historical moments of crisis the Afrikaans churches found themselves divided for the simple reason that the Afrikaner people were divided. Reference has already been made to the refusal of the NGK to support the Great Trek. At the time of the 1914 Afrikaner rebellion, the Afrikaner churches were again thrust into crisis with their members and leaders divided in their support for rebel and government causes. The Council of the Dutch Reformed Churches, comprising delegates from all three of the Afrikaans Reformed churches, was called into session to consider this conflict and eventually resolved that theologically it was unable to condemn rebellion *per se* or censure those who participated in the rebellion. Yet neither was it prepared to state that this particular act of rebellion was legitimate. It argued that in addition to its theological responsibility, it also had a unique responsibility to the Afrikaner nation, which required it to reconcile the conflicting parties.[12] When the militant *Ossewabrandwag*, in turn, engaged in anti-government activities and sabotage during World War II, the Afrikaans churches were again divided. Prominent dominees (ministers) and church leaders joined the *Ossewabrandwag*, while others sided with D. F. Malan's National Party in its eventual condemnation of the movement. Officially the churches provided no direct support to the *Ossewabrandwag* and ultimately aligned themselves with the rejection of the movement by Malan's party.[13]

The Afrikaner churches saw their primary role to lie in maintaining Afrikaner unity, providing extensive moral and ideological support for the Afrikaner cause. Their concern not to take sides between the different factions within the Afrikaner community resulted in these churches not being able to provide the unequivocal leadership in the Afrikaner quest for power which the more zealous leaders desired. All political hesitation, however, gave way to uncompromising support *for* the policies of the new regime after the 1948 victory of the National Party. Since then the Afrikaans Reformed churches have provided theological legitimation for apartheid legislation and the maintenance of Afrikaner rule. It was this legitimation which eventually led to a declaration of heresy against the NGK and the NHK by the World Alliance of Reformed Churches (WARC) in 1982, the Gereformeerde Kerk never having belonged to this ecumenical body.[14]

In more recent times, as the Afrikaner people have again divided in the face of political crisis, similar divisions are again to be seen in the ranks of these churches. Even the cautious and hesitant refor-mulation of NGK policy on apartheid which occurred with the adoption of the General Synod of the *Kerk en Samelewing* docu-ment in 1986 has led to schism by the more conservative members who have established the Afrikaanse Protestantse Kerk, and to the appearance of the Nederduitse Gereformeerde Bond within the NGK as a pressure group opposed to the revised position. The implications of *Kerk en Samelewing* are discussed in chapter 5. Here it is enough to observe that, as in earlier years, the Afrikaner church continues to reflect the political division of the Afrikaner people. It reflects the split between the cautiously pragmatic stance of P. W. Botha's ruling party and right-wing conservative groups. United and powerful when Afrikanerdom has shown a measure of political homogeneity, in crisis the Afrikaner churches have found it impossible to choose between the warring factions.

The Afrikaner church, so often perceived to be at the vanguard of Afrikaner nationalism, is shown by history rather to be more concerned about contributing to the maintenance of the unity of the Afrikaner *volk* than providing specific guidance beyond a particular national or moral dilemma. Critical of the marriage between the Afrikaner church and Afrikaner nationalism, it is this factor that has in the past separated the English-speaking churches most decisively from these churches, as they have resolutely refused to side explicitly with any one group within the complexity of South African society. (Although, in *practice* the English-speaking churches have in their own way also reflected their particular social context.) The Afrikaans Reformed churches have furthermore consistently refused any direct link with the SACC, essentially because of its sustained protest against the apartheid policy of Afrikaner nationalism. In so doing, the Afrikaans Reformed churches have separated themselves from all the other major churches in the country.

Black Churches

The other major ecclesial group is the black churches, which have come to symbolize the black quest for liberation—a position which stands in contra-distinction to both the English-speaking churches and the Afrikaans Reformed churches. The black churches differ from one another in a variety of ways, but in each case were born out of racial conflict and/or differentiation.

The black churches can be divided into three groups: the *black mission churches*, the *historic black churches*, and the *African Indigenous Churches*. Because the African Indigenous Churches have, however, separated themselves from the traditions of the established churches in a way in which the former two have not, this ecclesial group is considered under a separate heading.

Unlike the black converts of the English-speaking churches who were incorporated into these churches, the converts of the Afrikaner Reformed churches, some other mission churches (such as the Lutheran church) and certain missionary societies were formed into separate churches—always under the watchful eye of the white missionaries—and remained economically dependent on the white churches. The American Methodist Episcopal Church (AME), the only major historic black church in South Africa, had a different history. It was brought to this country as a separate black church, established by black Americans in protest against the racism prevalent in American Methodism. After an attempt to establish union with the emerging Ethiopian Church it ultimately established itself as a separate denomination while maintaining links with the AME Church in the United States.

The black mission churches of the Afrikaans Reformed churches constitute the major grouping among black mission churches and emerged as a result of white racism and political expediency. What theological argument was produced in relation to separate churches can only be rejected as a legitimation of white domination and "nothing but a heresy."[15] It is difficult to identify precisely when and where race and class became dominant factors in South African history. Certainly they were present in some form from the arrival of the first white settlers and were a formative influence in the relationship between slaves and slave-owners. Class and racial stratification intensified when middle-ranking settler farmers who were unable to compete with large estates worked by slaves left the western Cape for the frontiers of the established white colony where Christianity and skin color became the criteria of group exclusivity. And as white opposition to *gelykstelling* (social egalitarianism) intensified yet further, "the crucial battlefield was the church."[16]

There was initially a measure of church integration in the major centers of the Western Cape. On the frontier and rural areas even the most limited form of integration was unacceptable, and in 1801 armed insurrections broke out when missionaries sought to evangelize blacks in the Graaff-Reinet district. Charging that "the heathen" were being "instructed in reading, writing and religion and thereby put upon an equal footing with the Christians," the insurrectionaries demanded that the missionaries be barred from using church property.[17] When rural and frontier congregations began to demand separate facilities and services for black converts, theological tradition initially prevailed and baptism was affirmed as the sole theological qualification for church membership. The 1829 Synod of the NGK insisted that holy communion be administered to all members "without distinction of color." But in time social discrimination between slaves and slave-owners, frontier farmers and the indigenous population and generally between black and white gained the upper hand, and in 1857 the Synod revoked its earlier decision. It allowed that where the "weakness of some impedes the furtherance of the cause of Christ among the heathen, the congregation from the heathen . . . shall enjoy its Christian privileges in a separate building or institution." The social divisions of dominant white society were shaping the identity of the church, and soon the 1857 concession to "weakness" became the norm, with separate mission churches emerging as a result of NGK mission work. In 1881 the Sendingkerk (Mission Church) was established for so-called "colored people." The first synod of a separate church for blacks, the NGK in Africa, did not meet until 1910 to unite those separate black congregations which had been established as part of the mission activity of white congregations in the Orange Free State. The first Transvaal synod met in 1932, followed by the Cape in 1951 and Natal in 1952, with the four separate synods being combined in a general synod in 1963. This was, in turn, followed by the establishment of a separate church for Indian people, the Indian Reformed Church (later called the Reformed Church) in 1968.[18]

The white Nederduitsch Hervormde Kerk (NHK) has, in turn, spawned its own separate black church with a clause written into its constitution which excludes blacks from membership in the white church. The Gereformeerde Kerk with its ultra-Calvinist theology was convinced that God had decreed the separation of races. The first Gereformeerde missionary to the black community was not ordained in this church until 1910, and black converts were ministered to in separate congregations. "Officially," says Gereformeerde theologian Professor Spoelstra, "the Gereformeerde Church rejects any suggestion that racial discrimination should be legitimated in the church. In practice, however, problems as the result of non-ecclesiastical factors led to a renunciation of the principle."[19] In 1860 a congregation of the Gereformeerde Church in the Orange Free State declared: "We did not learn in the Word of God that we had to allow them [blacks] to share in the same social rights. Given the nations which surround us here, such a policy will lead to the political downfall of whites and the corruption of blacks. Thus we consider it imperative for both us and them that they keep their religion separate and that their spiritual needs be met in a special way."[20]

The policy of separate churches for separate races within the Afrikaans Reformed Churches began to harden into a theologized form of Afrikaner nationalism in the 1920s and 1930s as these churches struggled to establish a common mission policy. Confronted with demands by blacks for equal rights as Christians, the Afrikaans Reformed churches rejected *gelykstelling* and from this emerged the theology of apartheid.[21] It was this policy that became the ideological basis of apartheid laws to be implemented in 1948 with the victory at the polls of the Afrikaner National Party.

Racial divisions between the Afrikaans Reformed churches continue. And when the *Belydendekring* came into existence in 1974 it had as its goal the unity of the different racially-based churches within the NGK, NHK and the Gereformeerde Kerk. The white leadership within these churches, however, rejected this move, suggesting that it had its base in political radicalism. The *Belydendekring* has gradually shifted its focus away from formal unity to the affirmation of a confessing movement based on a profession of faith which relates the gospel to the prevailing violations thereof in the apartheid structure. The work of the *Belydendekring* in many ways reached a level of pre-eminence with the 1982 WARC decision declaring the theological justification of apartheid to be heresy. The theological stance of the *Belydendekring* had been justified, and the same year the *Belhar Confession*, which affirms the rejection of apartheid and the eradication of all forms of social injustice as an inherent part of that church's confession of faith, was referred by the Synod of the NG Sendingkerk to its local congregations for consideration. In 1986 the Synod of that church officially adopted the Confession as a part of its theological identity. With this decision apartheid came to be regarded as false doctrine at complete variance with the gospel of Jesus Christ. What is more important, however, is that henceforth any divergence from this position would place the person or group concerned at variance with "the integrity of our communal confession as Reformed Churches." Bluntly put, the *Belhar Confession* states as a matter of confession that it is impossible to be a Christian in the Reformed tradition without being opposed to and working for the eradication of apartheid and all forms of social justice in society.[22]

As the social context of whites shaped the theology of the white NGK, so the political oppression of the black community has defined the parameters of the ecclesiology of the Sendingkerk. The NGK in Africa is more dependent on white missionaries and funding from the white church than the Sendingkerk, and this has resulted in a more cautious rejection of apartheid by this church.

Recently, however, this church has shown itself to be more outspoken in its opposition to white NGK theology and more resistant in relations with that church. It has not adopted a theological stance similar to the *Belhar Confession,* but has formally agreed to study the implications of the *Belhar Confession* for its own ministry. It has also in 1987 issued a joint statement with the NG Sendingkerk on church unity. The Reformed Church, a small separate church for Indians established in 1968 to counter any moves by Indians to join the congregations established for other racial groups, has, in turn, experienced several secessions by member churches precisely because this church has turned away from adopting a theological position similar to that of the Sendingkerk.

The challenge facing these churches is whether they will succeed where other churches have failed in producing a common front against the state. The option for so-called coloreds and Indians to participate in separate parliamentary structures and the reality of Bantustan politics has imposed divisions on the black community. The Sendingkerk has taken the lead in rejecting these moves within the black community, but as black resistance heightens and state

oppression increases, the battle for these churches can only intensify. For the present the black churches within the Afrikaans Reformed family of churches have, in spite of their varying responses
to apartheid, acquired a character which has come to symbolize the
theological repudiation of apartheid—a position largely due to the
high profile given to the stance of the Sendingkerk by the *Belydendekring* and the election of Allan Boesak, a minister (and Moderator) of this church, as President of WARC.

Another group of black mission churches emerged in the nineteenth century as a result of Scottish and European mission work.
Committed to the establishment of independent churches among
converts, the Scottish missionaries founded the Bantu Presbyterian
Church (today the Reformed Presbyterian Church). The Swiss
established the Tsonga Presbyterian Church (today the Evangelical
Presbyterian Church), and the American Board of Missions was
responsible for the emergence of the Bantu Congregational
Church. Other missionary boards followed suit. In each case these
churches were dependent on the settler churches. The Bantu Congregational Church has since become part of the United Congregational Church of Southern Africa, while other churches continue to
exist as independent black churches.

The struggle for the allegiance of these churches by conflicting
political groups is no less intense than is the case with black
churches within the sphere of the Afrikaans Reformed churches.
And, given the extensive membership of these churches within the
Bantustans, there is reason to believe it could become even more
intense. As the cohesion of the Afrikaans Reformed mission
churches centers around the Belydendekring, so the other black
churches have found their center in the Alliance of Black Reformed
Churches of Southern Africa (Abrecsa)—although this latter
group also includes NGK and other black Afrikaans Reformed
church members. More recently, as the focus of the Belydendekring
has shifted away from discernible unity between the NGK churches
to a more radical focus on a confessing movement, cooperation
between Abrecsa and the *Belydendekring* has become an increasingly obvious move. The possibility of a confessing church movement which extends beyond both Abrecsa and the *Belydendekring*
could in turn envelop both these movements and radically alter the
identity of the different protest movements within all the churches.

Such possibilities have not yet, however, taken sufficient form to be adequately assessed.

The AME Church, as already indicated, is a different kind of black church. Rather than having been born in segregation, the church, which is largely given to personal evangelism, had its origin in rejection of racism in the "non-racial" Episcopal Methodist Church in the post-Civil War period in the United States of America. Demonstrating a rejection of apartheid in much the same way as the English-speaking churches, the AME in South Africa has not provided an institutional alignment which has placed it unequivocally on the side of the black liberation struggle anymore than have the English-speaking churches or some other black churches. Yet in more recent times, as black resistance has intensified, this church too has found itself pressured to declare its stance more clearly in relation to the prevailing political struggle within the black community. One consequence has been the kind of internal conflict experienced in most churches.

The black churches, given their nearly exclusive black membership and immediate involvement in black suffering, have responded directly and spontaneously to the intensified demands by blacks for liberation in recent decades. This has thrust these churches in a less equivocal way than other churches "onto the side" of the black struggle, providing the struggle with the kind of religious support afforded white resistance by the white Afrikaner Reformed churches. Forced to respond to the shooting of their children in the resistance campaigns of 1976 and thereafter, these churches have nevertheless been reluctant in many instances to ask what it might mean in explicit terms of a political program and praxis to promote the cause of black liberation. Reluctant to side openly with any particular political ideology they have, for example, condemned all forms of racism but, like all other established churches which are part of the economic infrastructure of the existing order, they have not challenged the economic basis of racism. They have refused to declare themselves with regard to participation in the tricameral parliament or Bantustan governments and have ultimately given expression to the internal divisions within their respective communities rather than resolutely seeking to weigh up the different political and economic options of the day against the demands of the gospel. Torn between the kind of otherworldly religiosity characteristic of many of their oppressed members and the more political commitment of other groups within their membership, they have produced a majority of politically restrained members. The radical voices within these churches are in the minority in much the same manner as they are in other churches.

What makes these churches different is that they provide a constituency of people with first-hand experience of suffering. Schooled in the stories of the suffering of the people of God in the Bible, they are a people ready to respond to the leadership of those who offer to lead them out of their oppression. As such, they are sensitive to the appeals of those who relate the challenge of the gospel to the political challenges facing black people. However, the missionary theology that separates spiritual concerns from material needs continues to co-exist with the theology of the *Belhar Confession* in these churches—and in many instances it dominates. This militates against the instinctive response of the oppressed community to the challenge of liberating theology. Sustained state persecution of those leaders who *do* translate a spiritual message into programs which address the basic needs of the people, in turn, results in few leaders who provide the kind of spiritual leadership sought by the oppressed within the different churches.

African Indigenous Churches

The failure of the established churches to meet the spiritual aspirations of indigenous African people has enticed them to look beyond the established churches for their salvation. This has given rise to the phenomena of the African Independent or Indigenous Churches. There are varying estimates of the numerical strength of these churches in South Africa today. In 1982 the SACC estimated that more or less one-sixth of South Africa's more than fifteen million African Christians belonged to approximately 4,700 separate indigenous churches.[23] Government figures supplied in 1980 estimated the total number of churches at that time to be 3,500, with 29.3 percent of the African population claiming membership in these churches (in comparison with 18.6 percent in 1951).[24]

Trevor Verryn lists seven basic factors which contributed to the emergence of the indigenous churches: 1) The determination of white leaders in the established mission churches to exclude blacks from leadership positions; 2) race prejudice in the established churches; 3) the use of disciplinary measures to control black aspirations and what white leaders regarded as insubordination; 4) the example of Western schismatic and denominational practices; 5) the subordination of women; 6) personal leadership conflicts; and 7) the commitment on the part of African Christians to incorporate their own cultural and traditional religious ideas into their churches.[25] Shaped by the dominant white colonial-capitalist culture of the time, the mission churches were experienced by black converts as being as foreign as colonialism itself.

Thus the indigenous churches were born as structural alternatives to the traditional Western, white, European-type structures found not only in the English-speaking churches but also in the black churches. The defeat of nations and the destruction of their basic political and economic structures has throughout history produced major cultural and religious realignments, and southern Africa is no exception. Evidence suggests that within the present political conflict in South Africa indigenous churches could grow stronger unless the established churches address themselves more vigorously to the spiritual, cultural and material needs of the oppressed people in the country.

Allowing that the character of the numerous indigenous churches is vastly heterogeneous, certain broad trends can be discerned within various groupings of these churches. The work of Glenda Kruss, which seeks to relate the emergence of these churches to the changing socio-economic and political trends of colonization and industrialization, is important in this regard.

The *Ethiopian Movement*, a name which acknowledges the presence of Christianity in Africa before the arrival of British and European missionaries, consists of those churches which broke away from the established churches out of a desire to exercise control over their own affairs. The conquest of the black indigenous population by the British colonizers resulted in traditional, pre-capitalist forms of production being replaced by a capitalist economy. During this period of time the Ethiopian churches began to appear. Their leadership tended to come from the African elite, including chiefs and moderately wealthy peasant farmers, able in some way to benefit from the emerging new economy. Evidence suggests that during this early colonization period "civilized," educated and Christianized Africans could be incorporated into the mercantile sector as equals. In time, legislation would deny even this option to the African population, but in the late nineteenth century there were possibilities for black self-affirmation.

These churches, suggests Kruss, represented the early religious phase of the African nationalist response to the colonization process, a response which affirmed what was African in an irreversibly new political and economic milieu. What Africans were not afforded in the mission churches and movements of the settler churches, they were forging for themselves in their own churches. For Verryn, "Ethiopianism is the offspring of the nuptials of Christianity and African culture."[26]

The first Ethiopian Church was established in 1892 by Mangena Mokone, a preacher who became alienated from the Methodist Church. He was joined a while later by another Methodist, James Mata Dwane, whose energy and vision resulted in the emergence of several additional congregations. In 1896 the Ethiopian churches decided to seek affiliation with the AME, a church which had gone through its own struggle for independence in America. It was a marriage which was never quite consummated. Some Ethiopian members were absorbed into the AME church; others resisted what was seen as absorption rather than unity with the AME church. In time Dwane was ordained Bishop of the Ethiopian Order of the Anglican Church.[27]

The *Zionist Movement* affirms a different synthesis between Christianity and African traditional values. It is a movement with origins among peasants unable to benefit from aspects of the emerging capitalist system.

With the implementation of the 1913 Land Act and other items of legislation which drove Africans off their land in an attempt to ensure cheap labor in the mines, a new wave of protest was unleashed. (The emergence of the African National Congress (ANC) can, for example, be traced back to this period.) Intensifying forms of resistance to white domination and the destruction of traditional values were prevalent both inside and outside the churches. A series of religious groups with Zion in their title began to emerge during this period. In 1904, with the help of the Christian Catholic Apostolic Church of Zion in the United States of America, the Zionist

Churches were established in Johannesburg. Also referred to as the churches of "Zion and the land," their goal was to establish self-supporting communities on the land. It is this emphasis that is symbolized in the terms *Zion* or the *New Jerusalem*.

Zion Cities emerged in different parts of the country, although today many have lost their initial commitment to egalitarianism and economic self-realization. The best-known contemporary example is the Zionist Christian Church of Bishop Barnabas Lekganyane at Moria near Pietersburg. The community of farms, shops and small businesses built around the church today form part of a large enterprise owned by the bishop rather than by the community. It is an aberrant form of the early socialist ideals of the movement—with a bishop who invited P. W. Botha to address his Easter congregation. This constitutes a long journey from the initial activity of protest against white rule within which these churches were born.

The *Churches of the Spirit*, largely the Zionist-Apostolic churches and similar groups, constitute what is essentially a religious-cultural response among the black working class. They have been strongest in the post-World War II period as the socio-economic contradictions within the capitalist system have become obvious. Confronted with the stark realities of urban dislocation and impoverishment, industrial workers and others have turned to traditional culture and religion to find resources for personal and collective survival. Theirs is a cultural and religious protest, and therefore a potential subversion of the dominant white forms of Christianity in white-ruled South Africa.

As is historically so often the case, the initial *raison d'etre* of these churches has often tended to become less explicit as they have become institutionalized. In many ways the indigenous churches have acquired an apolitical aura, while their historical origins continue to protest against the socio-economic and cultural identity of the established churches. The seeds of their origins, which are coterminous with the awakening of black nationalism, continue to be manifested as a potential form of resistance. Itumeleng Mosala's observation is a compelling one: "The African Independent Churches and especially the Zionist churches are, in fact, in contra-distinction to all 'mainline churches,' strictly speaking black working-class churches."[28] Accepting this assessment of these churches, they too constitute in a more radical manner than the black mission churches an oppressed community seeking to understand the gospel in relation to their own oppression. Herein lies a latent potential for possible institutional engagement on the side of revolutionary change, while the dominant popular theology of many of these churches provides for a more definite separation between spiritual values and socio-political reality than most of the established churches. It is this as much as anything else that has prevented these churches from developing into the kinds of movements which Mosala argues they can become.

Drawing on traditional cultural resources for survival in a Western-capitalist society, and in protest against those churches which symbolize this society, the indigenous churches contain cultural and theological seeds of resistance buried deep within their identity. It is these resources which some writers and activists within these churches are seeking to uncover.[29] Given the correct political climate, they could become receptive to the forces which radically reject the present order. Suffice it to say that, with a few exceptions, these churches have failed to realize this potential.

The English-speaking churches, as has already been suggested, find their identity midway between the Afrikaans Reformed churches and the black churches. They also exist, however, in relation to several other churches which for various historical reasons have not had the prominence or the influence of the English-speaking churches. These are the Roman Catholic Church, the Lutheran and Moravian Churches and the Conservative Evangelical Churches.

The Roman Catholic Church

Until 1804 Roman Catholics were prohibited by both successive Dutch and English colonial rulers from public worship in the Cape. For years after that their mission work to the indigenous population was hindered by the decidedly anti-Roman stance of successive governments as well as by the Protestant churches. The rallying call of the Afrikaner church-state alliance has traditionally included the warning of a "Roomse gevaar" (Roman danger) along with the affirmation of the "black danger" and "red peril." This resulted in a restrained witness by this church on social and political issues, at least until the 1950s. In 1957, in response to the intensification of apartheid legislation, the Southern African Catholic Bishops' Conference became the first church body to *theologically* reject apartheid in its entirety. In declaring it to be "intrinsically evil," they prepared the way for a series of declarations both by themselves and by other churches which anticipated the important "Apartheid is a Heresy" declaration in 1982 by the World Alliance of Reformed Churches (WARC).[30]

It was essentially during the period of industrialization, as blacks were driven off the land and lured to the mines, that the Roman Catholic Church became involved in actively proselytizing the black population in the cities and elsewhere. This process did not, however, affect the institutional character of the church: "This massive influx of blacks into the previously white church did not ripple the tranquil waters of white Catholicism. Relatively few blacks entered the priesthood, and those who did ministered to black parishes. Even fewer became bishops and when they did it was in the 'reserves' or the surrounding countries of Lesotho or Swaziland. Black and white churches were separated—not by law but by custom."[31]

In recent years the Roman Catholic Church has for a variety of reasons moved more readily into the caldron of church-state relations in South Africa. With ecumenical resistance to apartheid intensifying, the Roman Catholic Church, responding to the initiatives of post-Vatican II theological developments requiring the church to show a "preferential option for the poor," intensified its opposition to apartheid. The Southern African Catholic Bishops' Conference has, for example, systematically declared itself opposed to apartheid and related legislation. The South African government has, in turn, been obliged to adopt a more tolerant response to Catholicism than has traditionally been the case, a stance not unrelated to the large influx of white refugees supportive of the South African government from the former southern African Portuguese colonies. Promoting this shift in attitude and hungry for international acceptance, P. W. Botha, for example, undertook an unprecedented step for an Afrikaner leader and visited Pope John Paul II in the Vatican in 1984.

The predicament facing the English-speaking churches is paralleled in the Roman Catholic Church. Drawn out of the isolation in church-state relations in which it found itself in past decades, the Roman Catholic Church has been forced to confront racism both within its own ranks and in the nation as a whole. The position of the church in this regard is well documented in a series of pastoral letters from the Bishops' Conference. Standing in an international tradition of non-racism, and sustained by a theological tradition which affirms the inherent dignity of all human beings in a less qualified manner than in Protestantism, the Roman Catholic Church has proclaimed a message of equality for all. But as the present political demands intensify, requiring the church to accentuate its proclamation of reconciliation and concern for the oppressed, white resistance to this message has also intensified. Obliged to minister to the needs of both black and white members, and trapped within the apartheid structures, the Catholic church fails in praxis to measure up to its own theological ideals of human dignity and that option which requires the church to declare itself to be on the side of the poor and the oppressed.

Yet it is within the imposed institutional unity of blacks and whites in the Roman Catholic Church, as in other non-racial churches, that one senses the reality of a social dimension representative of the mixed social and racial identity of South Africa.

The Lutheran Churches

Like the Roman Catholic Church, the Lutheran and Moravian churches did not come into the forefront of the struggle against the apartheid regime until fairly recently. Ideologically they are located midway between the Afrikaans Reformed churches and the English-speaking churches. Racially divided, they are not burdened by the cumbersome "theology of apartheid" which characterizes the Afrikaans churches. Yet, unlike the English-speaking churches, they have been unable to unite in a single church.

The distinction of providing the first European missionary sent specifically to minister to an indigenous population belongs to the German Churches. In 1738 the Moravian George Schmidt established a mission station at Genadendal to convert the Khoikhoi. He was soon forbidden to administer the sacraments and his work was hindered because his evangelical piety clashed with the Calvinist orthodoxy of the Dutch church. Clearly his work was also seen as a threat to the social life of the settler community; his mission work was closed and he returned to Europe in 1744. It was not until 1792 that the Moravians were allowed to reopen Genadendal, a mission which still exists today as a memorial to Schmidt's work.[32]

The white Lutheran churches were established with the arrival of successive German and Scandinavian settlers. The black Lutheran churches, in turn, emerged as a result of various European and American Lutheran missionary societies, and apart from Schmidt's pioneering work, the emergence and development of the Moravian churches took place along much the same lines.

It took until 1966 for any decisive step toward unity among these churches. In that year the different Lutheran and Moravian churches and synods formed the Federation of Evangelical Lutheran Churches in Southern Africa (FELCSA). But the white churches resisted an attempt to unite black and white Lutheran churches into one united church, and in 1975 four black synods broke away to form the Evangelical Lutheran Church in Southern Africa (ELCSA). With this move the latent racial division within this family of churches became explicit, locating Lutherans neither within the Afrikaans Reformed church family nor within that of the English-speaking churches.

The tension within the Lutheran family of churches came to a head in 1977 with the adoption by the Lutheran World Federation (LWF) of a statement of "Confessional Integrity," calling on white Lutherans to "publicly and unequivocally reject the existing apartheid system" as a matter of confession (*status confessionis*).[33] Then in 1984 the LWF Assembly meeting in Budapest went a step further and suspended the membership of the white Lutheran churches in South Africa and Namibia for their failure to respond positively to the 1977 appeal.[34]

Conservative Evangelical Churches

The word *evangelical* is a cherished one in theological circles. All churches claim this appellation as a necessary part of their self-identity. The group of churches referred to here are those churches which explicitly claim not to be involved in socio-political issues. They argue that it is the task of the church to confine itself to "spiritual matters." With political tensions militating against the unity of all the mainline churches, the numerical growth of these churches, especially among whites, witnesses to the appeal of a religion in the midst of socio-political strife focusing attention on the affairs of a world yet to come.

White Pentecostal and Apostolic churches submit to the existing socio-economic and political order while claiming to separate religion and politics. In so doing they are attracting members from both the Afrikaans Reformed churches and the English-speaking churches who are opposed to the involvement of their respective churches in political affairs. Other churches in this group openly support the apartheid order. Included in this ecclesial group are also "new" charismatic-type churches whose gospel ranges from the offer of material prosperity and social success to a religiosity which provides an escape from the pressure of the prevailing crisis.

However, this group also includes the Baptist churches, some of which have in recent years begun to rediscover a measure of social concern in keeping with their historic Anabaptist and English nonconformist origins. It also includes Pentecostal and Apostolic churches. Some of these, especially black churches within these traditions, are addressing the stubborn realities of racism and oppression in church and state in significant ways. The response by a number of individuals within these churches to the *Kairos Document*, entitled *Evangelical Witness in South Africa*, is but one instance of this development.

Collectively these churches probably constitute the fastest growing ecclesial group in the country. Generally speaking, they do not overtly choose to involve themselves as institutions in the present political crisis. It is this that separates these churches from the ecclesial groups to which reference has already been made. Because they refuse to place political issues high on the agenda of the church, the crisis within the country is not a constitutive part of what it means for members of these churches to be Christians in South Africa at this point in history. In many instances this aspect of life is, in fact, deliberately excluded from theological enquiry. As such, captivity within the racial and economic edifice of apartheid is neither troublesome nor disturbing to those whose self-identity is formed by these churches. It is, however, precisely this that makes these churches important agents in the battle for the soul of the Christians in the white struggle for hegemonic survival.

This group of churches is not theologically, socially, economically or politically homogeneous. It is this which accounts for the internal contradictions within this ecclesial group. The different and at times theologically extraneous agendas of various right-wing religious groups often find fertile ground among these churches. Yet, as indicated, some social groupings within these churches have come to understand the significance of the gospel for the South African conflict in a manner that is as potentially "revolutionary" as that found within any grouping within any of the other churches.

THE CHURCHES IN DIVISION AND AFFINITY

To discern the character of the English-speaking churches in South Africa, it is necessary to locate them within this larger ecclesial matrix. Tolerant and liberal, these churches are influenced by historical processes as well as by their racial and class composition to make certain choices which distinguish them (sometimes quite clearly and at other times less so) from the other churches on the South African scene.

The similarity between the churches is found in their ideological links to specific social and racial groups. The Afrikaans Reformed churches, for example, with exclusive white memberships, and the black churches with predominantly black memberships, each cater to the spiritual needs of the communities of which they are a part, and they are shaped by contexts which happen to be on different sides of the apartheid divide. What ecumenical contact may be experienced across this divide is institutionally limited. The English-speaking churches, on the other hand, are required to relate to the needs of both black and white members at the same time. It is this that locates them at the nexus where all Christians, including those in the exclusively white Afrikaans Reformed churches and the black churches, are obliged to discover the nature of a faith which doctrinally renders all distinctions void. This is what makes the English-speaking churches, as a microcosmic instance of the socio-ethnic composition of the broader South African identity, a focus of important study.

Yet the more the major churches differ because of the constituencies of which they are a part, the clearer is the affinity of values between them. Influenced by their respective memberships and committed, for theological as well as socio-economic factors, to maintaining the unity of their communities, their social function is essentially a moderate and cautious one. Yet deep within their common memory lies a restlessness which disturbs their complacency and obliges them to recall a theological obligation to live justly, to show mercy and humbly to submit to the declared will of God as made known in the scriptures. From within this memory emerges a will that requires the church to show a special concern for widows, orphans, those who are in distress, prisoners, the poor and the oppressed—the marginalized people in any society. It is this that has constituted a disturbing reality in even the most domesticated and self-satisfied churches in history, making for resistance amid conformity.

The question is whether the churches can free themselves (or better stated theologically, be freed!) to realize their declared theological goal of genuine unity, realistic reconciliation and a just society. A related question is whether the Christian church in its contemporary form has the theological and social motivation to realize this goal, and ultimately whether it has the will to realize the biblical imperative to set free the oppressed in the land. Before considering these questions, however, it is necessary to consider the history which has shaped the contemporary nature of the English-speaking churches.

Chapter Two

Imperialists and Missionaries

Perhaps the single most powerful social movement in the encounter between the settlers and the indigenous peoples in South Africa was the replacement of the Dutch by the British as the colonial power in the Cape. A more powerful and dynamic force than the Dutch, pulsating with the energy unleashed by the Industrial Revolution and driven by an imperialist dream, the British used military might to sweep away any obstacle to their goal, whether the Xhosa on the eastern frontier, the Zulu in Natal or the Afrikaner republics in the north.

Within this milieu of colonial expansionism the birth of the English-speaking churches took place. Military might and the acquisition of land historically altered the subcontinent in the name of progress, under the benign protection of God's providence and the Union Jack. It is a little like the story of the chicken and the egg to ask which came first: the missionaries, the traders, the explorers or the military. What can be said with confidence is that the missionary societies and immigrant churches planted in Africa during this period, like all other social institutions, acted as carriers of the social, cultural, economic and political forces of the society of which they were a part, in this case imperial Britain.

It was not, however, entirely a one-way movement; the settler church was also exposed to certain African values. The church socially transformed the proseiytized, but the proselytized, in turn, although to a lesser extent, carried their values into the church. Hence the church became the locus of conflicting values between the colonized and colonizers, and also reflected certain latent conflicts and values derived from the disrupted African society.

IMPERIALIST CONQUERORS OR SERVANTS OF GOD?

The debate on missionary activity in southern Africa is a complex one. There are those who would argue that the missionaries were among the worthy and honorable pioneers who contributed to the quest for social justice in the development of the subcontinent. At worst, the argument goes, they were well-meaning, even if naive and misguided. Others contend that the missionaries were tacit, and on occasion conscious agents of colonial subjugation and apologists for white domination. "Conquerors or Servants of God?" asks Monica Wilson.[1] Still others stress the difference between those missionaries of the London Missionary Society (LMS) who, they argue, championed the cause of the indigenous people against the racial exclusivism of the settlers, and the mission activity of the white Dutch Reformed and Lutheran churches, which tended to overtly promote settler interests. The problem with all these assessments is that they tend to be misleading if not understood in relation to the fact that missionaries, no less than other members of society, were not exempt from the social fabric of their respective communities, and that the churches they represented were an integral part of the socio-economic and political structures of the time.

Any conflict between British missionaries and the white settlers must therefore be assessed in relation to this basic allegiance. Selope Thema observes, for example, that despite their differences, the attitude of both Boer and Brit toward indigenous people was essentially the same. African traditional society, says Thema, "was condemned by both missionaries and colonists as a life of laziness and indolence. They both agreed that the African should be taught the dignity of labour."[2] Indeed James Stewart of Lovedale Mission understood the gospel to be the basis of what he called Christian civilization, linking it to two other gospels: "work and commerce." "The gospel of work," he argued, "does not save souls, but it saves people. . . . Lazy races die or decay. Races that work prosper on earth. The British race, in all its greatest branches, is noted for its restless activity. Its life motto is Work! Work!"[3] John Philip, committed to the well-being of the indigenous people in a more aggressive way than many of his fellow missionaries, found himself as trapped in the ideology of imperialism as many a colonial administrator. Indeed, such is the power of colonial or state structures that even the most worthy of people become its obedient servants. Philip was no exception, and he unabashedly argued that the missionaries were, "by the most exceptional means, extending British interests, British influence and the British empire." Among the tasks of the missionary, he contended, was to "teach them [Africans] industrious habits, and create a demand for British manufactures." And the mission stations, he argued, were "the cheapest and best military posts that a wise government can employ to defend its frontiers against the predatory incursions of savage tribes."[4]

The missionaries were fervently convinced that *the* most important gift they could impart was the gospel. From this, they believed, all else of good and worth would follow. Their gospel, however, was closely linked to the ideology of British colonialism, and what they perceived to be the fruits of the gospel could scarcely be distinguished from the values of the Empire. Their interests may well have been evangelical, but it is difficult to ignore the fact that they shared in promoting imperialist ideals. Being custodians of the religion of the status quo, the missionaries consciously and unconsciously served the prevailing ideology of imperial expansionism. "Conversion," it has been argued, "was . . . the initial phase in the subversion of African societies by Europeans." And Black leadership rejected such activity as treachery, coming to regard "conversion" as instrumental in creating the "psychological basis for a politics of colonialism."[5] *The Christian Express*, mouthpiece of the missionaries at Lovedale, was remarkably explicit in an editorial written in 1878, in defining the social goal of the Christianization process:

> We want to see the natives become workers. . . . And . . .
> we believe Christianity will be a chief cause of their becoming
> a working people. . . .
> How this . . . comes to be is twofold. Christianity creates
> needs. Generally speaking, every man will work just as much

as he requires to do and not more. There will be a constant relation between the time a man works and his necessities. . . . If you want men to work, then, you must get them to need. Create need and you supply stimulus to work; you enlist the worker's own will on the side of labour. Few men anywhere, and certainly no heathen men, ever work for the mere pleasure of working.

Now, the speediest way of creating needs among these people is to Christianise them. As they become Christianised, they will want more clothing, better houses, furniture, books, education for the children, and a hundred other things which they do not have now and never have had. And all these things they can get by working, and only by working.

But Christianity also teaches the duty of working, and denounces idleness as a sin.

So to Christianise a Kaffir is the shortest way, and the surest, to make him put his hand steadily and willingly to the work that is waiting to be done. This will make it both his interest and his duty to work, will enlist, besides his bodily appetites, his home affections, his mental powers, and his conscience, on the side of industrious habits.[6]

Notwithstanding their patriotic fervor, the central dilemma facing the early missionaries was how to minister to the needs and well-being of both the white settlers and the indigenous population at the same time. Clearly the missionaries sought on many occasions to act as the conscience of the settlers by speaking out on behalf of the indigenous people in the struggle for land, human rights and social justice. Yet because of their shared pastoral concern for the well-being of the settlers, commitment to the indigenous population was not unequivocal, and they were accused by discerning black opinion of capitulation to settler demands. With this sense of dual responsibility to both black and white, to both oppressor and oppressed, the die was cast for the internal conflict and compromise which still characterizes the English-speaking churches today.

It is this conflict which causes critical voices both within and without these churches to suggest that by definition these churches cannot unequivocally be on the side of the oppressed. It is further argued that due to a variety of social influences together with a theological propensity to legitimate the rulers of the time, these churches are being absorbed into the established order of white South Africa, offering little more than token protest against the violations of their most fundamental values.

This tendency is illustrated by a brief historical analysis of these churches within the pre-industrial age in this chapter, while the identity of these churches in the early industrial period is considered in the next chapter. As the course of South African history unfolded, contingent on the discovery of diamonds and gold, followed by the inevitable process of industrialization and urbanization, South African whites, English and Afrikaner alike, zealously committed themselves to the institution and maintenance of a politico-economic system which favored white supremacy. When these privileges were threatened, the South African English, despite their membership in non-racial churches, were drawn into an alliance with their white Afrikaner compatriots against the black majority, and against those black persons who constituted the dominant majority in the churches to which they belonged. It is this that causes radical critics of both the "left" and the "right" of the English-speaking churches to dismiss the non-racial image of these churches as a deception. And an increasing number of historians and social critics are coming to recognize that the tensions between the South African English and Afrikaners during the final decades of the last century and the first decades of the twentieth century were essentially squabbles between factions within an emerging broad-based ruling class, over against an exploited and oppressed majority. While the conflict between different white groups has at times emerged in vindictive political clashes, open rebellion and war, history has also shown that in the time of danger, when hearth, home and privilege are attacked, they bury their differences and unite to form a single resisting group. This, it is often said, is the natural and instinctive way for any group under siege to act. And if this is the case, any unity between blacks and whites in the English-speaking churches is necessarily most tenuous.

The Victorian Dream

When Queen Victoria came to the throne in June 1837, the free-trade philosophy of buying cheap and selling dear was well established, imperial expansionism was a reality, and within the wake of these developments British mission work was thriving throughout the empire, not least of all in South Africa.

The LMS, soon to be epitomized by such names as Johannes van der Kemp, James Read, Moffat, John Philip and Livingstone, had begun its work in 1799. In 1813 the Wesleyan Mission Society was established. Barnabas Shaw arrived in 1816, and in 1820 William Shaw, as chaplain to a settler party, initiated mission work that would lead to a chain of mission stations across the eastern frontier. Soon Wesleyan Christianity was entrenched among black people throughout the land. In 1824 the Church of Scotland established the Lovedale Mission, which was to become a formative influence in black education. Robert Gray, the first bishop to the Anglican community established in 1814, arrived in Cape Town in 1848.

It was the arrival of the 1820 English settlers, however, which reinforced the strength of the English-speaking churches and bolstered the Victorian synthesis of God, church and British Empire. In any settler church on the eastern frontier there was, and often still is, the "Union Jack co-existing alongside Cross and Altar, even when tattered and blood-bespattered from encounters with native and Boer in the service of God and Queen."[7] This was the age that saw the British Empire reach unprecedented power which not only subsumed the English-speaking churches in South Africa, but was appropriated and promoted by these churches. Mission education, evangelism and Christian "character-building" took on the values and assumptions of the Victorian era, and few missionaries doubted that the imparting of such values were to the inherent benefit of the proselytized. "Missions," writes Penelope Hetherington, "had seen little or nothing to respect or preserve in Africa, and were guilty of confusing Christianity with Western civilization and even with English social habits."[8] Indeed for some the image of the well-educated, monied English squire or financier who practiced philanthropy and attended church regularly was close to being the epitome of what it meant to be both civilized and Christian. Technological development, literacy, political sophistication and the supremacy of the British military all seemed to point demonstrably and objectively to the superiority of Western civilization. This was the era in which free enterprise had created a modern and industrialized England, and the benefits of this system were being widely extolled. It also produced conditions of grave oppression and new class structures every bit as exploitative as feudalism.

Many of the settlers had left Britain to escape the gravity of such industrial degradation. Given a "second chance" to make it within the new economic order—to "take root and grow"—with "restless energy" and "rugged individualism" they did precisely that.[9] For the more industrious settlers the sky seemed the limit, and philanthropists, missionaries and evangelists advocated clean living, hard work, and moral righteousness as a formula to the African indigenous population to overcome what most of the settlers believed to be the inherent inferiority of traditional African spiritual and material values. Even the enlightened William Wilberforce, addressing the House of Commons during the early 1800s, spoke of the need for Christian missionaries to raise "the heathen," and elevate the indigenous people "out of their present degraded state to the just level of their nature," freed from their gods which he described as "absolute monsters of lust, injustice, wickedness and cruelty."[10] For the practical-minded missionaries it was essentially "the gospel of work" that provided the means to this end, and this missionary-induced "work ethic" helped provide the vital spark igniting the emerging productive system at first in rural areas and then in the urban areas of colonized lands. It was an ethic hammered out and implemented in collusion with the colonial administrators and traders. One consequence was political legislation and economic controls designed to ensure a form of economic development made possible by the systematic exclusion of blacks from the benefits of the industrialized capitalist system. At the same time it involved the breakdown of traditional African social customs, subsistence farming and the loss of land and political power by African chiefs. In a word, for blacks the gospel went hand in hand with hard work, urbanization, exploitative labor, the lure of elusive material prosperity, and the loss of cultural identity and political power. For missionaries, a vested interest in preaching the gospel went hand in hand with their support for British hegemony. Missionary conquest was dependent on imperial protection, making missionaries both conscious and unconscious agents, along with traders, soldiers and imperial administrators, of the British domination.

Land and Taxes

In many ways it was Christmas Eve 1834, when twelve thousand Xhosa poured across the Fish River that fundamentally shaped the attitude of the English settlers toward the indigenous population. The Xhosa were fighting for their survival as a people, taking reprisal for being expelled from their land by colonial jurisdiction, which had assigned them to the eastern side of the river. This resistance was repelled by the settlers, and war brought to a head the direct clash of purpose and ideology between the indigenous and settler peoples. Any measure of cordiality or understanding that may formerly have existed between the two groups was gone.[11] Attempts by the missionaries to mediate were rejected, their philanthropic endeavors brushed aside, and slowly the missionaries' sense of goodwill toward the blacks deteriorated under the influence of an increasingly harsh colonial frontier policy. Two dimensions of this policy that became formative not only for the missionary response but also for the future social and economic placing of blacks within the settler-dominated social reality of the time were *land* and *taxes*.

Land meant survival itself to the Xhosa insofar as it meant cattle and cattle meant wealth, but it also formed an inherent part of their social structure. Land also meant agriculture, hunting and political power. The loss of land meant the loss of political identity and social cohesion.

The demand for more land by frontier farmers found common cause not only with the official colonial desire to dominate the Xhosa but also with the concern of missionaries to liberate the indigenous people from what the missionaries perceived as the reactionary power of chief and tribe, while exposing blacks to the "benefits" of western values and skills. With this the colonial settler-missionary syndrome came into its own. Historians writing from different perspectives tell the story differently. De Kiewiet, always favorable toward the missionaries, describes the syndrome as the "unintentional collusion" between the humanitarian desire of missionaries and some others, with the selfish, exploitative motives of others.[12] However altruistically conceived by liberal historians, the outcome was the same; black people were squeezed out of their traditional pattern of living and made dependent on the colonial economic system. The experience of the Zulu in Natal was little different, and the role of Governor Theophilus Shepstone in this regard is today readily acknowledged. "Quite simply he betrayed Cetshwayo in an effort to win support from the Transvaal Boers. The Zulu were conquered and annexed, subsequently they were divided against themselves, and then their land was parcelled out to covetous Natal colonists, leaving the Zulu with approximately one-third of their traditional lands."[13] Dispossessed black people meant a cheap supply of labor for settler farmers; for the colonial powers it meant the systematic destruction of rival political powers; and for the missionaries it meant the opportunity to incorporate such people into mission stations, arguing that this afforded them a measure of freedom from the restrictive influences of the chiefs.

> A system of individual land tenure would in their [the missionaries'] judgment do more than any other single innovation to disrupt the reactionary power of chief and tribe, and free the individual to expand the latent moral and economic powers which tribal discipline had held in thraldom. Only a small-hearted prejudice would refuse to recognize the liberal thought and generous intention that sponsored the system of individual land-holding in the Cape Colony. Yet the policy was not incompatible with a determination that as a reform it should not obstruct the flow of native labour. It was such a determination that ultimately robbed the policy of much of its value by withholding from it the additional land without which it could not be truly successful.[14]

De Kiewiet shows further that the land allotted on individual tenure in terms of the Glen Grey Act of 1894 was never intended as the sole means of family support. It was assumed that the women would cultivate the land while men labored elsewhere, and soon many of those eligible for individual tenure were laboring on white farms in return for squatting rights and a small monetary reward roughly equivalent to the government hut tax. Cochrane, in turn, shows that the demands made on blacks incorporated into mission farms and other enterprises were even more exacting than those of the farmers. "Besides taxes to the state, tithes were usually required for church buildings, educational facilities, ploughs, new seed, symmetrically constructed villages, and European clothes."[15] Lacking the sense of corporate responsibility and decision-making as practiced in the tribal system from which they had been removed, and at the same time motivated by the missionaries' inculcated sense of individual reward, many left these farms for more lucrative rewards in the form of wages on the labor market.

Whatever the complexity of causes involved, and in spite of the motives involved, the consequence was obvious. The traditional, communal, pastoral structure of African life was, for better or for worse, giving way to a dependent African peasantry and rural proletariat compelled to look to white bosses and ecclesiastical benefactors for survival. The acquisition of manufactured goods became the accepted mark of civilization and progress, often to the neglect of a sound economic and political infrastructure as a basis for self-reliance and esteem.

Little is to be gained in the search for motives and intent. It is enough to note that the missionaries seldom stopped to question their own values, the long-term effect of their endeavors, or to take seriously the African voices of protest. Cochrane sums up the milieu helpfully: "Missionary enterprise, remaining always beyond radical self-criticism, could do no other than transmit the values and structures embodied in British imperial colonialist expansion without sufficient awareness to distinguish firmly between what was intrinsically worthwhile and what could lead to long-term destructive consequences for precisely those people whom they believed themselves to be championing."[16]

The other major contribution to the emerging socio-economic place of the black population in the broader structuring of the country was the imposition of a wide-ranging tax structure. The "native taxation" was an important part of the more general taxation and economic policy of the time. The Immigration Board's efforts to bring white settlers to the British colonies of the Cape and Natal were being hampered by a scarcity of land, while at the same time landowners were resisting higher taxes. The story of "native taxation" cannot be fully understood without remembering this, for in part this taxation was a device to avoid heavier land taxes. At the same time it was presented as a device to release the labor force imprisoned in the tribal organization. Imported goods intended for blacks were taxed at a higher rate than those goods intended for the white settlers, while the total package of "native taxation" was wide ranging. There were hut taxes, marriage taxes, labor taxes on the unemployed and a poll tax. Few of the realized profits were returned to the blacks in the form of services.[17] When one takes into account that missionaries cooperated with the colonial authorities in collecting taxes and in other aspects of the economic hegemonic process, it is not possible to exonerate the missionary enterprise from the process of subjugating the black people.

There is, of course, another aspect to the story of the role played by the churches in the development of the country. This is the story of the establishment of hospitals, social services and schools. This cannot be denied and ought not to be belittled. What is argued here, however, is that the churches shared in the sustained destruction of African traditional society, while failing to integrate those whom they estranged into the full benefits of Western industrialized society. In this sense they were, at times quite deliberately and at times by default, part of the colonial process which specifically marginalized Africans in the burgeoning economy of the time. A more radical interpretation suggests that they were part of a systematic program designed for "underdeveloping Africa."[18] Those adhering to this position identify a direct link between the spread of colonialism and communal poverty, suggesting that during this period poverty in Africa increased rather than diminished and disease increased rather than diminished (citing the emergence of newly-introduced diseases like tuberculosis and venereal infections with hospitals being unable to contain these diseases, and mission stations failing to cope with the effects of malnutrition).

Missionary education has generated a great deal of debate, but it cannot be adequately understood apart from a definite shift in educational policy which occurred at places like Lovedale and Zonnebloem in the latter part of the 1860s. Earlier policy prescribed a classical curriculum which included Latin, Greek, English and at least one additional modern European language, as well as science and mathematics, in addition to an industrial education. The shift in the 1860s was away from the classics to a more general and practical education aimed at a broader cross section of the community.

At Lovedale, for example, this transition took place in 1869 when Dr. James Stewart replaced Dr. Alexander Duff as principal of the Lovedale Missionary Institute. The emphasis in the seminary was changed with a view to producing black preachers and teachers equipped to meet "the wants and conditions of Africans," many of whom "were wholly illiterate." In the elementary and secondary schools the emphasis shifted from a classical curriculum designed for equivalent schools in Scotland to instruction in the vernacular tongue with as adequate an understanding of English "as possible."[19]

Janet Hodgson shows how Zonnebloem College in Cape Town was established in 1858 to provide an education for an African elite. A primary aim was to separate the sons of chiefs from the "heathen and barbarous" influences of their traditional culture and equip them as enlightened (and anglicized) leaders of the future. A change came, however, with the Education Act of 1865. Frontier educational institutions provided comparable facilities, and Zonnebloem was compelled to draw its student body from a wider constituency. In the process its character changed significantly. Despite the gross limitations of an earlier elitism, the changes opened the way for a very different kind of mission education. In 1877 Dr. Langham Dale, the Superintendent General of Education, epitomized the shift in a cynical observation: The "kid-glove era" at Zonnebloem, he observed, had come to an end and "the saw, plane, hammer and spade had taken its place."[20]

Mission schools had, of course, always been of a mixed quality, and after the change in policy this difference continued to be manifest. There were the more successful schools, such as Lovedale, Adam's College, Healdtown and St. Peter's, but there were also others. Control of schools was often heavy-handed, paternalistic and rejected by black leaders as a means of promoting Western values and desires. It was only with the collapse of traditional African societies that mission education began to be sought instead of shunned. The kind of education provided by the missions also varied from elitist to basic literacy and industrial or manual education—which included cleaning gardens and repairing roads —equipping blacks to perform subservient tasks in the emerging new society.[21] To this discussion we return in chapter 5. It is enough to indicate here that the glorification of mission education in liberal circles is not substantiated by careful analysis. By far the majority of black children received no education at all, petitions were sent to the authorities from some school situations asking for state intervention, and the role of mission schools in the planned subversion of African power and the destruction of traditional values is yet to be considered.

THE ROLE OF THE MISSIONARIES

When one asks the inevitable questions concerning the social function of the missionaries in the struggle between blacks and whites for hegemony in the nineteenth and early twentieth centuries, and the discontinuity between a traditional African subsistence economy and imperial capitalism, certain dominant attitudes are discernible.

First, it is clear that the English missionaries had little doubt concerning the superiority of their culture, and from a Western perspective their values and resources were superior. There is a narrow line, however, between a regard for the virtues of one's own religion and civilization and a disregard for the values and achievements of others. It was this latter attitude which caused missionaries to dismiss the African way of life as evidence of religious and cultural depravity; it was to be replaced by their gospel and their civilization. Converting souls to Christ meant, for missionaries, a complete rejection on the part of blacks of the African worldview and a denial of traditional social custom. They sought to replace, argues Elphick, what they perceived to be the "false consciousness" of the indigenous people with "true consciousness" ensuring that the "old order" would give way to a "new order." A result was that "the kraal was becoming the scene of disagreement, of arguments, of indecision, where authority for patterned behavior was lost."[22] It was this kind of systematic disintegration of culture and political cohesion which was probably the most destructive function performed by the missionaries in Africa. They "condemned African customs and institutions and taught the social norms of nineteenth-century Europe as though these crystallized a moral code of universal validity."[23] Ancestor veneration, polygamy and tribal solidarity were condemned by the missionaries, and converts were obliged to turn their backs on the corporate responsibility inherent in each of these cornerstones of African society. Near blind allegiance to a belief in the superiority of imperial culture resulted in their imperial mission acquiring a soteriological character. Lincoln, for example, suggests:

> Colonial expansion is . . . cast as an altruistic crusade, bringing hope of salvation to those otherwise irrevocably lost. . . . Salvation is thus presented as an exclusive club, admission to which is European-controlled. . . . We see an ideology that serves the interests of the dominant party, spread by an institution that the dominant party supports, and this [is] . . . the hallmark of the religion of the status quo.[24]

Missionary "superiority" of this kind systematically changed an independent black peasantry bound together in tribal cohesion into a dependent proletariat. Trapped within the colonial-capitalist ideal, the missionaries' sense of religious and cultural superiority also left them quite indifferent to African religious ideas. Methodist missionary Samuel Broadbent, working among the Barolong people, spoke of the latter's "gross ignorance of spiritual subjects" and concluded that "they had literally no God; and having had no intercourse with the colony, they had no knowledge of God."[25] Robert Moffat of the LMS came to similar conclusions arguing that "a profound silence reigns on this awful subject" of salvation and God, requiring the missionaries "to prepare for the gracious distribution of the waters of salvation in that desert soil, sowing the seed of the word, breathing many a prayer, and shedding many a tear, till the Spirit of God should cause it to vegetate, and yield the fruits of righteousness."[26] So uncompromising was the missionary attitude on such matters that P.W. Harrison, writing in the early 1900s, was constrained to redress this wrong: "Missionary work," he told his colleagues, "is no enterprise of pity in which we of the smug and self-satisfied West take a superior religion, and hand it down to poor miserable and degraded heathens."[27]

The imposition of Western religion and culture caused black converts to be torn out of their traditional social structure and left to hover between two religions and two social systems. Black converts would at times imitate the habits of the missionaries, thrusting aside their own customs as vestiges of their former ways of darkness. If "white" and "Western" were to be aspired after as inseparable parts of the gospel, "black" and "African" values were to be despised and rejected. This cultural assimilation of blacks imposed an aura of whiteness on the missionary churches which still hovers over the English-speaking churches like an albatross. Desmond Tutu sums up the dilemma emerging from the cultural arrogance of the missionaries, while pointing to the remarkable persistence of "Africanness," in saying that they "consciously or unconsciously sought to Europeanize us before they could Christianize us. . . . Christianity has failed to be rooted sufficiently deeply in the African soil, since [Western Christians] have tended to make us somewhat uneasy and guilty about what we could not alter even if we tried till doomsday—our Africanness."[28] Locked into their own sense of superiority, the missionaries were simply not able to distinguish between the message of the gospel and the cultural baggage of imperialism, and the English-speaking churches continue to show a reluctance to engage with Africa in a serious manner, leaving many African Christians ambivalent about their Africanness.

The social function of missionaries in the transition from one culture to another is further discernible in a second characteristic directly related to cultural superiority. This concerns social *paternalism*, which motivated many an imperialist and not a few missionaries. Peter Hinchliff points to a particular form of this paternalism at the center of the missionary structures of the churches. It had to do with the ecclesiastical authorities in England being of a different social class and, as a rule, enjoying a higher education than the rank-and-file missionaries sent to the colonies. The result was the imposition of the English structures onto the emerging African church, with missionaries in the field being treated with firm, benevolent paternalism by their superiors at home. The missionaries were obliged to account for every decision made and every item of expense incurred. The outcome was that when missionaries dealt with their black converts, they tended to respond to them with the same paternalism prevalent in stratified British society. When indigenous leaders and ministers began to emerge, they were treated in the familiar paternalistic manner, and in turn learned that this was the manner in which they were to treat their parishioners. Hence an authoritarian and paternalistic ecclesial structure emerged which relegated the "ordinary" grass-root members to a servile status requiring social submission. "My own view," says Hinchliff, "is that it was this paternalism, developed originally by the English churches with regard to their own missionaries which rubbed off, as it were, on the whole colonial church."[29] It was partly this condescending attitude toward the indigenous people, together with concomitant forms of nationalism, which led to the establishment of the Ethiopian Order within the Anglican Church, and the emergence of a large number of African Independent Churches.

A third feature of the emerging English-speaking missionary churches in South Africa was the sense of missionary *deference to civil authority*. The Anglican Church was the state church in England, and in the British colonies of the Cape and Natal it was the church of the government, showing political support for and conformity to the status quo, at least until the time of political union between the British colonies and the Boer Republics in 1910.[30] In spite of Methodist involvement in the causes of the working class in England, Methodists tended, with the notable exception of trade union activity, not to be involved as an institution in political affairs. In nineteenth-century southern Africa they were not actively engaged in political dissent. When John Ayliff was in conflict with the Grahamstown magistrate about chaplains visiting prisons, he was told by his superiors in the Methodist Church that "preachers have been tried before conference for saying so much."[31] Yet, it is also clear that Ayliff worked in active cooperation with the authorities to impose their "native policy," while William Shaw, the superintendent of the Wesleyan Mission, was instrumental in depriving the Basuto chief Moshesh of parts of his land.[32] Scottish missionaries similarly abstained from overt critique of the government.

Hinchliff argues that the one exception to this deference was the LMS missionaries who, he suggests, were acting in keeping with their nonconformist heritage in responding with less submission to the authorities. Certainly van der Kemp, Philip and others laid the blame for racial friction and the frontier wars to the account of the settlers. And there is much evidence to support their good intentions. Johannes van der Kemp had, for example, intended to work among the Xhosa but turned to assist the Khoikhoi only because he perceived their immediate needs to be so much greater. The advance of the colonists had reduced them to a most miserable condition. They found themselves either landless wanderers or near-slaves on settler farms. The need van der Kemp witnessed was socio-economic not evangelical, and he committed himself to strive for the political and economic rights of the oppressed. The settlement established at Bethelsdorp was intended to give the Khoikhoi a measure of economic independence from the settlers and to ensure their economic advancement. The acrimony he engendered among the colonists, in turn, needs to be attributed to his apparent success in diverting their labor market and the poignancy of his contention that the Khoikhoi had the same rights as the settlers. Seeking to locate himself on the side of the oppressed, he found himself locked in conflict with the Dutch governor, Janssens, writing: "I could not forbear to warn him of the displeasure of God who most certainly would hear the cries of the oppressed."[33]

John Philip found himself every bit as unpopular with the white community as van der Kemp. Fellow LMS missionary Robert Moffat criticized him for being too political. He was drawn into controversy with the Wesleyan missionaries, and more particularly William Shaw, for similar reasons. Philip argued that it was the task of the missionary to "defend the weak against the strong," which the Wesleyans realized meant taking sides between blacks and whites. It could even mean missionaries "placing themselves at the head of one of the contending parties." To be partisan, the Wesleyans argued, would mean they could not become mediators.[34]

The Philip vs. Shaw conflict, of course, anticipates a similar debate which racks the English-speaking churches still today. For some a ministry of "reconciliation" means standing apart from and above a particular conflict, for others it involves participation in the struggle, showing solidarity with the oppressed in their struggle for liberation, knowing that reconciliation can only be negotiated from a basis of social equality.[35] The Wesleyan mission-aries were partisan when the issue involved defending the political rights of a chief with Methodist sympathies against one who failed to show such sympathy. They objected, however, when Philip extended such attitudes to black-white conflicts, and when such partisanship involved them in a consistent social location against the dominant power of the Empire.[36]

Despite the concern of van der Kemp and Philip for the weak in their conflict with the strong, there is little evidence to suggest that they were any less enamored with the virtues of imperialism than some other missionaries. To fail to allow for this conflict within the most dedicated missionaries is to fail to understand the pathos of the early missionary movement. It is a pathos that finds the noblest of missionaries rejected by their own colleagues and churches and trapped within the very structures which those whom they sought to help needed to overcome. Majeke, for example, shows that while Philip promoted the cause of the indigenous population, it was always within a presupposed feudal relationship to the settlers: he remained unswervingly loyal to imperial economic interests. Philip is quoted as arguing that in "adopting a more liberal . . . policy" the African population would not only be more productive and become a better market for British goods, but that "taxes will be paid and the farmers will have no cause to complain of a lack of labour." In a similar way van der Kemp is shown to have cooperated with the authorities in using the Bethelsdorp Mission Station to lure Khoikhoi people away from the rebellion led by Klaas Stuurman. He also provided a military outpost in the war against Ndlambe's Xhosa, collected taxes for the government, and organized a flow of labor for the farmers in his region.[37] Uzoigwe, in turn, shows how Moffat, who became assistant commissioner for what was then Bechuanaland, assisted Cecil John Rhodes in persuading Lobengula, the hitherto uncooperative chief of the Ndebele, to sign documents forbidding him to enter into treaty obligations with any other foreign powers and to cede the mineral rights on his land to Rhodes.[38] It was on the basis of this agreement that Rhodes eventually occupied Mashonaland, Lobengula was driven into the wilderness and in spite of a regrouping of the forces of the Ndebele and Shona in 1896, the Matabele kingdom was effectively destroyed. The long rule of white supremacy in what was to be known as Rhodesia had begun and was to last until the birth of an independent Zimbabwe in 1980.

It would be quite wrong to suggest that through their involvement in imperialist designs these missionaries were not committed to their *evangelical* task. On the contrary, it can be argued that it was a romantic and naive understanding of evangelism as the immediate answer to all socio-economic and political problems which prevented the missionaries from grasping the full reality of the biblical doctrine of salvation, making them the functionaries of British colonialism. It has already been shown that for the missionaries evangelical conversion was subsumed into the imperial socio-economic and political transformation process. Uzoigwe shows that even those political protests in which the missionaries were engaged were usually motivated out of fear that government policy toward the indigenous people would hamper their evangelical task.[39] And Hetherington concurs, showing that "many missionaries believed that the future stability of their societies, and the ultimate success of their work of evangelization depended on more positive action by the British government to prevent exploitation in Africa."[40] In similar vein it could also be argued that the social services provided by the different missions in the form of hospitals and schooling were not provided in a disinterested manner. Such services provided a context for evangelization and were at times quite deliberately and exploitatively used to this end.

What the missionaries provided was a buffer between the implementation of imperial demands and the disintegrating tribal society, making the transition for Africans caught in the trajectory of imperial politics a little easier. The missionaries needed the support of the government to succeed in their work, and the government, in spite of periodic quarrels with the missionaries, soon realized that the missionaries were essentially allies in their cause, able to act as intermediaries, motivating blacks to play their part in the emerging economic order and incorporating them into the social milieu of the Empire.

The impact of this interdependency only strikes home when one considers the extent of direct missionary involvement in the subjection of African chiefdoms. This was achieved both by indirect and direct involvement in military action against the indigenous tribes, and also by participating in the process of dividing the territory of the chiefs into magisterial districts within which the local chiefs were subordinated to the magistrate. Missionaries functioned both as intermediaries in this process and often as agents of the cause.

Knowing that the success of their proselytization was largely dependent on the break-up of the traditional social structure of

African society, missionaries became part of the process which destroyed African political power in the region. African chiefs particularly resented, for example, the missionary practice of dividing their people into "converts" (*Kholwa*) and "heathens," which contributed toward breaking down the cohesion of the tribe and the traditional structures of authority. Not only, in the words of Colenso, did missionary demands "fill their whole tribe with anarchy and confusion," but chiefs could no longer count on those of their subjects who were converted to obey their commands or show loyalty in time of crisis or war.[41] Yet once the collapse of tribal cohesion was a reality, whether due to attacks from other tribes, forced migration or the deliberate disruption of tribal existence by the imperial administration, missionaries were often welcomed to assist with the necessary transition to the emerging new order.[42] The problem is that having facilitated the disintegration of the old order, the missionaries could not provide the necessary resources to integrate blacks into the new order.

This ambiguous role of the missionaries notwithstanding, some did act as the conscience of the settlers. For all the connivance between missions and government, missionaries have been "notorious in South African history for their interfering ways."[43] To quote Welsh: "However much the settlers might rant and rave and vilify the missionaries, they could not ignore them, and they were forced to try to justify their conduct in the light of the values which the missionaries held."[44] Bishop John Colenso, for example, stood firm in his fight to secure justice for blacks in Natal. There were, however, many missionaries who did not act as the conscience of the settler community. Colenso's condemnation of the Anglo-Zulu war of 1879 was in stark contrast to the intelligence work on the Zulu undertaken by some missionaries for the British forces and administration, and he also stood alone in condemning vengeance in the wake of the British defeat at Isandhlwana.[45] He insisted that the Anglican church (the Church of the Province of South Africa) maintain the closest possible ties with the Church of England as the state church in England, and that the Church of England in South Africa which emerged as a result of his conflict with Bishop Robert Gray be inherently tied to the Church of England. This position revealed both his ecclesial loyalty and his essential political allegiance. He never failed, however, to criticize many of the actions of the military and government, and it was this that ultimately cost him the support and friendship of the leading Natal official, Theophilus Shepstone.[46] In the eastern Cape, William Shaw in turn appealed to the stated values of the settlers, relating these to their new environment and reminding them that "they came from a land of freedom . . . and that they had learned there personal liberty is the birthright of every man."[47] Yet he too, as already indicated, worked in direct cooperation with the imperial administration. The missionaries were the conscience of settlers and administrators alike, but always a conscience operating within the accepted structure of colonial domination.

To be the conscience of the state is an accepted part of the self-understanding of the English-speaking churches. From the earliest days the representatives of these churches sought to be this conscience, although with moderation, neither harsh nor rigorous. This, if for no other reason than that they were trapped into the very structures they sought to redeem.

The conscientizing role of the English-speaking churches within this period, always cautious and inevitably within the framework of their imperial loyalties, becomes most clear in the Anglo-Boer War at the turn of the century. *Some* English-speaking clergy and missionaries intervened as the conscience of the British, both with regard to the cause of the Boers and with regard to counselling blacks to have no part of the war. The major preoccupation, however, was British supremacy, and the English clergy and missionaries were as imperialist in outlook as most other colonists. Cuthbertson argues that in this instance it was the LMS which did most to generate the myth that the Anglo-Boer War was waged on behalf of the black population. Even John Moffat, who championed African interest during the war, insisted that most important was "the preservation of British influence and civilization in South Africa."[48] It took Hobson, writing in the *British Weekly*, to make the point which the missionaries failed to comprehend:

> Let those who believe that this war is going to result in benefit to the natives read the avowals of native policy made by leading capitalists of the Rand, expressing their intention to reduce Kaffir wages, and to introduce hut and labour taxes,

in order to compel natives to offer large quantities of labour to mining companies.[49]

When the war was over some clerics saw fit to advocate that the former republics be returned to the Boers but saw no reason to support black participation in the affairs of government. And during the war missionaries who felt constrained to vacate their stations when war broke out in 1899 often became chaplains to the British forces, reinforcing the popular imperial myth that the war against the Boer forces was the "Lord's battle," fought by the "soldiers of Christ," with the aim of bringing "glory to his name."[50]

Despite the perception of white missionaries and clerics that the war was being fought "on the behalf of black people," black discontent within the English-speaking churches manifested itself throughout this period in the rise of Ethiopianism and other separatist independent black churches. The church synod and assembly records both during the war and after the cessation of hostilities show that the English-speaking churches were more concerned about these divisions than they were about the number of blacks killed in the war or the number of Boer women and children who died in British concentration camps.

Despite the cautious and reluctant engagement of the English-speaking churches in the politics of the post-war period, a significant number of black Christians within these churches, both clerical and lay, exercised a pre-eminent influence in the South African Native National Congress (SANNC) (later to change its name to the African National Congress) from the time of its inception in 1912 until its banning in 1960.

Hinchliff sums up the socio-political function of the English-speaking churches in the late nineteenth century and the early 1900s by identifying a tension "between the duty to obey the powers that are because stable civilization is a good thing, and the duty to be critical of both government and society because of the need to act as the nation's conscience."[51] What these churches refused to do was to ask the question that would strike at the fragile unity between their white and black members—whether the de facto government of the day was a morally and theologically legitimate government capable of providing the kind of stability required. Or was it that the captivity of the English-speaking churches within the imperial dream rendered them incapable of posing this question?

This captivity would be reshaped but also intensified with the discovery of gold on the Witwatersrand, and it is necessary to consider the role of the English-speaking churches in relation to the political and economic development within the early industrial period. To this we now turn.

Chapter Three

Gold, Politics, and the Churches

In the previous chapter it was argued that the imposition of the imperial free market system on the South African region was among the more important factors which shaped and redrew the demographic map of the area while formatively determining the character of the English-speaking churches. In this chapter it is shown that the discovery of gold on the Witwatersrand during the latter part of the century was the dominant factor in the socio-economic and political identity of the region, and a factor which further shaped the identity of the English-speaking churches.

The 1886 gold rush was significantly different from similar stampedes for wealth in other parts of the world in one respect. In order to mine this gold it was necessary to penetrate layers of rock and sink vertical shafts into the subterranean depths of the earth. The scene has been sketched as follows:

> Imagine a solid mass of rock tilted . . . like a fat 1,200 page dictionary lying at an angle. The gold-bearing reef would be thinner than a single page, and the amount of gold contained therein would hardly cover a couple of commas in a book.[1]

Although extensive, the reefs were deep in the bowels of the earth and the gold-ore was of a low quality, demanding a massive deep-level mining industry. Capital was needed, labor had to be found, and the cost restraints associated with an internationally fixed gold price had to be met. A consequence was the generation of wealth and its distribution in a highly uneven manner. Industrialization and urbanization produced an array of social and political problems, with racial and economic solutions being proposed which entrenched the black population in a dependent and vassal role. This led to intensified racial and social stratification in South Africa, and provided a firm foundation for the eventual emergence of the apartheid system. Shaped by these forces, the church would be trapped in a socio-economic system which contradicted its own theological identity.

It would be wrong to romanticize pre-industrial African society. It had egalitarian features, but political and economic differences were manifest between the chiefs and the people, between different groups among the people, between men and women, and between generations. It would, in turn, be disparaging to regard traditional African society as static and incapable of generating change from within, and evidence suggests that African pre-industrial society was interrupted by colonial forces at a time of crucial transition and expansionism. Be this as it may, colonial dispossession and incorporation into an emerging capitalist economy was clearly not imposed onto an idyllic, homogeneous society—and many blacks found some of the qualities of the capitalist-imperialist alternative more attractive than those of their traditional societies. It would, however, be categorically wrong to regard British imperialism as distinctively humanitarian. There was little benefit derived by blacks from a policy of trusteeship and protectionism. Indeed, whites gained both economically and politically from the effects of colonial intervention, and indigenous societies suffered. In time the dual loyalty of the missionaries to both settler and black interests began to crumble under the impact of South Africa's industrial revolution. It was a period in which the English settlers came to regard their future best served by an alliance with the Afrikaner population rather than with blacks, an impact that would be felt throughout the church.

INDUSTRIAL SOCIETY

If issues of land and taxes determined the socio-economic place of blacks in pre-industrial colonialism, it was the intensified emphasis on these factors in the period following the discovery of gold that deepened the gulf between whites and blacks. The focus of the confrontation between the races had shifted from the frontier to the mining towns, where the major requirement of the newly-founded deep-level mines was labor, plenty of it, as cheaply supplied as possible. This, concisely stated, became the issue around which pass laws, job reservation and other laws anticipating the modern panoply of apartheid laws emerged. These laws included the notorious Land Act of 1913 which assigned 13 percent of the total land area in the country to blacks for permanent residence.

The essential background to this process was the demand for maximum profits coupled with a fixed gold price. The only solution seemed to be minimal labor costs. Skilled labor which was imported largely from Britain, amounting (in 1898) to 11 percent of the 93,000 labor force, was essential but expensive.[2] These white workers in fact absorbed half the wage bill, but pragmatic factors prevented any reduction in size or confrontation with this constituency of workers for the present. The mine owners needed the political support of the *uitlanders* (immigrant workers) in their own conflict with the administration of the Boer Republic in the Transvaal. Confrontation with the white workers would come later, but by then other factors would be operative. The immediate solution was to cut black wages, remove any possibility of competition for labor among employers, and ensure a steady flow of black workers to the mines. The divide between black and white workers was impassible. This story is found in many other sources, and need only be briefly outlined here.[3]

The ground had been prepared in the pre-industrial period by tax and land laws to ensure the availability of black labor—black subsistence farmers and peasants, many having left the mission farms. Others unable to pay taxes and attracted by the lure of riches flocked to the mines. Yet still more labor was needed. "We must have labor," contended the President of the Chamber of Mines established in 1887, a year after the discovery of gold on the Reef. "The mining industry without labour is as bricks would be without straw or as it would be to imagine you could get milk without cows."[4] The way to obtain labor had already been tried and tested. It had to do with imposing taxes and possessing land.

The complete implementation of this strategy, however, did not get systematically underway until after the Anglo-Boer War (1899-1902), a war grounded in economic aggression, that marked the high-water mark of British imperialism. "The laws that made Africans into helots," says Thomas Pakenham, "were now to be applied with an efficiency that the Boers had never been able to muster."[5] The British tightened up bureaucratic controls over blacks on the Witwatersrand, refusing to grant any political rights to blacks in the defeated Boer republics. The Chamber of Mines was assigned the task of organizing the recruitment of labor and of taking "active steps for the gradual reduction of native wages to a reasonable level."[6] Lord Milner's eleven-member Lagden Commission met from 1902-1905 and produced a report on black labor which, in the words of a conservative imperial journal, strongly favored the interests of "well-to-do land and mine owners, representatives of an acquisitive society hardened by pioneering experience and eager for economic development."[7] The Native Recruitment Corporation was established in 1912 to ensure non-competitive and regular supplies of labor from the "native reserves" at a fixed wage and under contract, which prevented workers from leaving the mines to sell their labor elsewhere. The 1913 Land Act followed, and African breadwinners were compelled to look to the mines for employment as migrant workers. At the same time a variety of complementary laws and practices ranging from pass laws to reduced wages were imposed on black workers to ensure the smooth running of the system.

There was, of course, protest against these practices by the workers. Working conditions were poor and dangerous, workers resented the long and restricting contracts demanded by the mines, and wages were low, especially after a reduction of wages in 1902 and subsequent years. The only avenue of protest open to blacks was for them to withhold their labor, a policy which the mine owners tried to overcome by replacing the former with Chinese workers. The Chinese workers were, however, also discontented with the low wages and conditions. The "experiment" failed and the workers were eventually repatriated to China. In the meantime black wages dropped still further, conditions on the reserves deteriorated further, other industries offered working conditions that were no better than those of the mines, and black migrant workers were compelled to continue to rely on the mines for the larger part of their meager income.

Another area of defeat for black unskilled workers came from the actions of skilled white miners who established unofficial trade unions and involved themselves in political parties to protect themselves against the actions of mine owners who employed unskilled and semi-skilled workers (many of whom were Afrikaners) at lower wages in "skilled" positions. In an attempt to counter white labor dissatisfaction and meet its growing demands, the government passed the 1911 Mines and Works Act, reserving thirty-two areas of employment for whites. And when further conflict between white miners and mine owners resulted in the 1913 strike, the government again intervened. White trade unions were officially recognized, and the first steps toward a closer working relationship among management, government and white workers were taken; strikes by black miners did not enjoy the same response from either management or government. The 1914-1918 war was followed by further mine management attempts to negotiate with white unions as a result of further demands being made on the state and industry by returning soldiers. Black workers were, in turn, gradually being drawn into the hitherto rather elitist membership of the ANC, and the ground was being prepared for a new phase in black-white conflict. At the same time black resistance emerged in rural areas, and a series of strikes and protests against pass laws occurred in the cities. It was a period which saw "the largest number of workers on strike in South Africa's entire history."[8] The concern of the Chamber of Mines was essentially with white miners, however, and more especially with the breakdown of union-management negotiations which led to the 1922 strike. Fighting broke out between the striking white miners and the police, and the Prime Minister, General J. C. Smuts, called in the army and the air force to quell the fighting.

Rejected by both Afrikaner and English workers for its support of capitalism and management, the Smuts government was defeated in the subsequent 1924 general election. The Pact government of the Afrikaner National Party and the Labour Party supported by English-speaking workers came to power with Colonel Creswell (leading the Labour Party) and former Boer general J. B. M. Hertzog (the Nationalist leader) agreeing that the greatest danger facing South Africa was "big finance."[9] The English were a minority without any hopes of significant immigration after Union to tip the scales numerically in their favor, and Milner's aggressive attempt to Anglicize Afrikaners had failed. Their only other option was to throw in their lot with black workers, but that was for them no option at all. The privileged position of white workers was enough to convince them of that. Afrikaner workers were thrust reluctantly into the industrial age with many of them constituting the "poor white" problem in the cities, but given the legislation favoring white workers, an alliance with English workers was their obvious choice.

The 1924 Pact government made it clear that white workers wanted job protection against the threat of cheap black labor. The government provided this, and mine management was ultimately forced to accept the quid pro quo of protecting white worker privileges in return for their support against black demands. The economic division between black and white, present from the earliest encounters between these groups on the frontiers of the British colonies, had taken its toll and the breach between black workers and a white "labor aristocracy" was irreparably widening.

A major turning point in South African history had occurred in the previous century when industrial entrepreneurs and farmers found that blacks could be incorporated into the capitalist mode of production without undermining white domination. Economically exploited and politically deprived of their land, blacks became the vassals of white landowners and industrial bosses. It was a process in which the economic and political practice intensified racial oppression. In the 1920s and 1930s this practice was translated into a legal system.

Afrikaner political power was growing rapidly throughout this period at the expense of the predominantly English-speaking Labour Party. Among the more interesting explanations of this is that offered in Dan O' Meara's *Volkskapitalisme*.[10] His basic thesis is that the rise of Afrikaner nationalism is the outcome of the "concrete processes of class formation and class struggle." Allowing for the different regional manifestations of Afrikaner nationalism in the 1930s, when D. F. Malan's Purified National Party was formed, he shows how opportunities hitherto blocked to Afrikaners in business and the civil service produced a broad alliance of Afrikaner workers, intellectuals, clergy, farmers and business people committed to economic well-being based on a sense of national unity (*volkseenheid*). The rallying cry was apartheid, which functioned as a basis for protecting Afrikaner interests against black domination while inevitable competition for job privileges developed between the traditional English industrial workers and the emerging alliance of Afrikaner nationalism.

The South African English were politically marginalized by the rise of Afrikaner power, and the social influence of the English-speaking churches waned rapidly. They continued to affirm a position of non-racism. Their membership continued to be essentially black and their leadership almost entirely white. The economic and political alliance between Afrikaners and the South African English-speaking workers in the 1920s resulted in the English-speaking churches showing concern for the entrenchment of the oppression of blacks. But ultimately—if only by default—they allowed a system to gain dominance which entrenched racial segregation and imposed statutory economic servitude on blacks. The rise of Afrikaner nationalism marginalized the limited sociopolitical influence of the English-speaking churches still further, and any possibility of these churches realizing their theological commitment to non-racism required concerted commitment to political struggle and ultimately civil disobedience. Such action would have required a radical break with the cautious and politically subservient tradition of these churches. They were not theologically equipped for such action, and as institutions lacked the desire to throw off the yokes of their captivity. One consequence was white members of these churches having more in common with whites in the other churches, and not least the segregated Afrikaans Reformed churches, than they had with black members of their own churches.

THE RESPONSE OF THE ENGLISH-SPEAKING CHURCHES

It was several decades into the industrial age before the English-speaking churches reassessed their position in relation to the black population—the *other part* of their traditional commitment both to white settlers and the indigenous black population. When the

General Missionary Conference met in 1904, its concern was with "heathenism" and "Romanism"; no serious attention was given to the advent of the industrial age. When the conference met again two years later, a plea was entertained to "watch over the interests of Native races, and where necessary to influence legislation on their behalf." But not until 1928 (four years after the election of the Pact government) did the theme of the Conference address the plight of blacks in the prevailing situation. The Conference committed itself to the "realignment of native life on a Christian basis," and yet no attempt was made to propose ways of changing the nature of church or society with a view to attaining this end.[11] The emphasis was still on evangelism and other traditional missionary concerns such as education, and again state and church found agreement in the need for blacks to become an effective labor force. Missions had traditionally given attention to technical training, but faced with the equally traditional problem of the unemployment of skilled and semi-skilled black workers, the churches warmed to the idea of blacks being equipped for specific jobs in the mining and industrial sector. In so doing the churches, as was the case in the pre-industrial missionary era, again allowed existing labor needs, dictated as they were by political interests, to shape their mission policy. They were being drawn a step further in the direction of Verwoerd's Bantu education policy designed to equip blacks for servitude, ensuring that there would be no place for them in white society "above certain forms of labour."[12]

In later decades, when their own black mission schools were threatened and finally closed as part of the Verwoerdian educational policy for blacks, the English-speaking churches would protest, but in vain; the die had been cast already. Industry needed black workers with certain limited "skills," and the churches were in the early decades of the century cooperative in facilitating the supply and distribution of efficient cheap black labor to meet the growing demands of the cities.

The English-speaking churches were committed primarily to a doctrine of personal salvation. Concerned with ministering to the individual social needs of blacks and ready to protest against the harshness of legislation affecting blacks, the churches paid little attention to the fundamental structures of exploitation and control, thus ministering to the symptoms rather than the essential causes of black suffering. Archival research undertaken by James Cochrane on the English-speaking churches during this early industrial period shows that the leadership of these churches, exposed to a black majority membership, "felt and understood the anguish and resistance of the indigenous people," and although not "being able to speak and act in solidarity with them nevertheless understood the need to take some responsibility, provided that the colonial 'white supremacist' structures were not radically undermined." Yet faced with the reality of an increasing proletarianization process—exploitative wages, labor controls, underdevelopment of the reserves, and dislocation in the urban areas, the churches were quite overwhelmed. "Like most if not all settler-dominated institutions benefiting directly or indirectly from the situation, they perceived the threats involved in the proletarianization process, especially if some reasonably secure outlets of Africans were not allowed."[13] The major response of the English-speaking churches to the suffering of blacks during this period was one of special pleading and an appeal for a liberalization of restrictive legislation.

There is, in fact, little evidence to suggest that the English-speaking churches' response to the economic and social problems of the pre-1948 period differed significantly from the ruling ideology of the time. The response of these churches to the 1913 Land Act, the foundation stone of the entire apartheid system and the fundamental cause of the impoverishment of the indigenous rural population, was at best ambiguous and inconsistent. Their response showed the customary concern for individual suffering, focusing on the exclusion of blacks from access to land which they could afford. They regarded it as "too restrictive," but failed to concern themselves with the fundamental ideological intent of the legislation. It was this muted and restrained response which distinguished the English-speaking churches from the more perceptive (although at the time cautious) response of the SANNC (later ANC) and other political groupings, as well as that of the fast-emerging African Independent Churches. Morally obligated to their large black membership and contextually in a position to hear their complaints, the English-speaking churches were sensitive to their anguish. They provided aid where and when possible and spoke on behalf of the black population to the authorities, but because of their obligation to minister to whites as well as blacks, they were unable to locate themselves unequivocally on the side of the oppressed majority. The structures which both produced white affluence and black exploitation had entrapped the churches.

The 1920s witnessed a new period in the country. World War I was over, imperial concerns less pressing, manufacturing on the increase. Urbanized black workers and especially educationists demanded more say in the churches, and a number of black clergy and prominent laity joined the ANC. The white miners' strike of 1922 was followed by the Pact government and, as already indicated, legislation favoring white workers became the basis of the emerging political alliance of Afrikaner nationalism and white labor, while the equally significant strikes by black workers produced the opposite effect. A new sense of concern began to emerge in the churches with the legalization of job restrictions for black workers becoming the focus of attack by the English-speaking churches. Protest was formal and of little avail. Their affirmation of liberal values, trusteeship and the incorporation of "civilized" blacks into "civilized society" having been violated, they found themselves at loggerheads with the Afrikaans Reformed churches whose support for a series of Hertzog Bills was seen to be tantamount to support for a feudal system grounded in a form of bad Calvinist doctrine. English-speaking clergy were, however, in several instances equally critical of the response by the ANC to the legislation. Despite its caution, some clerics found it "immoderate and intruculent."[14]

Clearly Hinchliff is too optimistic in identifying this as a period "when the Church really discovered what its function was in social and political affairs."[15] The structures were sufficiently entrenched to ensure that fundamental change would not come by protest alone. And the values of the churches constituted a form of liberal idealism which failed to become the basis for meaningful programs of social or economic alternative strategies at a crucial turning point in South African history.

By this time momentum was with the Afrikaner rise to power and, with the breach between the English and Afrikaans-speaking churches deepening, the English-speaking churches began to speak of the need for "mature" blacks, those able to "discharge the responsibilities which citizenship involves," to be given access to the socio-economic benefits of the industrial society. The motivation for this shift in emphasis was, according to the 1929 conference of the Methodist Church, to produce "a Bantu citizenship in South Africa, good in character, economically efficient and contented . . . a blessing and not a menace in the land."[16] Whatever might be read into these words, it was the beginning of increased strain between the state and the English-speaking churches. The nature of the conflict was essentially related to the way in which the government imposed and executed its policy, which persons were included in the privileged class, and which persons were fit to discharge the responsibility of citizenship. The churches essentially saw the norms of Western culture and capitalist economic interests as the measures against which to decide who should be included within mainstream society. The "dignity of work" continued to be of primary concern, and the mine compounds seen as unique opportunities for evangelism. Theological identity continued to be founded in nineteenth-century mission thought and moral values in British social and theological debate, while racially discriminatory practices continued to be left largely unchallenged by church leaders.

When the Christian Council of South Africa was formed in 1937 (to become the South African Council of Churches in 1968) the rift between English-speaking churches and the Afrikaans Reformed churches began to widen. And as indicated in an earlier chapter, by 1941 the only Afrikaans Reformed churches to have joined the Council, the white NGK together with the Sendingkerk in the Transvaal, resigned to form the Federal Missionary Council of the NGK. With this, any hope of church unity across the language barriers was gone. The reasons for the breach were numerous: the desire for coordination or control of mission work within the NGK group of churches, the failure within the Council to give the Afrikaans language equal status to English and, as becomes clear in Gerdener's discussion on the breach, "questions affecting the relationship between Europeans and Natives."[17]

The Afrikaans churches applied themselves with fervor to their work among blacks, with evangelization high on the agenda, while ensuring that racial segregation—in accordance with established segregationist practice—was maintained in their churches. It was this last factor more than anything else which motivated accusations that mission within the Afrikaans churches was a means to "indoctrinate a people into servility."[18] The essence of what is argued in the pages of this book is, however, that a similar accusation can be laid at the door of the English-speaking churches.

The English-speaking churches had from the earliest times opposed government legislation discriminating against blacks, and even when allowing themselves to be instrumental in the implementation of such legislation, they had sought to soften the impact of such restrictions on the black population. Their protest changed few laws, while perhaps making life a little more palatable for the black members of these churches. This spirit of protest can be attributed to a number of things, not least of all to an inherited spirit of liberalism and missionary paternalism, but above all to the presence of a numerically predominant black membership. The harshness of race and class exploitation was a daily reality for the majority of their members. This resulted in the churches protesting virtually every piece of discriminatory legislation to have gone into the statute books from the earliest laws effecting land distribution. South African liberalism is displayed at both its best and its worst here with the churches demanding equality before the law and yet showing conformity to certain imposed standards of Western individualism and achievement. This is nowhere more clear than in the 1930 Anglican Synod of Bishops' statement: "We believe that the rights of full citizenship in any country are not dependent on race or color, but on men's fitness to discharge the responsibilities which such citizenship involves."[19] It is the latter part of this statement which, given the history of missions in this country, portrays the familiar paternalism and sense of trusteeship of the English-speaking churches.

The Afrikaner National Party victory at the polls in 1948 introduced a new phase to the relationship between the English-speaking churches and the state. The general tenor of the response of the churches was to express views that racial discrimination and prejudice were irreconcilable with the gospel, while many within their ranks expressed an understanding of the enormity of the task facing the new government—with not a single church supporting universal franchise. The stated position of the Anglican church in this regard is a fair reflection of the stance of the other English-speaking churches as well:

Giving the vote to all non-Europeans would not only be a danger to the European, but a very grave danger to the non-Europeans themselves. In South Africa, the population is not only overwhelmingly black but, except in a few rare instances, overwhelmingly ignorant. We welcome qualified Africans as responsible citizens, but the time is not ripe for universal enfranchisement.[20]

Many voices were heard within the English-speaking churches urging that the rulers be given a chance and that a concerted effort be made to build relations with the Afrikaner community. But as legislation systematically deprived blacks of the few rights they had left, the English-speaking churches, confronted with the suffering of their black membership, felt themselves constrained to intensify their protest. The Afrikaner churches, in turn, found their loyalty to kith and kin requiring loyalty to the Afrikaner government which they had helped to elect, and the tension between these two groups of churches intensified.

However, when the response of the churches to the Defiance Campaign launched by the ANC on 26 June 1952 is considered, it becomes clear that even the intensified protest of the English-speaking churches was mild and cautious. The ANC's membership rose from a few thousand to over 100,000 members during the course of the campaign, and thousands of volunteers were arrested. Individual clerics such as Michael Scott who had left the country two years earlier, Canon Collins who was living outside South Africa, and Trevor Huddleston supported the popular movement, but they were clearly in the minority. The campaign was rejected by the churches as excessive and responsible for unnecessary suffering. Unable to exert influence on an Afrikaner government and unwilling to align themselves with the radical forces of opposition to this government, the English-speaking churches were locked into protesting the activities of both sides.

There is little doubt that these churches, and more so the Anglicans than the others, have consistently produced resilient and determined opponents of the apartheid system. Names such as Trevor Huddleston, Michael Scott, Joost de Blank, Geoffrey Clayton, Gonville ffrench-Beytagh, and more recently Desmond Tutu, have come to symbolize Anglican resistance. But the other English-speaking churches have also produced their prophets and leaders: Albert Luthuli, ANC leader and Nobel Peace Prize winner; Robert Sobukwe, the founder of the Pan-Africanist Congress; Seth Mokitimi, the first black elected leader of an English-speaking church in South Africa; and many others. De Gruchy has observed: "There must be few comparable instances in the history of the Christian church where such a sustained protest has been waged over such a long period against state legislation and action."[21] Monica Wilson, speaking of an earlier generation of the English-speaking churches, affirms the need to praise this lineage of ancestors, in the knowledge that in so doing we follow the *amasiko* (tradition) of the Xhosa people.[22]

This celebration of the few has persuaded some that the resistance of the English-speaking churches has been more influential than what critical analysis allows. There is, in fact, little evidence to suggest that the witness of the prophetic individuals within these churches, or the suffering of many Christians who remain unrecognized by these churches, has in any significant manner changed the social character of the institutional churches.

The Mixed Marriages Act was, for example, seen by the English-speaking churches as unnecessary interference with the lives of individuals, while the Afrikaner churches found biblical and theological cause to support it. Yet ultimately the English-speaking churches required their clergy to abide by the legislation, despite its disastrous consequences for some of their own members. Their theological response to the legislation was hesitant and equivocal. Recognizing that "the contracting of marriages between partners of different races is not contrary to the law of God as declared by Jesus Christ," a joint statement by those churches opposed to the legislation (including the English-speaking churches and the Roman Catholic Church) allowed that "such marriages [were] inexpedient and likely to produce unhappy results. . . ." The Presbyterian Church, while opposing the Mixed Marriages Act, concluded that mixed marriages are "an evil" because of the suffering imposed on children. The Methodists thought the Act to be an unnecessary restriction on individual liberty, placing an "unfair" responsibility on marriage officers. The Anglicans alone saw fit to explain that the "undesirable" nature of the Bill was directly linked to "the conditions determining the interrelationship of races in

Southern Africa."[23] None of the churches, however, sought to tackle the fundamental cause of such legislation or to redress the prevailing social milieu which caused children of mixed marriages "to suffer" in an apartheid society.

Within four years of the passage of the Mixed Marriages Act a series of education bills ended the churches' traditional role in black education, and this too was accepted with little more than due protest. Blacks were forcibly moved from areas declared "white," compelling churches to engage in massive building schemes in newly proclaimed "black" areas, with the practices of the state becoming the practices of the church. The Methodist Church, for example, took until the late 1970s to remove from their statutes a *legislated* discrepancy in stipends between white, so-called colored, Indian and black ministers. And still today it is the marked exception rather than the rule that ministers of different races receive the same stipends, or that congregations in any of the English-speaking churches are integrated. It is "this gap between word and deed," argues de Gruchy, that "has been exploited by the government as blatant hypocrisy. Many a deputation to the state has floundered on the mere fact that the churches' own lives have not been beyond reproach. Indeed, on occasion the state has exercised a prophetic ministry to the churches. For example, the churches soon learned that they could not justly criticize wage discrimination between whites and blacks in society or in state employ because there was similar discrimination in the churches."[24] Unable to justify this contradiction the churches have slowly become increasingly cautious in their critique of specific details of a structure of which they are a part. Theologically having condemned apartheid as a heresy, and having made no serious attempt to consider an alternative economic or political program, the English-speaking churches have found themselves trapped in apartheid.

It is this that suggests that although there is a difference in theology and rhetoric between the Afrikaans Reformed and the English-speaking churches, at the level of praxis they are essentially the same, a point further developed in a later chapter.

THE CHANGING CHARACTER OF WHITE HEGEMONY

"The more these *Engelse* and Afrikaners differ the more are they the same," suggests the Afrikaner writer W. A. de Klerk, reflecting on race and class relations in the South African context.[25] They have, however, differed within their alliance of privileged whiteness, and often intensely so. The Afrikaner rise to power which culminated in election victory in 1948 marks the zenith of such animosity. Yet within thirty years these two groups within the white dominant class were once again finding more to unite than to separate them, a process seen most clearly in white voting trends with an increasing number of English-speaking South Africans electing to support a predominantly Afrikaner ruling party. This process has direct implications for the churches located on either side of a no-longer-so-rigid divide. It will be shown in chapter 6, for example, that the NGK has in its most recent General Synod opted for a less rigidly dogmatic stance in support of apartheid (although resolutely refusing to reject it). The English-speaking churches as institutions have, in turn, come to find themselves divided against the more radical voices within their own constituency as seen, for example, in their response to the *Kairos Document*. A consequence of these developments is the chance of *toenadering* (rapprochement) between these two dominant church groups becoming increasingly likely. In order to understand this possibility, which is a corollary to political developments, it is necessary to consider those political and economic factors which have contributed to the changing character of English-Afrikaans relations within the dominant class of privileged whites.

Poignantly stated: Why the collapse of the 1924 alliance between Afrikaner nationalism and the English-based Labour Party? Why the subsequent apparent split within the ranks of the ruling class? The answer is complex and cannot be dealt with in much detail here. A matrix of components seemed to come together: cultural, racial, religious, institutional, political and economic. O'Meara has explained this in terms of a class struggle which saw a coalition of Afrikaner interest groups hitherto excluded from dominant positions in commerce, industry, management, cultural organizations and trade unions, striving to occupy these places. A consequence was the inevitable confrontation with those who had traditionally occupied these positions within white society—the South African English.

The numerical strength of Afrikaners placed them at a distinct advantage over the English, but hegemonic struggle requires a particular group within a ruling class coalition, or a ruling class as a whole, to preserve and consolidate this dominant position. To this end maximum support is sought for the values and internal cohesion of this group or class, and consolidated opposition to individuals, groups and movements directly or potentially threatening its dominant position.[26] Given the economic strength of English capital in relation to the limited economic resources of Afrikaner nationalism in the 1920s and 1930s, Afrikaner hegemony required the mobilization of its cultural and nationalist resources as a basis from which to make inroads into the power of the English mining entrepreneurs and skilled labor aristocracy. Afrikanerdom was obliged to close ranks in its quest for economic and political hegemony if it was to consolidate its newly acquired ruling-class position and not slip back into the marginalized position it had occupied in the wake of the Anglo-Boer War—consisting (at least outside of the Cape Province) essentially of subsistence and tenant farmers, and semi-skilled or unskilled mining and industrial workers.

Stanley Greenberg explains this hegemonic imperative which faced the Afrikaner in the 1920s and 1930s by locating it within what he discerns as a broader pattern of development in capitalist economies. His thesis is that capitalist development initially intensifies racial barriers while at the same time creating contradictions which threaten to dismantle them.[27] In the South African context this intensification of barriers and the process of evolving contradictions helps explain both the recent internal adjustments to race relations within the dominant class as well as the full circle which has again brought Afrikaans and English-speaking South Africans into an overt relationship of co-existence. It is a process involving essentially three interrelated and overlapping phases.

The *first phase* is one of racial intensification during which the dominant class (in the case of South Africa, the white settlers in their capacity as commercial farmers, entrepreneurs, mine owners, business owners and trade unionists) demand total control over the subordinate population. A consequence was conflict among the major factions within the dominant class. Farmers required subordinate labor in the rural areas, while mine and industry recruitment agencies demanded a regular supply of cheap labor to meet their needs in the cities. Trade unionists sought to create areas of protected employment, while the employers' concerns were to substitute "cheap" semi-skilled labor for costly skilled labor. Despite different economic interests, initially at least, an excess of unskilled labor was able to meet the needs of farmers and industry, providing sufficient reason for commercial farmers, industrial entrepreneurs and trade unionists all to support the dominant class and its oppressive policies. A consequence was the destruction of subsistence farming in the rural areas, the creation of a cheap and regular labor force for industry, and the protection of skilled jobs for white workers exclusively.

This alliance of white interest was soon eroded by the complicating factor of Afrikaners being confined to less privileged positions within the ruling class. It was this factor as much as any other that accounted for the collapse of the alliance of Afrikaner nationalism and English workers, resulting in the more exclusive nature of Afrikaner rule in the post-1948 period. A consequence was the temporary suspension of the coalition of Afrikaner-English socio-economic interests as Afrikaners systematically occupied those spaces in the civil service, trade unions, business and elsewhere formerly held by English-speaking South Africans. This was a process which contradicted English liberalism which was in theory opposed to all forms of distinction between humankind—even though their own ideology of trusteeship gave only the most anglicized blacks access to the full benefits of "civilization."

The *second phase* involves a crisis of hegemony among the different constituencies within the dominant class. We have already seen this emerging in the relationship between English- and Afrikaans-speaking South Africans. There is, however, a more fundamental dimension to this crisis. It is a phase which began to emerge in the 1960s in South Africa and which in many ways continues to influence contemporary politics.

Each separate privileged constituency within the dominant class has, by this time, become dependent on the racial order for its privileged position. *Total* dependency on race is, however, no longer a criterion and attempts are made (if only to counter protest from the dominated classes) to move away from traditional to more tempered structures of domination, more appropriate to the needs of expanding markets and labor demands. The main actors in the dominant classes, while continuing to cling to the rewards of class and racial privilege, have in the meantime become firmly entrenched in their privileged position and are less dependent on elaborate state involvement in their affairs. Big business, having become a dominant political influence and less dependent on government "interference" in the economy (built on the realities of racial privilege), is more interested in labor stability and a growing market than labor repression. Economic necessity has, in turn, initiated a movement of subordinate workers into some industries with a consequent splintering of the labor movement. All of these factors contribute to less intensified support for unbending racial barriers in the labor market.

In brief, the class character of the racial order becomes more explicit, while the racial ideologies established within the earlier period of racial intensification militate against any attempt to eliminate the racial characteristics of the class structure. This, in a word, is the internal hegemonic crisis facing South Africa.

A variety of factors ranging from economic crises to political resistance and a sense of impotence on the part of whites in the face of the black rise to power has required virtually every constituency within the dominant class, from labor to business and church to state, to address the question as to whether the present disrupted system can be deracialized without relinquishing power.

It is this question which has torn deeply into what were hitherto the most homogeneous of constituencies within the white-ruled South Africa, with the options for "reform" constituting the single most divisive factor in contemporary politics. Rejected by some as the thin end of the wedge that will open the floodgate to the black dominated classes, while dismissed by others as a ploy to entrench the present system of white privilege, a concerted effort is made by a broad-based alliance of business and political leaders to build a new moderate economic and political center around which to prevent fundamental change. Because the churches are part of the social fabric, this division is found in their midst no less than elsewhere. The English-speaking churches above all others, given their propensity for moderation, are instinctively inclined to support these moves. They find it difficult to understand how at precisely the time when the government is seeking reform it should be rejected as illegitimate.

A *third phase* concerns the realization that racial domination in

South Africa constitutes the basis of social privilege; the former cannot be tampered with without striking at the latter. It is *this* which constitutes the most contentious and potentially explosive problem facing the entire subcontinent. Emerging in specific situations at given moments in time to meet certain socio-economic needs, racial restrictions are not simply "surrogates for hidden, material forces: the dominant racial section does not dissolve into the bourgeoisie and the subordinate population into the proletariat."[28] Racial prejudice cannot simply be dismissed as superstructure or false consciousness! Race groups in a given situation have particular skills and needs, and manifest certain modes of behavior and production which have specific political and economic consequences at a given time. In the South African situation, the encounter between the subsistence economy of blacks and nineteenth-century imperial capitalism resulted in the subjection of blacks—a process perpetuated by generations of class differentiation. The difficulties facing even the most committed reformists within business and other circles who wish to deracialize the existing economic order stem from the realization that the complete dismantling of all racial legislation must inevitably result in the collapse of not only the capitalist order in its present form but perhaps the entire infrastructure of the country.

There are, in other words, fundamental internal contradictions within the existing order presently being manifested in conflict and crisis. So intense and far-reaching are these that some regard them as part of a *Kairos* (a moment in time when the salvation or damnation of a people is at stake) facing the churches in South Africa. It requires the English-speaking churches to face up to the implications of their theoretical declarations concerning the inherently evil nature of apartheid. These are declarations with far-reaching economic and political implications which the institutional churches have not seriously considered. These implications strike at the heart of the fragile unity which exists between the black and white members of these churches, as essentially those groups which constitute the "haves" with much to lose and the "have-nots" with little to lose. They also call into question the dominant values of the existing order within which the institutional churches are trapped.

The above analysis of capitalist development suggests the inevitability of a reformist phase in the class-race character of Afrikaner politics. A consequence was the partial relinquishment of Afrikaner exclusivity in order to explicitly re-establish class alliances with the English, more recently with "coloreds" and Indians through the tricameral parliament, and the possibility of the incorporation of cooperative blacks into the alliance. But this is a more recent development. Early phases were less obvious, and an important question concerns the role of the churches in this process. Faced with the influx of "poor white" Afrikaners to the cities, the Afrikaans Reformed churches showed an appreciation of the need for social reform and indeed espoused a form of socialism. The English-speaking churches had a different social experience. Not having had to cater to the needs of large numbers of impoverished whites, while not allowing black property to exert a formative influence on their social character, the English-speaking churches were seen during the industrial period to be aligned with mining and foreign capital against the workers. Mining magnates often belonged to the English-speaking churches and acted as their benefactors. These churches had long been involved in labor recruitment and training. Some of the most successful products of their mission schools had come to form an emerging black petty-bourgeoisie often co-opted by management and government. Their mission policies favored only the incorporation of "qualified" blacks into mainstream society, and their involvement in Lord Milner's anglicization policy in the post-Anglo-Boer War period isolated them from the dominant white labor constituency which was by this time predominantly Afrikaans. The concern of the English-speaking churches and especially of the Methodists in the early industrial age was essentially evangelical. Their uncompromising stand against alcoholism, prostitution and other dysfunctional forms of behavior was often seen by workers to be moralistic and productive of a middle-class character quite alien to both black and white miners and industrial workers. The *Methodist Churchman* as early as 1911 lamented that "the sons of toil are mainly conspicuous by their absence from church worship." A 1913 edition of the same paper reported striking miners as regarding English-speaking clergy ("formally trained" and often with educated English accents) as a "class alienated from the working man," showing "no sympathy with him in his struggle for what he believes to be his rights."[29] *The*

Anglican carried a letter which condemned the church because it was "not in touch with the working man," and did "not grasp or understand the working man's aims and ambitions" with "his surroundings [being] beyond the ken of the greater portion of her clergy." The letter continued:

> It is not sufficient that the Church should throw open its doors, it must go out into the world, mix with the people, learn of the bitterness and cruelty and oppression and wrongs that exist, . . . extract knowledge of the results of the iniquity and uncharitableness it now preaches so guardedly against, and then it will be in a position, if courageous and fearless, to fight the good fight.[30]

If only in relation to the "poor white" Afrikaner constituency in the cities, an important target group in the National Party's rise to power, the Afrikaans Reformed churches were able to establish a link with workers which made their agenda a part of the social concern of the church—and an important ingredient in that alliance of constituencies which ultimately brought Afrikaner nationalists to power in 1948.

It was an alliance which necessarily excluded all others in its initial thrust for power. In order for this to happen the rhetoric necessarily takes on a particular character, religious legitimation is required and the cultural symbols of the past are appropriated to facilitate the process. In so doing the English and their churches, together with all other groups—Jews, Catholics, blacks and foreigners—became the objects of attack. The consequent division within the broader white community was inevitable with the legal entrenchment of racial and economic divisions and the affirmation of separatism in every area of existence being offensive to the laissez-faire attitude of English liberalism.

There is, however, no evidence to suggest that the socioeconomic commitment of the English-speaking churches was essentially different from that of the Afrikaans Reformed churches. The English-speaking churches were not committed to social or economic egalitarianism among all sections of the population. The above analysis of the role of the English in the encounter between blacks and whites in this country confirms as much. Their response to Afrikaner nationalism was rather a reaction grounded in a form of liberalism which affirms the dignity and equality of all people, despite the obvious differences which the South African English identified only too clearly between themselves and other social and racial sectors of the population. Having at no time experienced the reality of being underdogs in the socio-economic order, a reality shared by Afrikaners and blacks alike, the South African English advocated tolerance, moderation and the acceptance of others, confident that some "invisible hand" of destiny would resolve any conflicts to the mutual benefit of all. Advocating "nothing harsh or rigorous," all that was required was the *cautious* "interfering ways" of a cleric or two to ensure that decency and respect prevailed.

What the English-speaking churches have not done is to address the need, in consultation with other groups which also seek to promote the well-being of the people represented by these churches (trade unions, political groups and community organizations), with a view to putting together a political equation that translates their noblest dreams into social and economic reality. It is this which locates the English-speaking churches wholly in what Heribert Adam bluntly calls the "failure of political liberalism." For him, "South African political liberalism has traditionally become associated with the idea of a single South Africa in which all its citizens regardless of race enjoy political rights based on universal suffrage," something which has never existed. It is an idea which reached its heyday with the existence of the Labour Party in the 1950s and 1960s, which at best had approximately 5,000 members, half of whom were black.[31]

As the impact of political polarization took its toll so the fortunes of liberalism declined. One form of nationalism lined up against another: Afrikaners exclusively clawing their way up the socio-economic and political ladder, and blacks realizing that the only way out of their dilemma is through an ideological commitment to power. In some ways the English-speaking churches have not yet moved beyond liberal idealism, taking comfort in a psychological and/or spiritual pay-off which convinces them that, in spite of their privileged and elitist position, they are at least in principle on the side of the oppressed. At the same time, driven by what has in an earlier chapter been identified as a residual theology of resistance, these churches are compelled to face up to the need to be what in their better moments they know a residual theological dimension of their tradition requires of them, that is, to show special favor to those of their members who are socially marginalized, economically poor and politically oppressed. The many resolutions of these churches over the years condemning each phase of racial oppression and exploitation in some ways signal an awareness of this responsibility. The dilemma of these churches, given their loyalty to people on both sides of the socio-economic divide and their own captivity within the economic structures of the country, is how to affirm these resolutions in practice.

A CHURCH WITHIN THE CHURCHES

The presence of a large black majority within the English-speaking churches constitutes a major contradiction to the social location of these churches, which is critically but essentially on the side of the existing order. In spite of the dominant white institutional character of these churches, a sustained black protest can be detected within them from virtually the time of their emergence at the beginning of the last century. It is a protest which identifies a church of resistance existing within those churches whose character has been molded and shaped by involvement and captivity within the dominant economic and political trajectory of the formation of the capitalist order in South Africa. The resisting church has, of course, also been shaped by its location in the social order. Consisting largely of the poor and dominated, essentially black and forged in the crucible of resistance and struggle, it has heard and in certain social situations appropriated that theology of resistance and liberation which survives within the tradition of the church.

"The symbolic value of the word black," says Buti Tlhagale, "is that it captures the broken existence of the black people and summons them collectively to burst the chains of oppression and engage themselves creatively in the construction of a new society."[32] A resisting church in South Africa is of necessity a black church, a basis for unity among the oppressed within as well as beyond the English-speaking churches. Despite the separation of the African Indigenous Churches, blacks within the established churches have shown a remarkable denominational self-consciousness and loyalty to the English-speaking churches. This has often been attributed to the mission activity of the church which contributed to the dismantling of African society while being unable to integrate blacks into the emerging capitalist society. Between this social disintegration and inability to penetrate beyond the margins of the capitalist structure, the church came to provide a substitute social location. And yet, as shown in chapter 2, it was a location which required blacks to yield to the restraints, character and moderation of the churches. Such restraints did not, however, result in the suspension of black economic or political ideals, nor were they able to prevent black members of these churches from participating in the broader black struggle for self-determination and liberation. Black members of the English-speaking churches, for example, exercised a major influence within the ANC (particularly from the 1930s onward) as racial legislation further entrenched the exclusion of blacks from the political and economic structures of society, and within the Pan-Africanist Congress (PAC) from its inception in 1959. The Rev. Z. Mahabane was president of the ANC from 1937-39 and Dr. A. B. Xuma president from 1940-49. Dr. James Moroka, a leading Methodist layman, was president from 1949-52 and Chief Albert Luthuli, a leading member of the Congregational Church, from 1952–60. An Anglican priest, the Rev. James Calata, was General Secretary from 1936–49. Z. K. Matthews, also an Anglican and involved in the activities of the SACC, the All Africa Conference of Churches (AACC) and the WCC, was president of the ANC in the Cape Province and a leading member of its national executive until the time of its banning in 1960. Oliver Tambo was a loyal member of Trevor Huddleston's Anglican congregation in Sophiatown until driven into exile. Nelson and Winnie Mandela are confirmed Anglicans, with the former receiving regular communion from a Methodist chaplain to Pollsmoor Prison; and Robert Sobukwe, a Methodist lay preacher, became the founding president of the PAC.

With the banning of the major liberation movements in South Africa and the subsequent silencing of virtually all extra-parliamentary organizations, a political vacuum has resulted. As a result black Christians have been constrained to carry their politics back into the churches where in some instances they first discerned a gospel of liberating power so often concealed and neglected within the more dominant theology of the church. This move has forced these churches to face issues they had been content to evade or address only in principle. White church members, faced with a different kind of socio-political context, have not experienced the same compulsion to address themselves to the political and economic implications of the theology they have become accustomed to affirming. This is the essence of the internal conflict within these churches. It is the difference between what the *Kairos Document* critiques as "church theology" and "prophetic theology." The former remains at the level of theory, failing to become a material force which grips the imagination of grass-roots members, mobilizing them to concerted action. As such it is a form of false piety. The latter seeks on the basis of analysis of the existing order to discover the meaning of theology for the particular situation, using it as a means of concrete socio-political action.

If racial division is located outside of the Afrikaans churches, with black churches pitted against white churches, this division is apparent *within* the English-speaking churches. It is this division, which constitutes both the weakness and the strength of these churches: a weakness which witnesses to the lack of unequivocal commitment to the liberation of the oppressed, grounded in the dual commitment of the churches to both blacks and whites; a strength which recognizes that, in spite of the attractions of schism and partition, this conflict is ultimately to be resolved *within* these churches in much the same way that South Africa's problems can only be resolved within a unitary state.

For this resolution to take place within church and state the aspirations of blacks need to be explicitly and aggressively affirmed and promoted. But blacks have, in many instances, internalized their structural oppression and carried into the churches a spirit of servility and oppression, and it would be naive to suggest that black Christians are less susceptible to the kinds of socio-economic and political forces to which reference has already been made.

Recent years have for a variety of reasons (the rise of Black Consciousness, a changing political climate, etc.) seen dynamic and determined black leaders elected to office, while the expectation that radical reform would follow created a new sense of expectation in the churches. But thorough-going reform within these churches has not happened. Blacks have not elected black leadership either consistently or in numbers equal to black church membership. Those elected have, in turn, not given obviously more radical leadership than white leaders, and in some cases have shown themselves to be as authoritarian and reactionary as white leaders. The structures have proved more powerful than individuals; structures which evolved in response to a liberal church tradition in a rapidly expanding industrial society tend today to envelop rather than be shaped by individual leaders. It is this which gives credence to the adage that there can be no "normal" church relations according to the declared theological principles of the English-speaking churches in an abnormal society within which ideological, racial and class divisions are entrenched by custom and enforced by law.

The church is and possibly can be no more than a microcosm of the larger political macrocosm. However, the theological commitment of the English-speaking churches is that they are one and undivided. This commitment, compromised and forgotten at times but relentlessly present as a disturbing memory, provides an incentive to persuade these churches to ensure that their practice is commensurate with their theology in both church and state. It is partly this restlessness within the English-speaking churches, rather than any overt commitment on their part to significant socio-economic or political change, that has made them the focus of government concern. This theological restlessness persuades those who are concerned to see an age of justice and peace emerge in South Africa that the church may have a role to play in this regard.

It is clear that the English-speaking churches have not yet demonstrated a willingness to appropriate this alternative theological stance which would radically transform their own identity as they engage, in solidarity and conflict with other social actors, in the transformation of a society which has become so much a part of their own identity. On the contrary, evidence suggests that when confronted with the internal contradiction between their theological affirmations and social practice, these churches have protested while reluctantly conforming to the social demands of the time; they have protested without resisting. This character of the English-speaking churches is illustrated in the next chapter in three separate incidents in which these churches have been tested and found wanting in terms of their own theological declarations in recent years. Or is it that they have simply declared themselves to be cautiously and reluctantly but firmly on the side of the dominant class—where some would argue the church has been firmly ensconced since the days of Constantine?

Chapter Four

Protest Without Resistance

Shaped by a dominant theology of moderation, formed by a history of compromise, and manipulated by conflicting power struggles both within their own structures and in the nation of which they were a part, the English-speaking churches soon found themselves trapped within their own history. Some individuals within the churches saw a vision beyond captivity, and Christian groups outside of the ecclesial structures rebelled against an ever-encroaching state tyranny. The institutional churches were left to protest without being part of the forces of resistance.

We have identified the involvement of the English-speaking churches in the history of pre-industrial racial and economic oppression. We have also seen that racial-economic exploitation was reinforced with the discovery of gold and how the English-speaking churches allowed themselves to become part of this process. Then in 1948 the present government came to power, transforming and intensifying the existing oppressive legislation into an uncompromising ideology of apartheid, destined to impinge on every area of church and nation. Although hesitant at first, the English-speaking churches protested this move and eventually condemned numerous pieces of racial legislation which passed through parliament. Yet only on one obvious occasion did this protest threaten to become resistance, and that was when Verwoerd introduced the famous church clause designed to impose racial segregation in the worship services of these churches. It was rejected by all the English-speaking churches. The Anglican Archbishop of Cape Town, Geoffrey Clayton, threatened to call his priests and laity to civil disobedience, and the other English-speaking churches supported the Anglican initiative.

Important as this stand was, when seen in relation to other apartheid laws it suggests a disturbing parochialism which allows for a narrow and restricted sense of the limits of bona fide church identity and religious freedom. Prior to the church bill and on numerous occasions since, the church has refused to regard laws affecting the broader ministry of the church as being quite as crucial, and the state has slowly but consistently convinced the church to accept that its primary task is confined to what happens on a Sunday within the walls of its own sanctuaries. More recently the churches again had occasion to threaten resistance. This happened in April 1987 when the Commissioner of Police introduced regulations making it illegal to call for the release of detainees. Seeing this as a violation of religious freedom, church leaders called on Christians to pray for the release of those in prison. "The state," said Roman Catholic Archbishop Stephen Naidoo, "is trying to take away our right to decide for whom we shall pray. With regard to public prayer, we will not accept it."

These moments aside, facing ever intensifying pressure from the state, the English-speaking churches narrowed their sphere of involvement in the affairs of the nation, voluntarily surrendering space which had traditionally been theirs. In this chapter three separate examples of this process are considered. The first instance is the response of the churches to the Bantu Education Act of 1953; the second, the churches' refusal to provide humanitarian aid to guerrilla fighters (many of whom were members of the English-speaking churches) engaged in 1970 in revolutionary war against the South African and other oppressive regimes; the third example relates to the hesitation of these churches to allow muted support for economic sanctions designed to bring pressure to bear on a government whose policy they have consistently condemned as being contrary to the will of God.

The English-speaking churches' parameters of engagement with the state and those opposed to it have since these instances narrowed even further. The refusal of these churches to actively support a campaign of prayers for the removal of the existing government from power or a theological declaration (the *Kairos Document*) which calls into question the legitimacy of the minority government is considered in chapter 5. The limited and reluctant response of the English-speaking churches raises an important question: On just whose side are these churches?

THE BANTU EDUCATION ACT

The Bantu Education Act (1953), which brought to an end a proud but not an unambiguous history of involvement by the English-speaking churches in black education, has been enshrined in the words of its architect, Hendrik Verwoerd:

> Education must train and teach people in accordance with their opportunities in life, according to the sphere in which they live. . . . Education should have its roots entirely in the Native areas and in the Native environment and Native community. . . . The Bantu must be guided to serve his own community in all respects. There is no place for him in the European community above the level of certain forms of labour.[1]

Bantu education was seen by the churches to be evil and insidious. Yet cold, calculated and ideological as were Verwoerd's words, introducing a new and oppressive form of education designed to ensure mental control and manipulation of the masses, Bantu education was not in *complete* discontinuity with mission education. The hesitant and cautious critique of the intentions behind the Act by at least some church leaders seems to verify this.

The demand by blacks for government intervention in black schooling had been going on for a long time. Mission education was often heavy-handed and paternalistic, and in most instances inadequately funded and administered. The ANC, for example, had called for free compulsory education to be provided by the state, and by 1949 eight hundred of the two thousand mission schools in the Transvaal had been placed under state control in response to demands by black parents.[2] However, the response of the Nationalist Government to the call for intervention, in the form of the Bantu Education Act, resulted in a second condition worse than the first. It introduced an ideological rigidity to black schooling which denied all possibility of educational reform.

From the time of the earliest white settlement in South Africa, black education had been used to serve a particular end. Protest against Bantu education grounded in liberal presuppositions that education should or can be ideologically free tends to ignore this point. The first school was established in 1658 to teach slaves the language, culture and religion of their masters; when the slaves were released in 1834, the need was seen for "more schools to instill social discipline." Sir George Grey, British governor of the Cape in 1855, identified mission schools as the key to making Africans "useful servants, consumers of our goods [and] contributors to our revenue," while the Natal Native Commission meeting in 1881 agreed that teaching Africans "to read and write, without teaching them to work, is not doing them any good." A submission to the same Commission is even more pointed: "As far as possible, I would teach at these schools every occupation that a servant is required to do in the colony. Why is it that I employ the red Kaffir boy as my groom and gardener? Simply because he demands half the amount that the educated boy does; he does his work as well, if not better, and is more amenable to discipline."³ D. D. T. Jabavu, a professor at the South African Native College at Fort Hare, writing during the first decades of this century in protest against the teaching of what was called "industrial" and "manual" education in mission schools, shows the extent to which these schools provided precisely the kind of education asked for in this submission: "In our schools," he complained, " 'manual labor' consists of sweeping yards, repairing roads, cracking stones and so on, and is done by boys only as . . . task work enforced by a time-keeper, and under threats of punishment."⁴ What the Bantu Education Act did was to entrench these traditional values in law. In so doing it resolutely eradicated the less subservient elements in black education. It was these dimensions within mission education, systematically exaggerated by Verwoerd, that have contributed to a romantic image of the mission schools. Mission schools, he argued, sought "to create a class of educated and semi-educated persons without the corres-

ponding socio-economic development which should accompany
it."

> This is a class which has learnt to believe that it is above its
> own people and feels that its spiritual, economic and political
> home is among the civilized community of South Africa, i.e.
> the Europeans, and feels frustrated because its wishes have
> not been realized.[5]

Verwoerd was partially right. Some mission schools were designed, at least prior to the 1865 Education Act, to produce an
African-educated elite. And even after the shift to a more practically oriented industrial education, graduates from mission institutions such as Lovedale, Healdtown, Adam's College, St. Peter's
and Fort Hare would become political leaders not only in South
Africa but well beyond its borders. This Verwoerd was not willing
to tolerate. It is equally true that there were simply no opportunities
in the racially defined industrial sector for skilled black workers.
The majority of black children, however, were not being provided
with an education by the existing mission school structure, and
most of those who did have access to these schools received an
education designed to pacify and equip them for "their place" in a
racially divided society—in much the way Verwoerd intended.

Verwoerd could with a measure of justification insist, "The state
is taking over from the churches to prosecute the same work *more
efficiently*."[6] Teacher training would henceforth take place only in
state training centers inside the "native reserves," and if churches
persisted in training teachers, their qualifications would not be
recognized for teaching purposes. Primary and secondary schools
were forced either to close down completely or to take a cut in
subsidy (which was enough to cripple their budget), teach only the
state syllabus and appoint only those teachers who received the
approval of state authorities. Private schools were initially allowed
to continue as independent institutions. But tougher legislation
followed, phasing out the subsidy on mission schools, empowering
the Minister of Native Affairs to close those schools which he
judged "not in the interests of the Bantu people," requiring all
existing schools to apply for re-registration, demanding that they
teach Bantu education, and compelling them to submit to regular

inspections by departmental officials. And in several instances registration was indeed refused. The die was cast. For all practical purposes the era of mission education was dead.

The churches responded with dismay. They protested against a philosophy of education which they saw to be in contradiction to their mission policy. The Anglicans condemned it as having "for its object the keeping of a particular racial group in a permanent position of inferiority." The Congregational Church and the Presbyterians "deeply regretted" being "unable to support the government in the theory underlying the Bantu Education Act," and the Methodists "emphatically declared" their opposition to "a policy which in effect aims at conditioning the African people to a predetermined position of subordination."[7] Protest was not, however, supported by everyone in the English-speaking churches; division concerning Bantu Education ran deep. The Anglican Bishop of Johannesburg, Ambrose Reeves, advocated total resistance, choosing the path of "death with honour."[8] Bishop Vernon Inman of the Natal Diocese, on the other hand, was less resistant, indicating that the church was being relieved of an enormous responsibility for which it was inadequately equipped. Having visited all the schools in his diocese to explain the significance of the transfer of schools to the government, he stated, "nowhere did I meet with the slightest opposition or spoken criticism."[9] Father Trevor Huddleston's observation is a telling one:

> Already, from within the mission camp, voices were heard whispering the insidious and fatal fallacies which so many ears were longing to hear. "After all, it may not work out so badly. . . . The inspectors are good men. . . . Verwoerd does not have anything to do with the working out of the plan. . . . African teachers won't teach inferiority. . . . Anyhow what can we do?" It was the voice of Vichy. It is that voice which, by and large, has prevailed.[10]

The will to resist as seen in Reeves, Huddleston and a few others within the English-speaking churches was itself resisted by the leadership of these churches. The protest which did emerge from these churches was related largely to two specific factors which impinged directly and narrowly on their own ecclesial activities:

One, that the churches would have less opportunity to pursue their evangelical work in the schools; the second was related to a cut in government subsidy.

A widely acclaimed address by Dr. Alexander Kerr, a retired principal of Fort Hare College, to the biennial meeting of the Christian Council which met in May 1954 shortly after the Bantu Education Act became law, admitted that "it has been difficult enough for the church to foster the spiritual element in the schools which it has controlled." At the same time he conceded that state involvement was essential if an increasing number of children were to gain access to schooling. His major concern in this address, however, was to ensure that the "spiritual element" be maintained in schools which were now under state control. To this end he argued that "it should be a prime consideration between church and state as to how best under a program of expansion of school facilities these spiritual values . . . can best be conserved." It was essentially *these* values, he insisted, to which mission schools had for more than a century applied themselves with "conscientious effort," while allowing for the "*unhurried development*" of blacks in other areas. He argued that instead of reducing the subsidy the state should have encouraged this work because the churches had been pioneers in "elementary training in agriculture, and in the arts and crafts like carpentry and building, blacksmithing, tin-smithing, wagon building, shoemaking, tailoring, weaving, domestic arts and first aid—all the services in fact which the African population, especially in the rural areas, has required."

What made this address important was its conciliatory tone. The importance of vocational training in mission schools was emphasized in much the same way as Verwoerd emphasized education "in accordance with the opportunities in life." Still more important was the emphasis that "it is a continuation of missionary duty . . . to give what help can be given in aiding a new and untried system of public education." The Council was impressed and asked that the full text of the address be immediately published.[11] And when the churches decided on their strategic response to the impact of Bantu Education, it was in accordance with the views expressed by Kerr. It was a moderate and cautious response which would come close to alienating that constituency of the church represented by Reeves and Huddleston.

Archbishop Clayton had informed the Diocese of Cape Town that having consulted widely with "a body of very experienced missionaries including both African and European clergymen, some of whom have devoted most of their lives to running educational institutions for native Africans" the advice was unanimous: The church should not refuse to lease their buildings to the Department of Native Affairs.[12] Notwithstanding the fact that Reeves had also consulted with clergy and educationalists in his diocese who counselled him to close the schools, the statement of the Anglican Episcopal Synod which met in November 1954 committed the church to a compromise position articulated by Clayton:

Both as to the religious and secular teaching it is our conviction that the Bantu Education Act will retard the true education of the African and the majority of us are of the opinion that the Church should not make itself responsible for taking part in such an educational system. All we are prepared to do is to lease certain of our buildings to the State. The majority of us think that in many cases it would be wrong to refuse to do so. Such a refusal would throw many teachers out of employment and leave many children without opportunity of any kind of instruction. It is incompatible with our duty to the African people to take action which might lead to such results. Here we are faced with a grievous choice of evils. We must choose the lesser. But this does not imply that we approve in any sense of an Act which will retard the progress of African education, and weaken the connection of such education with the teaching of the Christian faith.[13]

The Methodists adopted a similar position. Having rejected the policy of Bantu Education as "incompatible with the Christian principles for which the church stands," the Conference of the Methodist Church meeting in Queenstown decided: "Nevertheless, in order to provide for the immediate educational needs of the African people, the Church feels compelled to relinquish control of its schools to the State and to continue to exercise a Christian influence upon education wherever possible." Other churches like the Church of Scotland and the American Board Mission which controlled Adam's College in Natal followed suit.

The Roman Catholic Church decided to take a lonely alternative option and committed itself to keep open its schools with a reduced subsidy.[14] The judgment of the Catholic bishops as to what constituted the lesser of two evils differed from that of the Protestant churches. They raised a sum of one-and-a-half million rands during 1955, and by 1966 there were still 472 schools under their control (they ran 688 subsidized schools in 1954). At present this church still runs approximately 100 black schools, many of them still heavily funded from church resources and subsidized by income received from private white Roman Catholic schools.[15] However successful the bishops may have been in refusing to carry out the provisions of Bantu education, despite their commitment to keep their schools open and recognizing the continuing important involvement by the Roman Catholic Church in black education, they too became trapped in the labyrinth of apartheid, being forced by government legislation to teach a Bantu education syllabus.

The most radical form of ecclesial resistance came from the Anglican Diocese of Johannesburg. Reeves obtained a ruling from Archbishop Clayton which freed him from the Episcopal Synod's decision, and as Bishop of Johannesburg he wrote to the Minister of Native Affairs informing him that the Anglican Church would close all its schools throughout the Southern Transvaal on 1 April 1955.[16] Condemned by the state, Reeves also found himself isolated from his fellow bishops. Some respected his sincerity; others did not. The Johannesburg-based English newspaper, the *Star*, thought that it was the 10,000 African children in Anglican schools in the Diocese that were being "sacrificed as a gesture that might be admirable in other circumstances."[17]

Trevor Huddleston, whose name had become synonymous with black resistance, saw the Bantu Education Act as an expression of tyranny and chided the churches for capitulating to the view that "once a thing had become law it is wrong to fight against it."[18] The pathos inherent in his determination to resist is captured in his reflection on the struggle of the 1950s: "The hardest thing," he said, is ". . .to stand by the principle to the end and having done all to stand."[19] His description of the churches has proved itself as true thirty years later as when first written:

> The tragic mistake, as I shall always believe, lay in the failure of the churches to act together. I am convinced that had, say,

the Methodists, the Roman Catholics, the Presbyterians and the Anglicans united for once on this single issue, had they approached the Prime Minister and stated that, in conscience, they could not cooperate in the implementation of the Act, at least some major concessions would have been won.

While each church individually protested, argued against and condemned the rape of its schools, none apparently could take the initiative in urging a total refusal to surrender. . . .

Although the Anglican Church had condemned the Act as heartily as every other Christian body, when it came to the point of deciding how to translate her opposition into reality, it was another story.[20]

The English-speaking churches had failed to be more than moderate. Given to verbal protest, they failed to resist. Trapped within their own history they were predisposed to cautious compromise. For the Reeves-Huddleston option of total non-cooperation to have succeeded, the support of African parents, whose children would have been deprived of schooling, would have been required. This support could not have been assumed, but neither was it realistically canvassed, and those significant black voices which did support total resistance were ignored. Clayton had argued that "even a rotten system of education is better than that which young children pick up in the streets."[21] Father David Rakale saw it differently: "We are told," he wrote, "that half a loaf of bread is better than no bread at all. Those of us who agree with the Bishop's [Reeves'] decision say we would rather have our children starve than to even contemplate giving them as much as a slice of poisoned bread."[22]

The divide within the Anglican church was clearly the divide within the English-speaking churches as a whole. Dr. J. B. Webb, president of the Conference of the Methodist Church, insisted that there was a "common mind" among Africans that "although they hated this Bantu Education like poison, they still felt that a wreck was better than nothing at all."[23] The divide was between the majority of the church leaders and moderate African opinion which argued that some form of education was better than none, on the one hand, and those whose position was symbolized by Reeves and Huddleston, who kept faith with radical black opinion.

Black opinion outside the churches was also divided. It was a division carried into the ANC-led 1955 schools boycott campaign. The ANC favored "complete withdrawal" from the schools as a goal but could not agree on "what to do in the immediate situation." The National Executive Committee recommended a week's stay away from classes, but a conference called to consider the matter rejected the proposal and voted for an indefinite boycott. Various compromises were attempted, but dissension grew. Albert Luthuli, Z. K. Matthews and A. B. Xuma vacillated, while regional leadership in the Transvaal and eastern Cape, with the support of the acting ANC General Secretary, Oliver Tambo, called for the immediate withdrawal of children from schools. Dr. A. B. Xuma encouraged "teachers, sub-inspectors and supervisors to remain at their posts as allies of the people"—a position supported by teachers' unions and several black newspapers.[24] Professor Matthews advocated that teachers, members of school committees and school boards "discharge their duties in such a way as to make the system unworkable." At the same time he refused to condemn those whose strategies differed from his own or that of the ANC leadership, while militant voices within and outside of the ANC regarded those who agreed to participate in the Bantu education system for any reason at all "stooges, reactionaries, escapists and traitors." Popular support for the boycott was mixed, with the East Rand and eastern Cape supporting the call for a stay-away while other areas were less supportive. Ultimately the boycott failed.

A total refusal by the churches to allow the state to lease their schools in coordination with the ANC and other militant black groups could have forced the hand of the government. This point was made clearly by Huddleston. The fear of the churches was that their property could be expropriated, or that the entire black school-going population could be thrown onto the streets leading to a potentially revolutionary clash between the black population and the government. It was a possibility for which the churches were not prepared to take any responsibility. They were not ready for this kind of showdown with the state, and it was this that separated them so clearly from the ANC. Yet neither had the ANC actually planned for such an encounter, and their response to the crisis was inadequately organized. The National Executive Committee of the ANC was preoccupied with arrangements for the Congress of the People, Luthuli was gravely ill, several ANC leaders had been banned, concern was prevalent about the quality of alternative educational options offered by the ANC—and Verwoerd's threat that those children who did not return to school would be permanently expelled ultimately carried the day.

Bantu education was a fait accompli; any response seemed less than adequate and the most creative and imaginative responses from the black community were necessarily mixed. The inadequacy of the response by the churches needs to be seen in this context. What is perhaps most lamentable is that they ultimately abdicated all responsibility in the crisis. The churches were opposed to Bantu education. They were also opposed to the boycott, arguing that it was the wrong way to oppose the system. They believed that children would be required to pay the ultimate penalty, pointing to the 1952 Defiance Campaign as evidence of the kind of suffering that further resistance would precipitate. Yet they did not offer any form of support program to those teachers and administrators who decided "to remain at their posts as allies of the people." As a result, the resisting minority within black education, whether committed to "make the system unworkable" or simply to providing the best education possible within what Clayton had called a "rotten education," and Webb a "wreck," received ever-decreasing support from the churches. They provided no support for Trevor Huddleston's African Educational Movement which aimed to establish private schools, cultural clubs for the children of parents who could not afford private school fees and a home education program intended to meet the needs of children not attending school and those who wished to augment the education they received in school. Neither did they support literacy programs, night school incentives or attempts by teachers within the schools to upgrade the standard of Bantu education. Having decided to hand over their schools to the state since this was judged to be in "continuation with missionary duty," they abdicated educational responsibility both within and outside of these schools. The Institute of Race Relations, students on university campuses and various other secular groups sought in different ways to augment and offer alternative educational options, but not the churches. In so doing they took an important step in a process of narrowing their sphere of community involvement, allowing their religion to become less public and more private.

In time there were attempts by some to justify this move. The *Evening Post*, for example, quoted the president of the Methodist Church, Dr. J. B. Webb, who had earlier condemned the Act, as saying:

> The Bantu Education Act did not deprive children of Christian Education. . . . Our educational experts, having scrutinised the new syllabuses in so far as they have been published, regard them as an improvement on the old. . . . The African would have a far greater responsibility for the administration of schools under them than under the old regime. . . . But more important from the African's point of view, it is envisaged that within a comparatively short space of time, twice the number of children will be able to gain admission to schools than was possible at the commencement of the Act.[25]

The kindest comment to be made is that Webb was wrong. In his influential address to the Christian Council, Alexander Kerr had appealed to the state to allow for the "spiritual element" to be maintained in the former mission schools, and now Webb was claiming that this had been done. His definition of Christian education was pedantic and narrow, and he failed to address the question concerning the kind of education which "twice the number of children" were receiving. There was a great deal of confusion in some circles concerning an adequate response by the churches, but few within the black community shared Webb's optimistic reading of the legislation defined so bluntly by Verwoerd and other government spokespersons.

Today the black schools have become what some have called "sites of struggle" for liberation, and many difficult choices concerning boycotts, alternative education and participation within the black education system are being faced all over again. After thirty years of protest without resistance, the churches can provide no viable educational alternative to Bantu education. It is this that makes the resolutions of the English-speaking churches on the present education crisis seem all too hollow and ineffectual.

The churches had condemned Bantu education, but when it came to the point of deciding how to translate this protest into reality, they had little to offer. Of course their decision was a cruel and a difficult one, but an organic crisis in a nation—what Christians call a *Kairos*—demands a high price. The churches did not regard the implementation of Bantu education to be such a moment. They did not discern an opportunity to resist the ever-encroaching tentacles of apartheid as one not to be missed, refusing to accept that in so doing an opportunity would have been lost forever—for the church, for the oppressed people and for the country as a whole.

Huddleston saw the Bantu Education Act to be precisely such a moment. He described the Act as "by far the most important and by far the most deadly" of all pieces of apartheid legislation passed through parliament, comparing it to the appropriation of church and educational institutions by Adolf Hitler in 1935.[26] For him it constituted a stronger attack on the church than the "church clause" of 1957 which the church did resist.[27] He foresaw the implications of the Act stretching over many years, and he watched as the state acted against the churches in an unprecedented manner while the churches ultimately surrendered.

In the belief that the identity of the church was under attack, the churches did stand together in 1957 and resist an attempt by Verwoerd to prescribe who might worship in which sanctuary on a Sunday. They had refused to adopt a similar stance when relieved of their responsibility for the minds and character of the children in their care. It was this, suggests Huddleston, which could well have constituted the difference between what the government in fact did in 1953 and what they backed away from doing in 1957. Despite the lack of coordinated response from the different black teachers' unions and the inadequate planning that went into the ANC schools boycott, it is clear that these constituencies did perceive the urgency of the moment. The fact that the churches ultimately relinquished a public sphere which they had occupied for 150 years witnesses to a narrowing understanding of what they regarded as their most basic *raison d'etre*. The difference between their responses in 1953 and 1957 is precisely this point. It indicates that the churches, when under threat, regarded their primary responsibility to be *narrowly* spiritual, with a focus on what happens on a Sunday in a church building. The *broad* diaconal consequences of this spiritual center could be surrendered under protest.

There were many future issues which the church would protest against and find no viable manner in which to resist. Not least among these was the imposition of group areas legislation which resulted in the total destruction of congregations and the religious identity of perhaps millions of people in urban and rural removal schemes. Christian leaders were banned, imprisoned and exiled. It was a situation in which churches did not know what to do. Their own history and theology predisposed them to cautious and ambivalent protest. Perhaps it is Huddleston's experience, which less socially engaged members of the English-speaking churches find most difficult not to reject as hyperbolic, that captures the pathos of the response of these churches. A banning order under the Suppression of Communism Act had been served on Oliver Tambo, a graduate of St. Peter's College and a faithful worshiper at the Church of Christ the King in Sophiatown. The lack of response by the churches to the banning of one of their own, a prominent black leader, drove Huddleston to exasperation. His words published in the *Observer* under the rubric "The Church Sleeps On," haunt the English-speaking churches still today. He quoted Chesterton's "The Ballad of the White Horse":

> I tell you naught for your comfort
> Yea, naught for your desire,
> Save that the sky grows darker yet
> And the sea rises higher

"The church sleeps on," he wrote. "The church sleeps on—though it occasionally talks in its sleep and expects (or does it) the government to listen."[28]

ARMED STRUGGLE

The shots fired at Sharpeville on 21 March 1960 heralded a new era in black politics in South Africa. Protest hardened into resist-

ance, and blacks were forced to think in terms of revolutionary strategy. The significance of this phase of the struggle was
acknowledged throughout the world, and the English-speaking
churches, together with other organizations, were compelled to
address themselves to the ensuing struggle for black self-
determination with a new sense of urgency. What becomes clear is
that these churches were not prepared to cross the divide from
protest to resistance in 1960 any more than they were prepared to
do so in 1953. Nor were they in most instances able to show any
empathy for those of their own members who opted for the armed
struggle.

Twenty thousand people converged on the Sharpeville police
station in support of the campaign to defy pass laws on what was to
become a decisive day in South African history. Sixty-nine people
were killed, the majority apparently shot in the back while fleeing,
and a further 180 persons were injured. Two weeks later on April 8
the ANC and the PAC were banned under the hastily enacted
Unlawful Organizations Act. Several of their leaders went into
exile and others were banned and imprisoned, and the movements
were forced to pursue their struggle underground.

A new era had dawned. Anti-apartheid activity began to be
coordinated at a different level. Intermittent acts of counterviolence began to occur on a regular basis against the institutionalized oppression of the apartheid regime, and these were used by
the police as the necessary justification for further repressive violence. The spiral of violence had begun a process of intensification
which, despite periods of abeyance, has continued to intensify.
Events surrounding Soweto in 1976 resulted in approximately
seven hundred dead and far in excess of that number injured. In the
1980s people are being brutalized and killed by police and army
throughout the country.

The immediate response to Sharpeville by the churches was the
Cottesloe Consultation, meeting outside Johannesburg from December 7-14, 1960. Here representatives of the World Council of
Churches (WCC) and the eight South African member churches,
including the NGK synods of the Transvaal and the Cape Province,
met to conclude that apartheid could not be reconciled with the
teachings of scripture. But the NGK delegates, reprimanded by
Prime Minister Hendrik Verwoerd for allowing themselves to be

manipulated by the WCC were told to recant. They did so, enough of them to divide the Afrikaans churches from the English-speaking churches. Ultimately they isolated themselves from the world church by resigning from the WCC, and in 1982 their membership of the World Alliance of Reformed Churches was suspended.

The post-Sharpeville period witnessed the programmatic theological opposition of the English-speaking churches to apartheid. "The Message to the People of South Africa" rejected apartheid as a pseudo-gospel, anticipating the 1982 "Apartheid is a Heresy" resolution of the WARC by fourteen years, and several important statements of purpose and intent originated from these churches and their leaders during this time.[29]

It was, however, essentially on the international scene that the stage was being set which would strike at the moderate heart of the English-speaking churches and cause them to turn their backs on those of their number who resorted to armed struggle. The 1968 Uppsala Assembly of the WCC met in the wake of several successful liberation wars in Africa and the intensification of the war against Portuguese colonialism in Guinea-Bissau, Mozambique and Angola. The Civil Rights Bill had been passed in the United States and Martin Luther King, who was to have delivered the opening address in Uppsala had been assassinated; in South Africa the major liberation movements had been banned, with *Umkhonto we Sizwe* (the armed wing of the ANC) having been established since the previous Assembly met in New Delhi seven years earlier.

Confessing that it had done "too little too late," the Uppsala Assembly committed itself to the "elimination of racism throughout the world." A year later the Program to Combat Racism (PCR) was established, and the crunch came for the South African Church in 1970 with the establishment of a Special Fund "to support organizations that combat racism, rather than the welfare organizations that alleviate the effects of racism."[30] In effect it was a decision to shift the focus of the ecumenical church from protest and benevolence to resistance and support for those engaged in a liberation struggle. It struck at the heart of the character of the English-speaking churches; and the announcement that liberation movements (the ANC and PAC among them) committed to armed struggle to overthrow the minority and colonial governments in several southern African states were to receive monetary assistance from the fund found the English-speaking churches (as WCC member churches) thrown into major confusion. They rejected and condemned the WCC decision, while the South African white regime initiated a cry which was picked up around the world: "The WCC has committed itself to support terrorism!" The explanation by the WCC that their funding was "for humanitarian purposes consonant with the aims and policies" of the world body was lost in the heat of conflict. But perhaps the most soul-shattering realization for white South Africans with their feet firmly planted in the English-speaking and other churches was the realization that those whom they had all too easily dismissed as communists and terrorists were being affirmed by churches elsewhere in the world.

The WCC saw the grants as a "combination of political judgement and support for humanitarian programmes of a particular group or movement." It argued that it "does not and cannot identify itself completely with any political movement, nor does it pass judgement on those victims of racism who are driven to violence as the only way left to redress grievances and so open the way for a new and more just social order." In so doing it refused to identify "another better way to liberation" and submitted that any attempt to prescribe to oppressed people who had for generations tried other paths to liberation and reluctantly resorted to arms as a last resort would amount to insensitivity and paternalism.[31]

There were other issues which heightened the debate. Not least among these was the decision to accept the integrity of the recipients of the grants to *in fact* utilize the funds for humanitarian purposes, without instituting some kind of monitoring process. The Methodists thought this lack of control was "a condescending attitude and rather insulting to the recipients." But ultimately these debates within the larger debate concerning solidarity with oppressed people who resort to armed struggle were of lesser significance. If there had been any hesitation on the part of the WCC concerning its support for the liberation movements this was removed with the imposition of a further banning order on a number of individuals and organizations by the South African regime in 1977. The world saw this as a further indication of the unwillingness of the South African government to allow legal, non-violent protest and political opposition. It was interpreted as a vindication of those whose judgment it was that the last resort involving armed struggle had been reached.

The WCC used the words "brotherly solidarity" to explain the basis of its ministry to those engaged in liberation struggles which included armed struggle. "Our support [for these movements] is to be seen as a *sign of solidarity* which should be clearly distinguished from *identification* with a movement," argued Philip Potter, the General Secretary of the WCC at the time.[32] Whatever the semantics involved, the basis of ministry was seen to reside in a familial relationship within which those to whom one ministers are treated as brothers and sisters. Indeed, it was suggested at the time, if the church ministers to those who take up arms in defense of the existing order, it can do no less in relation to those who resort to arms in their struggle for justice.

The responses of the different English-speaking churches were similar in many ways, while several important differences in emphasis were to be noted. Despite the careful language used, most of the churches found themselves forced by dominant public opinion, fueled as it was by frantic anti-WCC propaganda unleashed by the South African media, government threats and their own considered responses to the WCC decision, into an alliance against that organization. They condemned racism in South Africa in their normal tried-and-tested manner, and all four churches decided to retain their membership in the world body while criticizing the WCC for what they regarded as its implicit support of violence. There was disagreement among the churches as to whether to withhold their affiliation fees to the WCC in protest against its decision to fund the liberation movements, but this was preempted by a decision of the government to prevent the transfer of such funds. Only the United Congregational Church decided to pay its affiliation fee on a regular basis into a savings account until such time as it would be possible to transfer funds to the WCC; the other churches either voted explicitly not to submit funds to the WCC or to accept the ruling of the government in this regard without protest.

The Anglicans expressed "appreciation for the WCC's Program to Combat Racism in so far as it is an expression of identification with those who are working for a just social order," but went on to stress that there is "not only one form of Christian obedience" which commits the church to "identify with any liberation movement, political party or government." It went further to respect "the fact that some Christians feel themselves called to be pacifists, others to defend the Republic of South Africa in the armed forces and others to leave its borders to take up arms to achieve what they believe will be a more just ordering of society."[33] Simply stated, the Anglicans refused to either take sides or to in any way indicate whether a particular stance by any party or group is more or less in accordance with the teachings of that church. Individual Christians were left to make their own political choices unaided by their church, and the church remained captive to a form of moderation born within and sustained by an obligation to minister without offense to both sides of the ideological divide in South Africa—a form of moderation which in this case led to an abdication of political responsibility and to ethical indecision. More than that, in failing to resist that process which was driving the churches further away from those issues which constitute the political conflict in the country, it lent direct support to the privatization of religion which constitutes an abdication of political responsibility. In so doing it played directly into the hands of the existing order.

The General Assembly of the Presbyterian Church of Southern Africa dissented from the decision of the WCC "to support nationalist movements," arguing that it is "no part of the Christian task to align the church with nationalist forces of any race," while urging that WCC funds be used "strictly for the relief of hardship"—a clause presumably to be read in opposition to the clause within the criteria governing the Special Fund of the PCR which commits it to support "organisations that combat racism rather than welfare organisations." In a separate resolution the Assembly further stated the need also to "dissent at least as much from the violence inherent in the racial policies of the South African Government." The Presbyterians no less than the Church of the Province were not prepared to face the fundamental issues involved in the PCR challenge.[34]

The United Congregational Church's response to the PCR grants was less critical than the responses of the other churches. The Assembly had responded positively to the decision of the WCC to aid "certain organisations in Southern Africa," while the Executive

Committee wrote to the General Secretary of the WCC (Eugene Carson Blake) expressing "grave concern that . . . one of the most serious implications of the grants was the fact that they might lessen the possibility of the World Council of Churches becoming the reconciliation agent and arbiter in conflict between black and white in southern Africa."[35]

The Methodist Church was, in turn, quite uncompromising in its condemnation of the PCR. Its Conference resolution on the matter assumes language which a comparison with the news media and government reaction at the time shows to be part of the dominant white reaction to the decision to provide humanitarian aid to liberation movements. The church expressed:

Its dismay at the indications of political partisanship in the allocation of grants by the World Council of Churches from the funds of the Program to Combat Racism. These allegedly humanitarian grants appear to go not to those who need them most but to those adhering to a particular political wing.

Its conviction that the struggle in Rhodesia/Zimbabwe and in South West Africa/Namibia is no longer between white and black, but is between those who desire a liberated and non-racial community but hope to gain it by consultation and reconciliation, and groups which seek their ends by the power of the gun.

Its impression that the World Council of Churches is attempting to heal the ills of mankind by human ingenuity and with human resources, without recognising sufficiently the penetration of all these by sin. . . .

Its urgent request that the churches having links with the WCC give serious consideration to the Council's proper functions. . . .

Its distress that this world-wide association of Christian Churches appears by its actions to condone the atrocities committed by guerillas on uninvolved non-combatants and humanitarian mission workers.

Its condemnation of injustice, cruelty and atrocities no matter by whom they are committed . . . established governments or guerilla fighters.

Its determination to continue and intensify its own efforts

to promote justice, non-racialism and power-sharing within
the structures of the Methodist Church and in the areas
within which it works.[36]

In conclusion the Methodist Church appealed to the WCC to
discontinue its "unconditional grants." The Methodists had
failed to engage in theological debate concerning the PCR call to
the churches to show a "sign of solidarity" with the oppressed in
their resolve to be free. An alternative reading of the Methodist
resolution suggests it could have been a deliberate choice to posit
the church against the liberation movements. Either way, their
response lent legitimation to a regime whose propaganda system
was geared to undermining the theological integrity of the WCC.
And when John Vorster, prime minister at that time, was approached by the churches to allow WCC officials to enter the
country for dialogue with the churches, he insisted that the purpose of such a meeting be "to confront" the WCC officials on the
grants to "terrorists in Southern Africa" as articulated in their
"respective resolutions against the abhorrent decision."[37] But this
too was preempted while the deliberations on the agenda were still
under way, with Vorster insisting that the WCC visitors be not
allowed to go further than the international hotel at Jan Smuts
airport, a position quite unacceptable to the WCC and the
English-speaking churches who initiated the invitation to the
WCC officials.

Debate on the details of the PCR decision is not what is at stake,
and certainly the apparent failure of the WCC to forewarn their
South African member churches of their impending decision left
these churches unable to anticipate the impending storm. What is
at stake is the failure of the English-speaking churches to seriously
accept their responsibility to minister to their own church members
who found themselves embroiled in a civil war against a regime that
their churches had condemned as having consistently disobeyed the
will of God. Some refused to allow for any moral distinction
between the conflicting forms of violence engaged in by the state
and the liberation movements; others stated that revolutionary
violence is wrong without making any comment on the oppressive
violence being resisted. Yet each of these churches has chosen to
continue to supply chaplains to the armed services of the South

African regime which are consistently used to ensure that the present government remain "in control." Herein is the glaring contradiction within the response of the English-speaking churches. Captive to the dominant ideas of the dominant class and trapped within a theology of moderation and submission to the existing order, they have at best submitted to those within and without their own ranks who contended (in the words of the Methodist resolution) that it is not their "proper function" to show solidarity with those who suffer if they resort to an armed struggle, nor to lend theological recognition to those whose goal it is to "combat racism" in a manner which their Christian consciences may dictate. In this context President Kenneth Kaunda, who had taken Zambia to independence a decade before the PCR storm broke, articulated the sentiments of many black South Africans when he called the decision to fund liberation movements "the WCC's visionary action . . . which may well be seen in the future as decisive for the church's fate in Southern Africa."[38]

Now, almost two decades since the first PCR grants were made to southern African liberation movements, new demands are being made on the churches. The *Lusaka Statement* which emerged from the May 1987 WCC conference on The Churches' Search for Justice and Peace in Southern Africa reads in part:

> We affirm the unquestionable right of the people of Namibia and South Africa to secure justice and peace through the liberation movements. While remaining committed to peaceful change we recognise that the nature of the South African regime which wages war against its own inhabitants and neighbours compels the movements to the use of force along with other means to end oppression. We call upon the churches and the international community to seek ways to give this affirmation practical effect in the struggle for liberation in the region and to strengthen their contacts with the liberation movements.

The SACC has since adopted the *Lusaka Statement*, voting against a resolution merely to "receive" the statement and refer it to member churches. The report of the Church and Society Department to the 1987 Assembly of the United Congregational Church captures the initial reaction of these churches in identifying the paragraph quoted immediately above as having "caused . . . consternation in some quarters." It further identifies the internal division within the churches in noting that "the *Lusaka Statement* is causing great distress amongst some Christians in South Africa, but it is hailed with joy by thousands of other Christians . . . as a sign the church really cares about the oppressed victims of apartheid." The Assembly "received" the statement and referred it to local churches, regional councils and the Church and Society Department "to consider the *Lusaka Statement* and the manner in which the Church can assist in the process of change."[39] "It is as far as the Assembly could go without tearing the church apart," said a senior minister and theologian of the United Congregational Church.

The Methodist and Presbyterian churches have received the document for further study, while the Anglicans, with certain qualifications, "accepted" the *Lusaka Statement* in the following resolution of their Provincial Standing Committee, the executive body of the church.

Understanding the pressures which have led the liberation movements to respond to violence with violence,

Aware that there is at present insufficient factual evidence on the effects of disinvestment to make an informed resolution on this issue or to use this issue as grounds for rejecting the Lusaka Document,

Recognizing the commitment to peaceful change laid out in the Lusaka Document, and

Acknowledging the urgent need to correct the Church's current abysmal failure to bring about meaningful change and an end to aggression:

1. Accepts the Lusaka Document and stresses the need for further meetings with the ANC and PAC to discuss the nature of South Africa beyond Apartheid to which we are committed.

2. Implores its members to explore to its fullest, means by which it can show Jesus' "Third Way" as a positive nonviolent way to change, despite the high cost of this way.

3. Appeals in the strongest possible way to its members, to

pledge the Church to learning about and adopting "The Third Way" of vital and active non-violent change.

ECONOMIC SANCTIONS

A third paradigm which portrays the moderate character of the English-speaking churches is the response of these churches to the call for economic sanctions—a call with which the WCC first confronted the churches in 1968, and one which still evokes spirited and recriminatory debate in both secular and ecclesiastical circles. If the tenor of this debate and the response of the South African government are anything to go by, the political potential inherent in the disinvestment campaign is significant.

The debate is an intense one which has produced its own nuanced distinctions between disinvestment, divestment, sanctions and boycotts of different kinds.[40] These important differences are not considered here, recognizing that the consequences of each of these options are, to differing degrees of intensity, potentially the same. The discussion that follows is with certain qualifications equally relevant to each of the above options. Total withdrawal from the South African economy in the form of disinvestment and/or mandatory trade sanctions, as discussed below, is also the logical consequence of the various forms of "economic pressure" being advocated.

There are no easy answers to many of the issues raised by disinvestment and related discussions. What follows is not intended conclusively to address these issues but rather to illustrate the difficulty facing the churches trapped in the dilemma of ministering to two constituencies—those who benefit from the economy and those exploited by it.

The essence of the argument put forward by those opposing the various disinvestment options is that blacks will suffer most and that, with the exception of a few radicals, the majority of black workers is against them. Opinion surveys among urban blacks, invariably conducted by liberal academics and quoted by spokespersons for foreign companies defending their economic engagement in South Africa, are purported to verify this. Research conducted by Mark Orkin, however, reveals that in many instances the questions posed in these surveys are ideologically biased and fail to take the realities of an oppressed context into account. Orkin's own survey shows that 73 percent of urban black workers favors either total or conditional disinvestment. It also suggests that black leaders (including church leaders such as Tutu and Boesak) advocating disinvestment who have so often been castigated in this country as radical mavericks are in fact important opinion makers in the black community.[41]

Archbishop Desmond Tutu has been cautious and modest in his support for disinvestment, explaining that neither he nor any other black leader specifically wants sanctions. It is, however, an option which he feels compelled to appropriate. "There is no guarantee that sanctions will topple apartheid," he insists, "but it is the last nonviolent option left." As relentless a campaigner against apartheid as Alan Paton, on the other hand, contends that the very thought of a successful campaign is a nightmare to him because it is blacks who will suffer most. The questions he posed about the then Bishop of Johannesburg's "political morality" and "Christian conscience" which could allow him "to advocate disinvestment . . . [and] put a man out of work" produced an extended debate in the South African press. A contribution to this debate in the form of a letter to the *Sunday Times* from a Mr. Makhagoane, living in a black resettlement area in Witsieshoek, focuses the debate:

> Disinvestment or not? The debate goes on and on. Bishop Tutu calls for the sabotage of the South African economy. It doesn't concern me. After all, it is not my economy.
>
> What bothers me is this sudden concern Alan Paton, T. Mopeli, Gatsha Buthelezi and all the rich are showing about me.
>
> I will be the first to suffer, I will be hit the hardest, they say.
> So they don't believe that we are already starving.
>
> Whites think they are living in the world of their own; that everything in this country is in its natural state.
>
> They think we are content with our hand-to-mouth life. They write from their cozy houses to question Bishop Tutu's morality and to express concern about me, should the disinvestment campaign succeed.
>
> I am among the masses of the surplus South Africans

deposited in the barren homelands to ensure I am cut off
from the country's economy.
I can't leave this homeland to look for work. I am un-
wanted.
The bishop calls for disinvestment to end this country's
abhorrent system. I will suffer even more, but at least it will
make whites aware that I am suffering.[42]

Briefly stated, the disinvestment issue in South Africa is being
debated from two very different perspectives. An editorial in a
student newspaper made a simple but pointed observation: "While
P. W. Botha might talk of a bloodbath that is to come, opponents of
apartheid . . . are pointing to the actions of police and the military
in suppressing opposition to apartheid throughout South Africa.
Their talk is of the bloodbath that is already occurring in townships
around the country, which disinvestment might in some way assist
in ending."

Of course it is possible to take the academic view and suggest that
the present extent of human suffering cannot be qualitatively compared to the extent of the blood that could flow or that a successful
disinvestment campaign might induce. It is, however, exceedingly
difficult to convince a parent whose child has been killed in a hail of
police bullets or left paralyzed by township brutality or who has
become the victim of malnutrition that the bloodbath is not already
here. To fail to understand this is to fail to understand the intensity
of black anger or the extent of black suffering and death presently
perpetrated by the apartheid system.

Most of the debate concerning disinvestment seems to ignore this
yawning gap in perspective. As is often the case when emotive
issues acquire high political profile, thoughtful analysis is ignored
while participants in the debate are so blinded by their interests that
it is difficult to assess their motives. It is impossible not to be
suspicious of the motives of some of the advocates of private
enterprise both inside and outside of the English-speaking
churches. The churches cannot easily throw off their long involvement in industrial and mining labor relations, and multinational
companies are suspect who almost overnight became avid advocates of the cause of economically deprived blacks, feeling the need
eagerly to support investment for "the sake of black workers"!

There are presumably also some American politicians who are more concerned about American foreign policy interests than what actually happens in South Africa, arguing that the United States as the leader of Western democracy cannot afford to be involved in any way with the messy and morally reprehensible South African situation. But because altruism and ambition are always mixed in history, there is probably little to be gained from trying to unravel various motives.

The disinvestment debate *is* a complex one and the options facing those who choose to disinvest are limited, with no evidence to suggest that companies are prepared to simply jettison their capital invested in South Africa. It is partly this kind of realism that persuaded Archbishop Denis Hurley, until recently president of the Southern African Catholic Bishops' Conference, to argue that "all-out sanctions" might force a change of government, but unless the major Western powers give sanctions complete support it would be "ineffective and a long drawnout struggle." It is the possibility of the complete destruction of the economy, further unemployment, poverty and misery for the country's black majority which has Hurley saying: "I find it very hard to be as enthusiastic as Archbishop Tutu . . . on this matter of all-out sanctions. I and my brother bishops don't feel quite the enthusiasm he does because of the possibilities which could result."[43]

The Catholic bishops have wrestled with the disinvestment issue in a manner that no other church in South Africa has done. They have found themselves haunted by the Mr. Makhagoanes of this sad land who simply contend "it is not my economy." Political struggle also suggests that ultimately it is those who have most to lose who are prepared to lose the least, and those who have least— when pressed—are ready to lose what little they have in their struggle for basic justice and the fundamental rights of their children. It is this which persuaded the bishops to weigh "the possibility of further unemployment" against the "present rate of suffering and unemployment . . . if apartheid is not dismantled." In so doing they resolved that "economic pressure *has* been justifiably imposed . . . [and] that such pressure should continue," while qualifying their call by cautioning that "intensified pressure can only be justified if applied in such a way as not to destroy the country's economy and to reduce as far as possible any additional suffering to the oppressed through job loss."[44]

In February 1987, having received the interim report of a commission appointed to monitor the effects of economic pressure, Bishop Wilfred Napier, president of the Bishops' Conference, concluded that "there is consensus among black people, those who are politicised and socialised in their views: these are definitely in favour of economic pressure." A press release from the Catholic Bishops' Conference read: "Bishop Napier and the Bishops' Conference still subscribe to the view that economic pressure was justifiable and should continue, but should not destroy the country's economy and cause further suffering."[45]

Without defining the nature of "economic pressure," the bishops found themselves torn between prophetic discernment and pastoral concern. Recognizing the need for some form of disinvestment as a means to change, confronted with the possible effects of their prescribed medicine, they warn that the treatment may need to be cut short.

The English-speaking churches, with the notable exception of the United Congregational Church, are less decisive despite the resolution of the SACC National Conference in 1985, the major ecumenical meeting point for the English-speaking churches. It resolved

that disinvestment and similar economic pressures be now called for as a peaceful and effective means of putting pressure on the South African government to bring about those fundamental changes this country needs;

to ask our partner churches in other countries to continue with their efforts to identify and promote effective economic pressures to influence the situation in South Africa, towards achieving justice and peace in this country and minimising the violence of the conflict.

It further requested the executive members of the SACC, its regional councils and church leaders to consider the implications of the resolution, "encouraging congregations to study and debate with them," while asking "member churches and individual Christians to withdraw from participation in the economic system that oppresses the poor, by reinvesting money and energy in alternative economic systems in existence in our region."[46] This resolution enjoyed little support from the official delegates of the English-speaking churches present and has since been virtually ignored within these churches.

Despite the outspoken position of Archbishop Tutu on the matter, Anglicans have not provided any directive either from the Synod of Bishops or at the level of its General Synod. The SACC resolution on disinvestment has been referred to the Department of Justice and Reconciliation for study. The Diocesan Synod of Cape Town has, however, noted that "the government of the USA has imposed wide-ranging sanctions on trade with South Africa," and expressed its belief that "it lies within the power of South Africa to dismantle Apartheid and so dissipate the international response thereto," resolving "to call for an end to sanctions" when certain demands are met. These include the release of political prisoners, the unbanning of political organizations, freedom of expression and association, and a living wage for all workers.[47]

The Presbyterian Church of Southern Africa addressed the disinvestment question in a paper presented to its 1986 General Assembly meeting in Harare. Recognizing that "punitive measures will continue to be taken against South Africa until the basis on which apartheid rests has been removed . . . the Assembly calls upon the Government to abandon its apartheid policies and so bring an end to sanctions and disinvestment." In so doing the Assembly resolved that appropriate action by members of the Presbyterian Church of Southern Africa *could* include "support [for] selective sanctions and disinvestment, particularly those which bring pressure to give recognition to worker rights and to improve the conditions of labour." Yet other options which the Assembly regarded as worthy of its support included support for "investments which are labour intensive," and a variety of less radical options such as white voters using their "democratic powers" and "being open minded about communications and negotiations between those who may hold very different points of view. . . . " The Assembly failed to express a single opinion on the disinvestment question.[48]

The United Congregational Church's response differed from that of the other English-speaking churches. It is the only church within this grouping of churches to have unequivocally supported disinvestment and comprehensive sanctions. A task force having been appointed to consider the issues of Economic Justice and Sanctions, the 1986 Assembly of the United Congregational Church adopted a resolution in favor of "immediate and comprehensive sanctions against South Africa."[49] The challenge facing this church, however, is essentially that which has bedeviled the English-speaking churches throughout their history. It has to do with translating theory into practice or, differently stated, the problem of how to mobilize people through their spiritual lives to realize the ideals which the highest courts of their churches have projected for them.

In considering the matter of sanctions and disinvestment, the Methodist Church found itself trapped in a theological anomaly which bespeaks the agony of theological debate and Christian obedience in South Africa today. The 1986 Conference of this church identified the gathering momentum of disinvestment and sanctions "*as part of the judgement of God*." It further recorded its belief that "the South African government . . . has the responsibility to take those steps necessary for the lifting of sanctions and the halting of disinvestment by immediately instituting those fundamental changes required to move South Africa from oppression to full democracy and justice." It was not sure, however, whether as part of the church of God it ought to support this judgment or associate itself with those who resisted it. *This* is ultimately the captivity of the English-speaking churches. Indicating a knowledge of the will of God, they are yet not sure whether to serve God or Mammon. The pathos of the Methodist resolution emphasizes the point:

> While our church is divided on whether or not to commend sanctions and disinvestment as a strategy to bring about change, we are persuaded that this kind of economic pressure is already bringing about a measure of self-examination and reassessment which may yet lead to repentance among privileged South Africans. We cannot condemn something that could succeed where the cries of the people and the pleas of the church have gone unheard.[50]

The dilemma facing the English-speaking churches, identified in an earlier chapter, dominates the disinvestment debate. Required to minister to both privileged whites and oppressed blacks they are torn within—not as if they stand above the conflicting groups unable to decide how to minister to both, but because their very identity is formed and shaped by these conflicting groups. More than that, it is an institutional identity that has only just started to shift from being predominantly white to the point where it must reflect the majority membership.

The Catholic bishops are aware that there is consensus among politically-aware blacks "definitely in favour of economic pressure." All the churches under consideration accept the reality of disinvestment and sanctions as having been imposed on South Africa as a result of the intransigence of a government disobedient to the will of God as made known within the scriptures and tradition of the church. The Methodists allow it "may yet lead to repentance among the privileged South Africans," but apart from the United Congregational Church none of the English-speaking churches is prepared to allow church policy regarding disinvestment and sanctions to be shaped by the informed opinion of those who suffer most from apartheid.

TRAPPED IN PROTEST

There is much within the tradition of the English-speaking churches which persuades them that it is not a primary task of the church to show solidarity with the poor and the oppressed as they engage in a struggle for their true God-given humanity and liberation. Such solidarity is therefore, from the perspective of these churches, negotiable. Their identity is formed by a dominant theology which has been shaped by the mores and meanderings of a long history of captivity within the socio-economic and political structures of white domination. A consideration of the ambivalent response of these churches to Bantu education, the resorting to arms by oppressed South Africans, and the call for disinvestment and sanctions also suggests that these churches have, however, been inwardly disturbed by that alternative tradition within their history of the church that calls true believers to resistance and in some instances rebellion. This tradition has, of course, been heard with differing degrees of clarity as the issues involved have impinged with differing impact on the interests of the privileged members within the ranks of the English-speaking churches. The Methodists, for example, were (however reluctantly) more or less ready to allow for the legitimacy of this tradition in relation to Bantu education, perhaps because their criticism of the Bantu Education Act had little immediate impact on the dominant members of society. They were less ready, however, to accept the legitimacy of the resisting tradition regarding armed struggle or disinvestment because of the obvious implications such actions would evoke among their dominant members.

Ecclesial character is tediously and tenaciously formed. The English-speaking churches have been born and nurtured in those things that are neither harsh nor rigorous. It is their character, suggests Edmund Bishop, "not to scare away the faint hearted."[51] It is this character, so clearly seen in the response to the issues discussed in this chapter, that leaves these churches critical of the harshly oppressive reality of apartheid but unable to affirm the radical options of those within their own ranks and beyond who are not only ready to pay a high price for their liberation but expect others who claim to share their vision to join them in paying that price.

The above analysis of the response of the English-speaking churches suggests not that these churches are necessarily "wrong" for not having supported the more radical responses in the contemporary history of struggle, but that they offered no alternative programs for the kind of fundamental change which their many resolutions and policy statements suggest. "We have condemned by bell, book and candle, the political doctrine of apartheid as being not according to the mind of Christ and not in conformity with Scriptural teaching," insisted J. B. Webb, in delivering the Peter Ainslie Memorial Lecture of Rhodes University in 1968.[52] Yet, in so doing the English-speaking churches have not only conformed to the system which they have so consistently protested against, but also been unable to translate that protest into significant resistance.

Having surrendered important space in the Bantu education crisis, these churches have refused to allow that it is the proper function of the church to provide humanitarian aid to oppressed people who resort to an armed struggle. They have also not seen their way clear to supporting disinvestment or suggesting a viable alternative strategy for change. And, as shown in the next chapter, they have not been prepared to pray for the removal of the present rulers from power, while most of the churches have not joined the *Kairos* theologians in seriously challenging the legitimacy of the government—this despite the fact that this same government is responsible for the policies which they reject as contrary to the will of God.

Chapter Five

Moderate and Restrained

Critics of the church argue—with substantial evidence to support their argument—that the church since the days of Constantine has been held captive to the ideas and interests of the rulers of each successive age. It has, they argue, neither the will nor the motivation to set the oppressed people free. The captivity of the church to moderation and restraint is the focus of enquiry in this chapter.

Sociologists argue that "it is not consciousness that determines life but life that determines consciousness." It is difficult not to concede that all ideas, while dialectically structured, are the product of a particular social structure.[1] Religious people are often more forgetful of this than most. Religious ideas, like any other ideas, do not fall from the sky. This means that the different social bases in South Africa inevitably produce their own understanding of the faith first brought to this country by white colonizers, settlers and missionaries.

Schism, sectarianism and internal church divisions in South Africa, as elsewhere in the world, can on this basis be explained as a direct consequence of socio-economic and political divisions in society. A consequent temptation is to ignore religious conflict as an issue in itself, believing that it will be resolved as a part of the political solution to society's problems, at which point the religious identity of the community will reflect its new social base. Religion is not merely an epiphenomenal reflection of social reality. It stands in a dialectical relationship to its social base, formed by that base but also shaping and determining the nature of the society from which it emerges. This inherent relationship between religion and society means that the dominant influences and ideologies of society at any given time are reflected in the structures and symbols of that society's religion, just as they are reflected in the society's newspapers, propaganda systems, cultural events and political programs.

Being part of the overall social self-understanding of society (what Durkheim has called the social *idea* and Marx the *superstructure* of society), religion, like any other aspect of this self-understanding, is dominated by the ruling class of a particular society. Simply stated, the rich and the powerful do most to influence society's perception of itself.

To ignore the religious identity of a society is therefore to turn a blind eye to the fact that religion is part of society's ideology of existence. In South Africa the Afrikaners' traditional theology of apartheid has, for example, undoubtedly contributed to the maintenance of racial exploitation and white domination. And, it is argued, *the religion of the English-speaking churches has contributed significantly to the entrenchment of a system of laws making racial and economic discrimination possible.*

Certainly there is sufficient historical evidence to suggest that the dominant religious practice of South Africa has, generally speaking, provided ideological legitimacy, whether implicit or explicit, for the prevailing oppressive socio-economic structures of the day. There is, however, also evidence of dissident forms of religion providing justification for political protest *against* the existing order. Religion, depending on its social base, can be regarded as an ideological support either for the maintenance of the status quo or for the forces of revolution. The question is not whether religion in fact renders this role in a given society—this point can be readily granted—but whether in terms of its own identity it ought to do no more. To this question we return in chapter 7.

The English-speaking churches have, as a rule, received favorable press concerning their response to apartheid. They are depicted as guardians of human rights, champions of the poor, and their martyrs are celebrated as representative of the churches to which they belong. The NGK, on the other hand, has been portrayed as anachronistic, bigoted and racist, guilty of a panoply of theological sins and finally, in providing a theological justification of apartheid, also of heresy. A closer examination of these churches shows, however, that although they *are* in many ways different, there are also essential similarities. They are both trapped within the socio-economic, political, and theological constituencies of which they are a part. And from this context there is no obvious way out. Theological protestations to the contrary, it is nearly impossible for a church to be sociologically different from the society of which it is part.

It has become a cliché to say that South Africa is in crisis. But somewhere beneath this cliché lies the truth that virtually every social constituency within South Africa is divided against itself. Each of these constituencies—which together form the social fabric of South Africa—experiences the trauma of crisis in different ways, and each in its own way pays the socio-political cost of resistance to change and the incentive for renewal. Yet at the same time there is within each constituency the inevitable clinging to some form of unity. The institutional churches within these groups are under enormous pressure, and no small amount of self-interest, to contribute to this cohesion and a sense of communal social well-being. Prophets are never welcome among their own, and certainly not when they contribute to the destruction of a society under siege.

Whatever the importance of the priestly function which heals the divisions within a given society, providing it with a center of belonging, religion without prophetic vision and courage is simply insufficient to successfully resist or transform the existing political and socio-economic structure of any society. The dogged determination of white South Africa is, in turn, such that it will take more than priestly counsel to institute the necessary transformation. The churches in South Africa have consistently balked at going beyond the point of priestly counsel, and this ultimately is the Achilles' heel of the English-speaking churches.

Both the NGK and the English-speaking churches make particular and at times admirable theological affirmations. These are inevitably qualified, however, by the social context of which the churches are a part. Social context is ultimately the hermeneutic through which the Bible is read and in relation to which theological ideals are attuned. Few are those within the church who challenge the prevailing milieu, and for all the efforts of outspoken prophets and social critics like Trevor Huddleston and Joost de Blank in the English-speaking churches and Beyers Naudé as an Afrikaner, little has changed within their respective churches. This raises the question whether Desmond Tutu, Allan Boesak and others can succeed in the immediate future where an earlier generation met with little success.

To speak of the social function of a church is not to speak of a romantic theological ideal of what theologians suggest it ought to be, or what its conservative adherents argue it is. Practice is the touchstone of authenticity for the Judeo-Christian tradition. The Hebrew Bible is adamant that it is those who *keep* God's commandments who will live (Lev. 18:5; Neh. 9:29; Ezek. 20:11), and the New Testament teaches that true believers are those who practice what they hear (Luke 8:21). Neither is the social reality of the church to be confused with some strong individual who symbolizes what the church should but has failed to be. Nor should the church be confused with a resisting group, marginalized by the ecclesial elite. The church is a social reality made up of divergent and different individuals who in conflict and mutual concern exercise a moderating and restraining influence on one another.

The South African church is necessarily heterogeneous. It is inspired neither by similar dreams nor motivated by common memories. This is especially so in the English-speaking churches, constituted as they are by people from different racial groups and social classes, with each group and class perceiving reality as it corresponds with its own social conditions. In this kind of church, members of the same denomination experience even their "common" theological heritage in a different manner.

It is perhaps here, as suggested in chapter 1, that the essential identities of the English-speaking and Afrikaner churches differ. Given the diverse nature of the membership of the former, the affirmation of any kind of theological absolute is a virtual impossibility. It is this that makes these churches most pragmatic and yet liable to vacillate in their response to social issues. The more homogeneous character of the latter, in turn, makes for a common perspective which allows for doctrinal and often doctrinaire absolutes. Yet in the final analysis both church groups, not necessarily explicitly and often by default, provide differing degrees of ecclesial legitimacy to the existing political order.

TOWARD A CHURCH OF MODERATION

The tensions found within the church in South Africa are not unique. They constitute a particular contextual manifestation or a microcosm of the macro-history of Christianity reaching back to the origins of the church. And in order fully to appreciate the pathos of the church in South Africa, it is necessary to locate this church within the larger historical quest by the Christian church for an identity in both theology and praxis.

Most scholars would agree that the origins of the Christian church were of a revolutionary nature. Indeed the insistence of the church that slaves and other social underlings were also created in the image of God, with immortal souls—that they were human beings, and that God showed them special favor—made a significant impact on the social order of the day. It gave rise to a community of people who sought to live in obedience to the message of Jesus which not only favored the poor and marginalized of society but also resulted in Jesus being found guilty of political agitation and treason. The nature of his deliberate concern for the poor and its implications for an ecclesiology in continuity with his ministry is discussed in chapter 8. For the present it is enough to note that for the first three centuries the church consisted largely of socially deprived people who were regarded by the rulers as politically subversive.

Then, as the Roman empire began to disintegrate, the character of the church changed as it gained adherents in larger sectors of society, including the army. In time the emperor found it expedient to negotiate with the church: The Edict of Milan followed in 313 CE and within a little more than a decade, as a result of a series of treacherous and bloody deeds, Constantine emerged as the sole ruler of the empire, with Christianity practically becoming a state religion. He "achieved by kindness," it has been suggested, "what his predecessors had not been able to achieve by force. Without a threat or a blow, and all unsuspecting, the Christians were led into captivity and their religion transformed into a new imperial cult."[2] Whatever the motivation, and it was probably what Machiavelli called political *virtu* rather than kindness, the outcome was the emergence of a new alliance founded in religious opportunism and political expediency. The centuries that followed saw the church transformed from a persecuted and impoverished social entity into a community of wealthy and powerful people. By the high Middle Ages it had become the single most despotic political force in Europe.

At the same time there were other economic and political forces beginning to shape the social identity of the region, and this too was beginning to take its toll on the character of the church, leading to the Protestant and Catholic Reformations. Whatever the fundamental cause of these reform processes—economic, the rise of nationalism and/or spiritual renewal—the consequence was the emergence of a bourgeois church. The control of the church, and certainly the Protestant church, had shifted from the imperial aristocracy to the bourgeois princes, with the peasants continuing to be marginalized and excluded from the socio-political identity of the church. This became most clear when in 1525 the peasants of Germany sought to extend the Protestant affirmation of spiritual freedom to socio-political liberation. Luther sided with the princes, counselling them to kill those peasants who were in revolt. What is important to recognize here is the shift in the ideological identity of the church from a church of the subversive poor to a church of the ruling classes, a concomitant part of which was the emergence of a religious individualism grounded in the Protestant emphasis on the individual's responsibility before God. This development would, in time, be reified through the period of the Enlightenment and the secularization process into the privatization of religion. One consequence was a type of religion which would identify Kierkegaard's "lonely" relationship between the individual and God as the essence of Christianity. From this it was a short step for some Christians to suggest that the church's engagement in politics constituted a dangerous deviation from its spiritual center.

Equally important, however, is that the church has never quite managed, at times at significant cost to itself, to deny or suppress a residual revolutionary theology in favor of the poor and the oppressed, traceable back to its earliest history. It is this "dangerous memory" (Metz) which contradicts its social location in society and which accounts for marginalized groups within the church being susceptible to revolutionary influences.[3] It is the special character of this tendency which, properly understood, prevents the church from entering into an altogether uncritical alliance with any dominant political group. Inevitably, when socio-political crises are most intense it is these revolutionary origins which are appealed to by those within the churches who reject the existing order. This double identity of the Christian church (social and theological) is portrayed in few places as vividly today as in the church in South Africa. It is an identity which often results in the ideological co-existence of two competing churches within one ecclesial structure.

This divide is often identified in terms of one group affirming a political gospel while the other claims not to involve itself in "politics." The truth of the matter is that both groups are political. The divide relates rather to whether or not a particular manifestation of the gospel or the theology of a particular period endorses, challenges or opposes the status quo.

The church has always been political. It cannot be otherwise. Initially it was fired by an active apocalypticism which understood the secular order to be in revolt against the divine order and, as has already been suggested, the church was born in confrontation with and persecution by the state. But already by the second century apologists were seeking to establish a truce between Christian apocalypticism and the imperial ideology of the Empire and, as indicated, eventually Constantine came to terms with the church. It was left to theologians to work out the compromise, and rather impressively they did just that. Yet throughout the history of this "compromise" the obligation of the church to resist tyrannical rule has been repeatedly acknowledged, although not readily translated into practice. This two-fold emphasis on church-state relations constitutes a continuing ambiguity within the history of the church and provides the historical context within which the inherent conflict of the church in South Africa is to be found.

Augustine laid the foundation for this ambiguity in his *City of God* by distinguishing between two realms in history, which he called the heavenly and earthly cities. The debate has long raged around this theoretical separation, but dominant groups in the West found within it justification for the desired compromise between church and state. Augustine certainly argued that it is the task of the Christian to bring the earthly city into conformity with the heavenly city, and he never doubted that a nation without justice could be no more than a band of robbers. Nevertheless, for him, the Christian's primary concern was to be found elsewhere.

The political order was to be endured as a period of passing significance, although he brought the political significance of the heavenly order repeatedly to bear on the earthly realm. It is to *this* dimension of his thought that appeal is made today by those Christians who affirm the radical significance of the church's eschatological symbols for daily politics.[4] Augustine had, however, done sufficient to allow subsequent generations to take the next short step of granting secular leaders unrestrained power in maintaining "law and order," or what Augustine had called the "peace of Babylon" in the earthly kingdom.

All the constituent aspects were there for a comfortable relationship of co-existence to be worked out between secular and spiritual leadership. The nuances and qualifications of his elaborate doctrine of church and state could conveniently be bracketed, with the church and state each being assigned their respective spheres of influence. Still today the tried and tested formula for the politically acquiescent church is to be found in the claim that the church should confine itself to spiritual things while recognizing the power of the secular authorities to deal with matters of politics, economics and society. It required only one further small step to provide theological legitimation for the view that secular leaders were placed in positions of leadership by God. Few dictatorships the world round have failed to avail themselves of this theological legitimation. And the church, recognizing sufficient of its own teaching in this heresy, while experiencing sufficient social and economic encouragement not to affirm the "other" part of its heritage which requires it to resist unjust rulers, finds itself trapped in the wiles of a "Constantinian" religion.

The story of this process from Augustine through nineteenth-century renditions of Luther's two-kingdom doctrine, via the privatization of religion to the coalition between state and church in the Nazi era, and the captivity of the church to state ideology in the West as well as the East, must not detain us here.[5] The more blatant and explicit examples of church cooption by the state in the theology of apartheid have been told in numerous other publications.

Our immediate task is to investigate the less obvious and more subtle involvement of the English-speaking churches, with their sustained theoretical rejection of white domination, in providing a soft or implicit legitimation of South Africa's apartheid regime. This is an "easy heresy" of praxis against the more obvious violation of the norms of the Christian tradition which led to the declaration of heresy by the World Alliance of Reformed Churches in 1982 against the NGK and NHK already mentioned. The English-speaking churches escaped this condemnation because they had consistently condemned apartheid as at variance with the basic tenets of the gospel, while accepting their primary task to be the salvation of souls in the narrow sense of a privatized religion. As will be shown, these churches have with equal consistency refused to call the essential legitimacy of the apartheid regime into question. In so doing, implicit recognition is afforded the minority regime, rejected by black groups within the country and questioned in a growing number of countries around the world. It is this cautious critique of apartheid by the English-speaking churches which is challenged in the *Kairos Document* which identifies the government of South Africa as tyrannical and illegitimate.

Criticism by the English-speaking churches of the prevailing order in South Africa remains at a level of liberal principle and fails to strike at what is analytically identified as the fundamental cause of social evil. As such it is not only tolerated by the present regime, but often welcomed as a sign of the existence of religious freedom and the right to democratic dissent. "Toleration" of the numerous church assembly and conference statements which "condemn apartheid" is continually shown. It is this which compels critics of the South African government to allow that in comparison with some regimes in other parts of the world there is a measure of religious freedom in South Africa. The kind of religion that comes to expression in the *Kairos Document*, on the other hand, is subjected to unprecedented attack by the government; liberation theology is caricatured as a thinly veiled Marxist-Leninist ideology; outspoken clerics and church workers are arrested; at the 1986 June 16 memorial services for victims of the 1976 riots, two entire congregations were detained; funeral and community worship services are banned on a regular basis. Those who affirm and participate in this kind of resistance contend that the church is the victim of state persecution; the government contends that religion of this kind is a cover for political agitation.

It is this impasse which reintroduces the significance of religious freedom in a revolutionary situation such as the one which prevails in South Africa. The irony is that this freedom has hardly been regarded as a central political imperative in recent instruments of human rights, and certainly it has not been addressed with the sense of urgency that enshrined it in the first amendment to the constitution of the United States of America.

In South Africa, where theology is a constitutive part of the social identity of the country, religion continues to be an important arena for ideological struggle. The pertinent question is whether when Christians mobilize people across the nation and abroad to pray that the present government be removed from power, and when the *Kairos Document* deliberately identifies the present regime as the anti-Christ, recognizing that Christians have traditionally resorted to arms to overthrow such tyrants, such action should be regarded as bona fide religious or political. And when these events lead to protest marches and the direct violation of laws regarded as unjust, the need for an answer to this question becomes urgent. It is a form of religion which has had direct links to the civil rights struggle in the United States, to the involvement of the Berrigan brothers in anti-Vietnam activities, to the protest of Christians in South Korea and the influence of Christian base communities in Latin America. The integration of religious and political symbols in liturgy and worship is addressed in chapter 7. For the present it must suffice to note that the churches, and especially the black and English-speaking churches which have been drawn directly into these developments, have found this integration of religion and politics as divisive and difficult to respond to as have other institutional churches in other parts of the world.

It is clear that these are the issues which could make for either the disintegration of the church as a social actor in the South African crisis and elsewhere in the world, or for its theological and political transformation. The church cannot remain unaffected by such influences. Indeed as the political conflict in South Africa intensifies, the churches experience divisiveness in their own ranks which, to the extent that their internal unity is to be maintained, necessitates increasing caution and moderation in matters political. And given the propensity of the different churches to bend their theologies to meet social expediency, it is likely that this passage too will be negotiated with moderation. A consequence will be ever-decreasing ideological homogeneity in any particular denomination, which can only minimize the differences which had hitherto existed between them. Certainly the English-speaking and other multiracial churches, given the diverse nature of their membership, can only experience further disintegration of the limited internal cohesion which they have built up over the years. The all-white Afrikaans Reformed churches are already experiencing the disintegration of the Afrikaner ruling class under the strains of political change. The black churches are torn between the increasing solidarity around the will to political liberation and the various less costly options offered to them by the state as compromise solutions. This choice makes the black churches the central ecclesial actors in the current political milieu. It makes traditional denominational divisions less significant and places theological options related to socio-political alliances which transcend denominations at the cutting edge of the current South African conflict.

CHURCH UNITY AND POLITICAL DIVERSITY

Dissident voices in the church in South Africa have long dismissed denominationalism as the hangover of extraneous sixteenth-century European ideological conflicts, quite irrelevant to the church in Africa. This is, of course, largely true. It does not, however, detract from the fact that similar ideological divisions in this country have continued to subvert any semblance of unity either within denominations or between them. It can, in fact, be argued that while the history of the church emerged out of conflict and hostility in South Africa, a significant level of cooperation and unity had emerged among at least the major denominations by the first decades of this century, with the Protestant churches meeting in the first General Missionary Conference in 1904. Then, with the emergence of apartheid and the consequent intensification of political fragmentation, this "unity" began to give way to discord, polarization, confrontation and political diversity which struck at the very identity of the different churches. The Christian Council of South Africa was, for example, established in 1937 and included the Transvaal synods of the NGK and NG Sendingkerk, but by 1942 the NGK and the Sendingkerk had withdrawn and the Federal

Missionary Council of the NGK was founded. In 1948 the National Party was elected to power, and the rift between the Afrikaner churches and the English-speaking churches had been entrenched.

This ecclesial division has continued to intensify ever since. It is a division existing not only between the white Dutch Reformed Churches, largely supportive of the government, and the English-speaking and black churches theologically opposed to its policies. It is also a division which, as already indicated, runs through the different churches, and more particularly the English-speaking churches whose identity is founded in a somewhat fragile union between different ideological and social groups. This is a union which, despite its deep social divisions, has proved to be surprisingly resilient. It is a union between different races, and in South Africa this necessarily constitutes a union between different classes. Indeed, it is a union between masters and servants—with domestic servants often belonging to the same church as their employers.

These tensions, more provocatively present in South Africa than in many other parts of the world, are a latent ingredient in all but the most homogeneous and parochial churches elsewhere. At the same time, theological incentives to unity so deeply imbedded in the identity of the Christian faith tend to take on a new urgency and dynamic in the South African context. This theological will to unity, however, has become in South Africa a pretext leading to the submissive acceptance of actual division under the guise of unity.

There is, nonetheless, a residual gospel radicalism buried deep within the tradition of the Christian church which affirms the unity of humankind as a powerful subverting factor in a church and society divided against itself. There is also a theological concern for the poor and the oppressed in the tradition of the church that contradicts the church's history of social acquiescence and stands in protest against the social reality of the church. It is a church within the dominant church which unites dissenting groups within different denominations and gives expression to its theological ideals in such statements as the June 16 *Call to Prayer for the End to Unjust Rule*, the *Kairos Document* and more recently the *Lusaka Statement*—documents discussed in chapter 6.

The ethos of the Christian church as manifest in modern history, and certainly in South Africa, has given rise to a Christian character which is significantly different to what we read of the early church in the Bible. Bluntly stated, the modern practice of the church is a subversion of the New Testament teaching concerning those who chose to follow Jesus. It is this which constitutes both the judgment and the hope of the church; judgment because the church has deviated from its own norms, hope because these norms remind the faithful within the church what they ought to become.

PRESCRIBED STATE RELIGION

There is a sense in which the state understands this challenge to the church to realize its New Testament norms better than the institutional church itself. It accounts for the state's apparent contradictory response to religious protest; the critique of liberal idealism is considered acceptable while the response to the *Kairos Document* is rejected. It also accounts for the kind of religion deemed politically useful by the state.

In fact, as the Christian tradition has become increasingly appealed to by marginalized groups within the churches as a basis from which to challenge the government's legitimacy, the state's perceived role for religion in the wider ideological framework of national existence has shifted quite dramatically. The traditional self-perception of the Afrikaner people, schooled by *dominees* (Afrikaner church ministers) and *volksleier* (popular leaders), is deeply religious, God-fearing, Christian and Calvinist. Obsessed with a Puritan sense of being an instrument in the hands of the divine Architect, Afrikaners applied themselves with a sense of urgency to build a nation with divine purpose and mission. *White* came to be regarded as "Christian," "moral," "civilized" and "of God," while such terms as "heathen," "immoral," "uncivilized" and "pagan" came to be synonymous with *black*. Biblical material was employed to substantiate the myth of white superiority, while national seers, prophets and priests identified the "hard evidence" of God's ratification of Afrikaner exploits. Today, as the zealous Afrikaner patriot looks back, history is seen to be punctuated with symbols of divine affirmation.[6] When the white South African republic was established in 1961, Dr. H. F. Verwoerd (prime minister at the time) could only conclude:

Perhaps it was intended that we should be planted here at the southern point within the crisis area so that from this resistance might emanate the victory whereby all that has been built up since the days of Christ may be maintained for the good of all mankind. May you have strength, people of South Africa, to serve the purpose for which you have been planted here.[7]

It is this kind of theologized nationalism which continues to inspire the religious right-wing of Afrikanerdom, accounting for the conflict within Afrikaner circles in both church and politics today—and it is the persistence of this "true belief" that distinguishes the Afrikaner from Puritans elsewhere in the world. Afrikaners did not move to the cities until the 1930s, and the normative process of secularization failed to make significant inroads into this community until very recently, with the economic and military dimensions of P. W. Botha's pragmatic-reformism replacing the older type of overt religious-based Afrikaner nationalism. A direct consequence of this socio-economic shift within the structures of the regime has been a parallel shift in the religious expectations of the state.

This shift is nowhere more clearly articulated than in two recent government Commissions of Inquiry appointed to investigate the role of the churches and the function of religion within the prevailing political crisis.[8] One is the Steyn Commission of Inquiry into the Mass Media (1981), which found it necessary to include 400 pages on the role of the churches in its published report. The other is the Eloff Commission of Inquiry into the South African Council of Churches (1983).

While arguing that "a personal relation between the individual soul and the Godhead" is the essence of religion, the Steyn Commission is quite explicit in its affirmation of white patriotic theology. In fact, the normative synthesis between religion and politics which lies at the heart of traditional Afrikaner theologized nationalism is actively promoted, while any theological critique of the political order, whether in the guise of black, liberation or the more traditional theology of the SACC is rejected as the consequence of a deviant gospel.

The Eloff Commission, on the other hand, dismisses *all* "political" theology, whether "for the state" or "against the state." The Commission finds that "in South Africa, where religious freedom exists and is indeed protected, the state is bound to recognize the right of the church, and church bodies such as the SACC, to express themselves on, to criticize and, if so persuaded, to condemn its policies or actions." But then, adopting a classic secularist position on religion, it proceeds to make this critique relative. Allowing that (a) there are so many conflicting religious views, (b) there is no obvious basis for choosing between them, and (c) there are no definite religious answers to complex political situations, the conclusion is drawn that it is best that religion be restricted to the private sphere. Giving evidence to the Commission, the Commissioner of Police insisted that the churches should focus on "personal salvation and conversion," while the Commission itself concludes that the true gospel addresses "only truly spiritual purposes," and that politics should be left to the secular forces of "national interest."

Despite the shift in the state's perceived role for religion in the total framework of national existence, the political continuity between the kind of patriotic theology advocated by the Steyn Commission and the privatized religion promoted in the Eloff Commission is readily identifiable. The former affirms a religion of personal piety which takes the form of other-worldly preoccupation accompanied by a social political theology of patriotism. The Eloff Commission, on the other hand, recognizing that many of the advocates of a patriotic theology are beginning to falter, while others have been unable to substantiate their claims against conflicting political theologies, has resorted to a strictly apolitical form of pietism. This latter stance allows for a social conscience to emerge in response to "a personal relationship between the individual soul and the Godhead," but insists that this be of a moderate and restrained kind. This permitting of a moderate social awareness is then, as already indicated, taken as evidence of the existence of religious freedom, while a prophetic witness which strikes at the root of state legitimacy is dismissed as the result of alien influences which have been allowed to corrupt the spiritual center of the gospel.

This suggested shift means that the present challenge facing the church in South Africa is not how to deal with a traditional theological justification of apartheid. The World Alliance of Reformed Churches' decision to declare this kind of theology a heresy led the way in this regard, and all the SACC member churches have followed suit. The NGK, in its 1986 Synod, has in turn seen the need to alter its theological stance, arguing that it is impossible to provide biblical or theological justification for any political program. This shift in policy, as explained in *Kerk en Samelewing* (*Church and Society*), is considered in relation to the recommendations of the Eloff Commission in the following chapter.

The white regime no longer needs the kind of explicit theological legitimation once required, and any attempt by the Afrikaans Reformed churches to provide this legitimation has become an embarrassment in both ecumenical and secular contexts. The social and economic structures of the present order are already firmly entrenched, and the religious motivation so vital during the initial period of building the apartheid edifice must be allowed to subside. All that is required of the church now is the assurance that these structures should not be undermined by theologically justified resistance and dissent.

The intensity of the present political struggle *for* change, however, is such that any attempt by the church to avoid taking sides in the conflict is no longer acceptable. This necessity to take sides, in turn, provides the context within which individuals and groups within the churches rediscover those theological resources which require them to be on the side of the poor and the oppressed. The contextual demand facing the church in South Africa may well result in any refusal on the part of the churches to engage in direct action against the state being judged by history to constitute the single most theologically irresponsible act by such churches in the latter part of this century. If the theological and political analysis in the *Kairos Document*, for example, is correct, then mere refusal to actively support the present order is not enough to excuse the church from complicity in the existing exploitation and oppression. Reluctance to become actively involved in the eradication of evil is enough to imply culpability.

This radical theological position stands in bold contrast to the moderate position of the mainline churches—including the English-speaking churches. Popular opinion continues to locate the English-speaking churches on the side of the opponents of apartheid, and the NGK continues to be supportive of government policy. As, however, the NGK cautiously moves away from the explicit theological legitimation of apartheid, and the "church theology" of the English-speaking churches is criticized by *Kairos* theologians, these churches may well move toward *rapprochement*. Alternatively, they could again be driven apart by oppressed groups within the English-speaking churches who affirm the residual gospel of resistance, and traditional Afrikaner ideologues on the other hand, who reaffirm patriotic Afrikaner theology.

The answer will presumably be provided, as has been the case so often in the past, at least partly by socio-economic and political developments within the social constituencies which these churches represent. Past experience also suggests that while the English-speaking churches continue to show equal concern for the aspirations of both blacks and whites, and the NGK continues to endeavor to affirm the unity of the *volk* in a divided Afrikaner milieu, it is unlikely that their political influence can be other than moderate and restrained.

Chapter Six

One and Divided

The *Kairos Document* has become to the English-speaking churches what *Kerk en Samelewing* is to the NGK. The responses of the English-speaking churches to the *Kairos Document* show these churches to be deeply disturbed by Christians (especially those from within their own ranks) who are less "moderate and restrained" than they are. And when the responses of the leaders of the English-speaking churches to the June 16 *Call to Prayer for the End to Unjust Rule*, published a few months before the *Kairos Document*, are considered, the troubled nature of these churches is confirmed. The *Lusaka Statement* which emerged from a WCC Consultation on Southern Africa in May 1987 has, in turn, given rise to similar concern within these churches. Unlike these statements, *Kerk en Samelewing* is an official policy statement of the NGK. Like the above statements, however, it too has revealed deep divisions within the NGK.

Both the English-speaking churches and the NGK have an appearance of unity, but there are divisions that penetrate deep into the ethos of their constituencies. Although one, they are divided by doctrinal and social differences which threaten schism to the "right" and the "left." In this chapter the responses of the English-speaking churches to the *Call to Prayer for the End to Unjust Rule* and the *Kairos Document* are considered, and brief reference is made to the *Lusaka Statement*. These responses need to be viewed in relation to the NGK's *Kerk en Samelewing* to be fully appreciated.

THE NEDERDUITSE GEREFORMEERDE KERK

Approximately 42 percent of South Africa's white population belongs to this church, and the majority of white political leaders in the country are among its members. This, together with various historic reasons, has made the NGK the single most politically influential church in South Africa.

That this church, therefore, should alter its traditional stance on apartheid as it did at the 1986 General Synod deserves the closest scrutiny. That its revised position accords with the general shift already discerned between the Steyn and Eloff Commissions is intriguing. It is a shift which deliberately abdicates direct political responsibility, while ensuring that criticism directed against the state is of a mild and hesitant kind.

The question faced by the Synod was how to incorporate into its official policy a shift away from direct and deliberate theological legitimation for apartheid, while ensuring that its theology could not become a basis for questioning the legitimacy of the state. Ironically it was the theological legitimation of apartheid which Verwoerd told Afrikaner church leaders it was their duty to uphold when they hesitated to do so in the Cottesloe Consultation together with other WCC member churches in 1961.[1] But this legitimation has cost the NGK dearly in ecumenical relations over the years.

The NGK's controversial 1974 report, *Human Relations and the South African Scene in the Light of Scripture*, which is intended to allay criticism of the racial stance of the NGK by providing biblical and theological grounds for its position, in fact contributed directly to the WARC declaration of heresy against this church in 1982. A new document entitled *Kerk en Samelewing (Church and Society)* was produced in response.[2] A great deal of what was explicit in the earlier document is implicit here and some implicit affirmations of the earlier document are explicit in the revised document; on balance the shift is toward a more moderate stance in relation to those aspects of the character of the NGK regarded as most unpalatable by the ecumenical church. It is the kind of moderation which would have been warmly welcomed in the Cottesloe era (1961), but it is hardly sufficient to convince critics of the white church today. It appears rather to be an attempt to move the church out of the

Verwoerdian-Vorster era of apartheid bolstered by theologized nationalism into a more secular age in which theology is allocated an explicitly apolitical function. As such, the Synod fails to move the NGK toward the complete eradication of apartheid in either church or society.

This "new" and ambiguous stance by the NGK is most clearly seen in three specific areas of the report:

Church-State Relations. Church-state relations in *Kerk en Samelewing* are established in relation to three formative principles with which few Reformed theologians would quarrel: First, the church is to be directed in all its ways by the Word of God; second, it has a prophetic task in relation to all areas of life, affirmed in relation to its priestly and royal tasks, with the latter constituting a celebration of God's righteousness over all forms of injustice, evil powers, ideologies and systems; third, the Bible provides no blueprint for the resolution of social, economic or political issues "whether this be apartheid or separate development, or a policy of integration."

Neither the 1974 biblical justification of "autogenous separate development," nor the elaborate exegetical argument which concludes that "ethnic diversity in its very origin [is] in accordance with the will of God" is found in the revised document. We are told that any references to ethnic diversity which are found in the scriptures simply refer to realities which existed at the time the particular text happened to be written. It is essentially here that the submissive "apolitical" stance of the NGK becomes most obvious. The prevailing political reality is affirmed both by default and by implication, and this in the name of a "non-political" gospel.

The "existing reality" of South Africa with its ethnic and cultural qualifications is left unchallenged, an assumption that continues to play a hermeneutical function in the latest report, although in a less explicit manner than in the 1974 document. We are reminded, for example, of the different ethnic groups that make up the South African population, although assured that "colour differences play no role in the Bible's judgement of people." The notions "volk," "culture" and "language" function as important categories in society, being allowed to escape the biblical injunction to unity and justice.

Avoiding the challenge of relating scripture to politics, the Synod simply refused to become directly involved in politics. This was nowhere seen more clearly than in the comment of the moderator, Professor Johan Heyns: "I cannot dictate to the State any particular form of political structure, I am a theologian and . . . cannot prescribe any [political] structure as such." Asked his opinion on the Group Areas Act, he replied: "This is a political issue. It is an open political question. I cannot see any explicit theological principle to maintain or abolish the law." Affirming only a slightly less cautious position, *Kerk en Samelewing* recognizes "the economic value of migrant labour" while suggesting that it be eliminated or minimized because of the social dislocation it causes; this is more or less in line with the 1974 position. The state's educational policy— despite a schooling crisis that has turned black townships into war zones—is left uncriticized; the document recommends that education take place within the context of one's own "culture and mother-tongue" on the basis of a "Christian-national" character.

Acknowledging the importance of both scripture and existing realities, ultimately it is the latter which shapes the former. Differently stated, while many of the cardinal theological principles found in the report are both acceptable and pleasing, they suffer significant ideological compromise when hermeneutically applied to the prevailing political dispensation.

Racism and Apartheid. The character of the Synod report becomes even more poignant when racism and apartheid are addressed. The document states quite adamantly: "Racism is a serious sin which may not be defended or practiced by any person or church." Despite the euphoria expressed in some liberal church circles concerning this statement, it needs to be remembered that the NGK has never exactly suggested anything to the contrary. Indeed the very basis of apartheid ideology as promoted by its most zealous theological proponents is that apartheid constitutes a morally defensible doctrine.

The pertinent question is not what the Synod says about racism but what it says about apartheid. And it is here that the true character of the document emerges. Apartheid is *not* defined as a sin, and neither is the theological justification thereof explicitly called a heresy. What is said is that "the conviction has gradually grown that a forced separation and division of peoples cannot be considered a biblical imperative. The attempt to justify such an injunction as being derived from the Bible must be recognized as an error and should be rejected." The resolution goes on to say that the implementation of apartheid "as a socio-economic system which treats people unjustly and favors one group over another is unacceptable on the basis of Christian ethics because it contravenes the very essence of neighborly love, righteousness and inevitably the human dignity of all involved." What the Synod has not done is to say that the present practices of apartheid are a contravention of Christian ethics; the Synod apparently allows that apartheid in itself is not necessarily an unjust system. In so doing it clings to the residues of traditional apartheid ideology which suggest that in principle it is a doctrine that is moral, of God and for the benefit of all. While many would argue that the *Kerk en Samelewing* statement is an improvement on any earlier affirmation by the NGK, it has incurred the unconditional repudiation of those who insist that apartheid cannot be reformed—it *must* be destroyed.

The retort by Dr. Hannes Adonis, a leading NG Sendingkerk minister, is a telling one: "By saying apartheid was an 'error,' the NGK was using a very clever means of getting away from what the Sendingkerk calls a 'sin.' When you say apartheid is a sin, you speak theologically." Certainly Adonis' uneasiness seems justified when, in referring to the resolution on apartheid in his moderator's address, Professor Heyns stated: "This synod did not give a political definition of apartheid . . . but criticised a policy which could lead to racism or discrimination whereby people could be exploited, and that this *negative* apartheid could not be defended on ethical and theological grounds." This statement illustrates the point already made in relation to the findings of the Eloff Commission. When a given political order is already firmly entrenched, it is not necessary to provide further legitimation: all that is required of the church is that it does not lend theological support to those forces opposed to it.

Church Membership. The stand of the Synod on church membership is only slightly less qualified than the issues already discussed. "Belief in the triune God as revealed in the Scripture" is given as the "only condition for membership of the church of Jesus Christ." This is an important theological point of departure. It means that by implication any church councils which apply any other measure in discriminating against a black person seeking membership could be subjected to synodical disciplinary action.

All visitors, "whose desire it is to hear God's Word within the fellowship of believers" are to be given free access to all worship services. In principle this means that the membership of these churches is open to all races. In practice, however, given social factors operative within these churches together with Groups Areas legislation and the ability of local church councils to prescribe the parish boundaries, it is highly unlikely that any black person (even if he or she should so desire) would become a member of a local white congregation.

This kind of ambiguity is further seen in relation to the *Church and Society* statement on church unity, and more especially with regard to those churches which form part of the NGK family in South Africa. Unity is affirmed as a goal while talks are called for to discover what this means given "the demands of both Scripture and practical realities." Again it is the "practical realities" which weigh most heavily. The net consequence is that the Synod, at least for the present, does not intend to merge with other members of the NGK family. On hearing the news of this decision, Dr. Allan Boesak, moderator of the NG Sendingkerk, responded: "What will be the sense of continuing discussions with the NGK when what we wanted has already been shot down by the synod right from the beginning?"

Has the NGK Changed? Locked into its own internal conflicts which represent the ecclesial face of those divisions which rack Afrikanerdom in every area of life, the NGK has not found it possible to align itself with the *Belhar Confession* of the NG Sendingkerk, which incorporates the fight against apartheid into its theological structure of belief. To say "racism is sin" and "apartheid is an error" is not sufficient to locate the NGK in the ecumenical family of churches which has judged apartheid to be a sin and its theological justification a heresy.

The Synod signals a desire to withdraw from explicit engagement in South Africa's political agenda, contenting itself with the affirmation of certain general principles of social justice—left unrelated to the prevailing exigencies of apartheid. In so doing the distance between the NGK and the English-speaking churches has been narrowed. The latter go further than the NGK in explicitly rejecting apartheid as a sin (and not a mere moral lapse or error), but the difference between these churches is not quite as decisive as once suggested. As will become clear in what follows, both the English-speaking churches and the NGK refuse to question the basic legitimacy of the state which is responsible for the existence and maintenance of apartheid.

Despite the cautious and ambiguous nature of the shift discernible within *Kerk en Samelewing*, it has nevertheless resulted in the emergence of the breakaway Afrikaanse Protestantse Kerk. It has also given rise to the emergence of a "right-wing" pressure group within the NGK, the NG Bond, committed to the elimination of certain revisionist clauses within the policy of the church. The willingness to allow that certain aspects of apartheid could be regarded as discriminatory and the possibility of black church members are regarded by these groups as the thin edge of the wedge of significant change. The reformist reading of these developments suggests that as the reality of apartheid continues to be subjected to theological and ethical critique, *Kerk en Samelewing* could come to be seen as a cautious step toward rapprochement with the English-speaking churches. A more critical reading suggests, however, that unless the NGK is able to broaden its social base to include a much wider constituency, any significant development beyond *Kerk en Samelewing* is unlikely.

Change in social praxis has never been other than slow, cautious and even tortuous in the history of the church. However, the urgency of the hour is such that an unequivocal signal of intent by the NGK is imperative. It has not yet been clearly given. What has emerged is a placid and moderate form of religiosity which refuses to condemn apartheid or constitute a serious challenge to the state.

THE ENGLISH-SPEAKING CHURCHES

Traditional "church theology" in the English-speaking churches differs significantly from that of the NGK. It carries evidence of sustained opposition to all forms of racism. And as already shown, since the National Party's victory at the polls in 1948 these churches have protested against apartheid. They have, however, in spite of their black majority memberships, also been obliged to respond to the needs of their white members who benefit from the apartheid system.

The resolutions against apartheid published by these churches must be attributed to their racially integrated decision-making process at conference, assembly and synod level. When prominent black leadership first emerged in these churches in the 1960s with Seth Mokitimi (the first black leader of an English-speaking church) elected as President of the Methodist Church in 1963, the debating halls of the English-speaking churches were stormy and polarized arenas of conflict. This period extended throughout the 1970s, coming to a head in 1980 when the SACC convened a Consultation on Racism at Hammanskraal. The black participants to this conference issued an ultimatum to "all white Christians to demonstrate their willingness to purge the church of racism," warning that "if after a period of twelve months there is no evidence of repentance shown in concrete action, the black Christians will have no alternative but to witness to the Gospel of Jesus Christ by becoming a confessing church."[3]

There never was much clarity as to what black delegates intended by this resolution, but clearly no significant black confessing group has emerged either within or in schism from these churches. The only sign of definitive black initiatives in the English-speaking churches are denominational black caucuses. When Stanley Mogoba, now the first black Secretary of Conference of the Methodist Church and a prime mover behind the black ultimatum, was asked several years later what had come of the 1980 resolution he replied that it had met with success in as much as blacks were beginning to gain control of the hitherto white power structures of the churches.

This process introduced a new complacency in the legislative halls of the English-speaking churches, and it is not uncommon to hear "new conciliatory spirit" spoken of in the official decision-making bodies of these churches, attributable to two factors: First, the recent emergence of credible black leadership; and second, the acceptance by whites of the inevitability of this process in churches with black majority memberships, churches that have consistently prided themselves on being non-racist. This black leadership has to some extent satisfied the demands of black caucuses and power groups within these churches, although the failure to make much progress in this regard has also resulted in a certain amount of sustained pressure. Black leaders have been required to operate within what is largely a white power structure and to be dependent on white funding, and this has resulted in the creation of a restrained and cautious black leadership. (The missionary origins of these churches as discussed in chapter 2 explain in part this phenomenon.)

While at one time a large section of the white clergy and laity were vociferously opposed to "radical" blacks in the church, they have learned to ignore the pronouncements of the latter. Differently stated, local white congregations have learned that they can maintain a character out-of-step with the official policy of their respective churches. A quiet *quid pro quo* has emerged. Conservative whites tolerate black leadership and black leaders are compelled to allow whites to continue in their former ways.

Suffice it to say, black leadership has not succeeded in enabling the English-speaking churches to narrow the gap between a theology which is critical of apartheid and a form of praxis which does not significantly differ from that of the white NGK. This invites the retort that while the NGK provides theological support for apartheid by failing to explicitly reject it, the English-speaking churches provide pragmatic legitimation by failing to live up to their own theological ideals. Trapped within their own history they are judged by their own policy formulations, and this ultimately provides the necessary theological incentive to change. Yet ultimately it is what places them in a strange analogical relationship to the present pragmatic-reformist milieu of South African politics. Cognizant of their own failings and striving for a measure of reform, they are neither willing nor able to sacrifice their own identity and influence in the broader South African context.

The cautious and moderate response of the NGK as seen in the 1986 *Kerk en Samelewing* document is complemented by the cautious and moderate stance of the English-speaking churches in relation to the state in two events which occurred in 1985: the *Call to Prayer for the End to Unjust Rule* on 16 June, and the publication of the *Kairos Document* in September. These events present the internal contradiction within the English-speaking churches in bold relief, witnessing to the reluctant and hesitant response of these churches to what they themselves have identified as the gross violations of justice perpetrated by the state.

Call to Prayer for the End to Unjust Rule

"Soweto, 16 June 1976" is among South Africa's most potent symbols of black resistance. The call for Christians to pray on the anniversary of that event for the "end to unjust rule" and the removal of the "tyrannical structures of oppression and the present rulers . . . who persistently refuse to heed the cry for justice," challenged the refusal of the English-speaking churches to relate their liturgy to the resolutions of their synods, assemblies and conferences condemning apartheid.[4] It was a challenge they responded to only with the greatest reluctance.

This point was perceived by Philip Russell, the then Anglican Archbishop of Cape Town, in what was by far the most thoughtful and candid theological response by a church leader to the controversy. The implications of the call to pray that God "remove the present rulers in our country are immense," said the archbishop. "It would mean that the thrust and wording of all prayers related to the state in both the South African Prayer Book and liturgy '75 would have to be altered."[5] What makes the response of the archbishop most interesting is his particular interpretation of what it means to pray *for* "all Christian Kings, Princes and Governors,"— an interpretation which epitomizes the sense of captivity of the English-speaking churches to the state. It seems to imply an obligation on the part of these churches to legitimate the government in prayer.

Few Western theologians have taken prayers for secular rulers more seriously than Karl Barth. He stressed that the church had more of an obligation to pray for brutally unjust rulers than just rulers. His concern was that in so doing the church does not become part of "the perversion of the power of the state" or church people become "traitors of their own cause."[6] Barth went so far as to suggest that prayers *for* "kings and those in authority" (1 Tim. 2:1-2 NIV) ought in certain circumstances to form the basis for the church to take the initiative in removing the government from power.[7] Barth recognizes, in continuity with the broad tradition of the Christian church (a tradition documented in the *Theological Rationale* published in support of the *Call to Prayer*), that political responsibility and possible confrontation with the state is inherent in one's obligation to pray for the government. For the church to take its prayers *for* the state seriously is to take the office of government more seriously than the government itself. It involves a commitment to ensure that authorities fulfill their God-given responsibility which is to do good and rule with justice (Rom. 13). In affirming this responsibility the *Theological Rationale* reads: "We have prayed for the government to change its policies. Now we pray for a change of government," recognizing that such "prayer cannot be offered without a corresponding commitment to work for good and legitimate government."

Archbishop Russell's response becomes still more pertinent when, despite his earlier reservations, he accepts that theologically "it is possible to pray for the removal from office of any government." He quotes a 1983 statement of the Synod of Bishops entitled "Romans 13—the Implications" in this regard.

> It can be argued that the state forfeits its authority over the individual progressively, to the extent that it departs from its role under God and pursues immoral ways, sectarian interests, or even its own glorification (which is a form of idolatry) rather than the purposes of God for which it has been established.

The crux of the archbishop's response was that "it is not for me as an individual to commit the Church of the Province of South Africa or to dissociate it from this radical stance of praying for the removal from office of the present government."[8] Hence he did not associate himself with those who called on the institutional churches to adopt such an attitude to the present rulers, and the Anglican Church has not regarded it as appropriate, despite the 1983 Synod of Bishops' statement on the theology of church and state and this church's numerous resolutions condemning apartheid and censuring the government, to express its mind on this matter. It has refused to take sides. Allowing in principle that a situation can emerge where a particular government should be removed from office, the Anglican Church was not prepared to express its opinion as to whether a government responsible for the advent and imposition of apartheid—which this church has rejected as inherently sinful—is illegitimate and needs to be removed. The result is a gap not only between the theoretical declarations of the church and its practice, but also a gap between the theological affirmations of the church and its liturgical life.

The Methodist Church was thrust into a similar quandary by this *Call to Prayer*, responding more ambivalently than the Anglicans but also more in line with their declared position on the relationship between politics and religion. The president of this church at the time, Peter Storey, was neither biblical nor prophetic in stating in a widely publicized report that one can pray that one's rulers be inwardly transformed but not that they be removed from office.[9] Yet despite Storey's rejection of *Call to Prayer*, the Conference of the Methodist Church later that year accepted it with "the clear understanding that Methodists believe that all men can be saved, that we place no limits on the grace of God and that He alone can judge when a person or group has persistently defied his laws to the point where repentance is no longer possible."[10] In practice, however, this church made no more of an effort to mobilize its people to pray for the end to unjust rule than any other church. It opted for a pragmatic hands-off policy in accordance with its "Guidelines on Politics and Religion." These guidelines remind Methodists that "it is as wrong to quote a part of Romans 13 in an attempt to suggest that all rule of such authority is 'of God' as it is to quote Revelation 13 in isolation from all other Scripture to suggest that all government authority is the incarnation of evil as symbolized by the beast." What it refrains from doing is to analyze the existing South African regime in relation to the Romans 13 and Revelation 13 options. Rather, it allows that in matters political, in keeping with its theological tradition, Methodists are obliged to think and let think, recognizing that there are widely differing interpretations of the precise way in which the justice of God may be manifest in political or economic structures.[11] At least with regard to these issues, Methodists resolutely refused to be other than ambivalent and ultimately unwilling to translate theology into political choices.

The statement on the *Call to Prayer* issued by the Presbyterian Church of Southern Africa responded directly to the confusion that had been regenerated by the response of the media and some church leaders in stating it had "not called for nor supported a call for prayer for the violent overthrow of the government. It has called for prayer for an end to unjust rule." The United Congregational Church's statement explained that it had not issued "a special call to prayer for 16 June as their statement issued after the Uitenhage shootings on 21 March 1985 [had already] called for prayer and action."[12]

Suffice it to say that none of the English-speaking churches organized official prayers for the end to unjust rule on June 16, and they made no attempt to mobilize support for this particular *Call to Prayer*. The ecumenical services arranged in several centers around the country were attended largely by marginalized Christians, people of other faiths and some church leaders (but with no clear institutional support from their respective churches). This internal contradiction within the English-speaking churches was turned into nothing short of an ecclesial furor by the government-owned South African Broadcasting Corporation and the liberal press.[13]

The churches had theologically declared apartheid a heresy, recognized their obligation to resist evil rule, and declared their intent in numerous resolutions to resist apartheid. But when a momentum built up within the churches to mobilize their people spiritually in prayer to oppose the existing order, the "will to resist" was seen to be no more than a formal protest. Not unlike the Afrikaans Reformed Churches, the English-speaking churches theologically allow for the possibility of resistance but are not prepared to identify the present crisis in South Africa as a *Kairos* demanding resistance. As such it has become difficult for an increasing number of people to view the liturgical life and the theological declarations of the churches to be much more than a form of false piety separated from an actual commitment to radical change.

The nineteenth-century atheist and philosopher Ludwig Feuerbach has identified better than many Christian theologians the need for this liturgical contradiction to be resolved. He states that "the ultimate essence of religion is revealed by the simplest act of religion—prayer."

Not the prayer before and after meals, the ritual of animal egoism, but the prayer pregnant with sorrow, the prayer of disconsolate love, the prayer which expresses the power of the heart that crushes man to the ground, the prayer which begins in despair and ends in rapture.[14]

Karl Marx had also seen the potency of religion, allowing that it is "an expression of real suffering and a protest against real suffering." "Religion," he said "is the sigh of the oppressed creature, the heart of a heartless world and the soul of soulless conditions." His concern was that prayer could become an escape from the world, and as such "the opium of the people."[15] Christians insist that prayer must never be escapism. It must also be more than a projection of human desire—but it cannot be less. It must flow out of the depths of human anguish, desire and commitment.

The great prayers of the Judeo-Christian tradition were born out of social, political and personal conflict, and engagement in life. They were a rediscovery of the intervention of God in the affairs of humanity as recorded in the biblical tradition. They remind us that this tradition knows no gap between the sacred and the secular, between prayer and social engagement, between commitment to eternal ideals and temporal goals, between communion with God and communion with the world. This is seen nowhere more clearly than in the prayer which Jesus taught his disciples to pray. The Lord's Prayer is, in fact, a spiritual manifesto of the Christian's engagement in life: to pray for one's daily bread is to affirm the dignity of work; to forgive sins is to recognize the importance of human relations; to request delivery from evil is to express resistance to evil structures and destructive people. To pray for God's kingdom to be manifest on earth as in heaven is to acknowledge an inherent relationship between prayer and social action. Prayer is a conscious reflection on one's place in life in response to God—the God of the universe and the Lord of history.[16]

Recognizing the "tensions which conspire against peace and even present a temptation to violence," the Latin American bishops meeting at Medellín in 1968 called on the churches "to be certain that preaching, liturgy and catechesis" are all related to existing social deprivations.[17] In this way the integration of the "contemplative life" with the "active life" became the basis of Christians being liberated, overcoming the passive role of mere objects and victims of the political process, acting as "subjects shaping their own history."[18] Prayer can never be a substitute for action, neither can it be an escape from responsibility. To quote de Gruchy, "in prayer the Christian does not turn *away* from the world but rather turns *with* God *to* the world."[19] Prayer involves encountering God within the crises of history. It involves carrying one's theological commitments and prayers through to their social implications. It is this spirituality of liberation which celebrates and encounters the divine within the midst of life that the English-speaking churches found so difficult to affirm in their responses to the *Call to Prayer for an End to Unjust Rule.*

The kind of prayer called for on 16 June was costly prayer. It was prayer that showed an understanding for the cost paid by black students and others who died in Soweto and elsewhere in 1976 and on subsequent dates. As a prayer it divides communities, separates people and unleashes a spiritual power which denies the essential identity of the English-speaking churches, given as they are to *nothing harsh or rigorous.* Yet ultimately institutional churches are inherently given to preventing geographical separations, doctrinal schisms and conflictive practice. It is this that seems to make the internal contradictions between the spiritual life of these churches and the resolutions and theology of their highest courts an inevitability. And it is this gap between declared intent and actual practice that has placed "church theology" under the spotlight in the *Kairos Document.*

The Kairos Document

Written as a "challenge to the church," and essentially the English-speaking and other liberal churches, the document allows that in "a limited, guarded and cautious way the theology [of these churches] *is* critical of apartheid." The concern is that this critique is "superficial and counter-productive because instead of engaging in an in-depth analysis of the signs of the times, it relies upon a few stock ideas derived from the Christian tradition" which are then "uncritically and repeatedly applied" to the existing situation. In a word, the stance of the English-speaking churches against apartheid is taken largely at the level of principle. Only with reluctance do these churches apply these principles (whether of liturgy, theology or synod and assembly resolutions) to the specifics of the oppressive situation in South Africa.

For our purposes, more interesting than the *Kairos Document* itself are the responses elicited by the document from critics within the English-speaking churches. Most of these responses are predictable, and perhaps valid from the perspective from which they are written. The response of university academics is, generally speaking, bookish and torpid; church leaders are defensive of "church theology"; and religious reactionaries make their own peculiar panoply of noises. Each group reflects its own particular social context. And theological dissidents? Most have apparently deemed it unnecessary to defend the document in print, although a second phase of the debate has started to emerge with a series of more systematic studies on issues raised within the *Kairos Document*.[20]

The official responses of the English-speaking churches to the *Kairos Document,* with the exception of that from the United Congregational Church, have been either restrained or critical. The Anglicans have made no official statement on the document, although the Board of Social Responsibility has conducted workshops and seminars on it. The 1986 Conference of the Methodist Church referred an initial response to the *Kairos Document*, written by its Doctrine Committee, to Methodist congregations for discussion. It warned against what it perceived as a tendency in the *Kairos Document* "to absolutise the evil and the good of opposing forces," suggesting that the implication of the *Kairos Document* is that within the present crisis "there are only two options—support for apartheid or for the strategy of peoples' organisations." "This," says the Methodist response, "we do not accept." The Methodists fail to offer any alternative beyond stating that "the church must continue its search for a mode of action appropriate to its subjection to the Word of God."[21] A further response by the Doctrine Committee of the Methodist Church a year later, in response to the revised (second) edition of the document and in response to representations made by Methodist congregations and individuals, adopted a more nuanced attitude. The second edition, for example, allows that strategies for change may differ but again stresses that there can be "no compromise" between the two options—one supporting the oppressors and the other the oppressed. The Methodists' response is to note that this "leaves it open for us to explore various courses of action," accepting that "sharp disagreements are likely to remain" between them and the *Kairos* theologians. Accepting the "sharp disagreements," the 1987 conference of this church has resolved to reassess the response of its people to the debate, and to evaluate such courses of action which may emerge during the next two years at its 1989 conference.[22]

The Presbyterian Church of Southern Africa, traditionally more conservative than the Methodists on social issues, "welcome[d] the initiative taken by theologians, mainly black, to bring about a theological debate on the issues arising for the church in the South African situation by the publication of the *Kairos Document*." Warning against the "polarisation of its peoples" and "a growing rift between white and black sections of the church," it urged its members to study the document "noting that the *Kairos Document* and the *Evangelical Witness in South Africa* (a declaration by Evangelical Christians) represent attempts at theology in South Africa from the contexts of the oppressed."[23]

The United Congregational Church, in turn, took cognizance of the fact that the church in South Africa and its own church is "still divided," with "the interests of the poor, oppressed and exploited masses" not being adequately represented in church forums." Identifying the *Kairos Document* as "a clear and unequivocal word of prophecy" and "a cry of the oppressed," it resolved to appoint a task force "to review the mission, ministry and structures of the United Congregational Church of Southern Africa in the light of the *Kairos Document*."[24]

The *Kairos* debate continues, and presumably the churches will in their own time respond further to the debate. What is important in our quest to identify the character of the English-speaking churches and more particularly the divide between establishment and voices of resistance within these churches is most clearly seen in relation to three specific issues: reconciliation, violence and state legitimacy. In each case a certain willingness to turn away from the consequences of their own theological declarations becomes apparent. In essence it is this tendency which justifies the perception which the *Kairos* theologians have of "church theology." English-speaking church theologians allow existing and oppressive social factors and incentives to shape and determine their response to contentious issues in much the same way as do the theologians of the NGK. Their social contexts are different, but ultimately they both locate the churches on the side of the existing order. Comment on the three issues just referred to makes this point:

Reconciliation. The *Kairos Document* is clear: "No reconciliation is possible in South Africa without justice." It further argues that we are not "expected to forgive the unrepentant sinner." Critics within the English-speaking churches have responded by saying that the document fails to give due emphasis to the unconditional free offer of forgiveness and reconciliation which God extends to sinful humanity. In similar vein, it is argued, Christians are obliged to offer and accept reconciliation within the human community in a similar unconditional manner.

God's offer of reconciliation *is* free and unconditional, but the human appropriation of this forgiveness involves a redeemed and transformed life. A consequence of repentance is necessarily a changed relationship with both God and humankind. This is not without considerable cost to the redeemed person, the origin of which is located in the act of human *metanoia* or repentance in response to God's grace. It is this cost, ultimately to be paid for politically, economically and socially in the South African context, which the English-speaking churches have not yet faced in an adequate manner. Indeed, the uneasy response by church leaders to the concern of *Kairos* theologians to stress the cost of reconciliation (which, in a political context, is social justice) is indicative of their unwillingness to face this challenge. At the same time they find themselves having to respond to the withdrawal of conservative whites from the English-speaking churches because of increased demands being made on these churches by the oppressed community that the "political" implications of the gospel be addressed. The outcome, suggests the *Kairos Document*, is the affirmation of a "justice of reform," "a justice that is determined by the oppressor, by the white minority and that is offered to the people as a kind of concession." It is this appeal to a reform from within the existing structures that must ultimately be judged as a deviation from the radical demands of the scriptures.

A word study of the Bible shows that the word *reconciliation* is used only sparingly in the New Testament, and that the Christian doctrine of divine and human reconciliation is a category developed in Paul's Epistle to the Romans (5:10; 11:15) and in the Corinthian correspondence (1 Cor. 7:11; 2 Cor. 5:18, 20), and referred to in Ephesians (2:11) and Colossians (1:20). The Greek word used to denote the concept of reconciliation is *katallage* (or *katallasso* and its derivatives) which is precisely the word used in the Septuagint text of Isaiah 9:5 to mean "restoration." (An accurate translation of this verse reads: "For every garment obtained by treachery must be repaid for by restoration/repossession. Those who had obtained goods in this treacherous manner will agree to do so, even if it should mean that fire needs to be used to bring them to this point.")[25] The concept of *katallage*, in turn, has a conceptual equivalent in Leviticus 25 where the process of *restoring* land by the landowners to the peasants becomes a central teaching on the Jubilee Year. This suggests that the New Testament doctrine of reconciliation cannot be understood apart from the teaching on restitution, repossession, and restoration as understood in the Hebrew tradition.

The intensity of the political situation in South Africa has compelled the *Kairos* theologians to look again into the theological tradition of the church to locate resources with which to meet the challenge of the times. In so doing these theologians may well have used language too strong for some palates. The Southern African Catholic Bishops' Conference (SACBC) attributes this to the "haste in the white-hot heat of the township unrest," while many Protestant commentators have seen fit to lose themselves in the niceties of a traditional theological response to avoid the challenge of the document. Bishop Tutu's observation in this regard is apt: "The language is excessive in places and tends to alienate some, but then prophets have traditionally done this."

The danger always exists that apocalyptic language can provoke blind fury. The *Kairos Document* guards against this, however, in concerning itself quite explicitly with an analysis of the prevailing socio-economic order, endeavoring to show that the nature of this order is such that it cannot be reformed. The churches, on the other hand, continue to call on the government to change its ways, arguing that the *Kairos* theologians wrongly assume that the government cannot repent. The *Kairos* position is not without biblical precedent—Pharaoh's heart was hardened by God (Exodus 10:20), and Jesus teaches that there comes a time when it is wise to shake the dust from one's feet and place one's evangelical energy elsewhere (Mark 6:11). As already seen in the response of the English-speaking churches to the call for prayers for the end to unjust rule, they are not prepared to support the suggestion of some that the present government is worthy only to be removed from office as a legitimate contextualization of these biblical positions.

The English-speaking churches have traditionally affirmed reconciliation between the races as a cornerstone of their belief. Their challenge is to become involved in a political process which is aimed at restoring economic, social and political relations. This is part of the cost of discipleship in the South African context, a demand which these churches are not yet ready to address in an unequivocal manner.

Violence. The burden of what the *Kairos Document* has to say on violence is related to the church's condemnation of *all violence*. The state, it is suggested, has appropriated the concept of violence exclusively to describe the behavior of people in the townships who throw stones, burn property and kill alleged collaborators. It refuses to allow that the "oppressive and naked violence of the police and the army" is other than in the interests of social order and good neighborliness. When the churches in this context simply condemn *all* violence, they merely compound the confusion. Such generalizations and abstractions invariably fail to address the fundamental problem involved. Even while including police and institutional violence in this general condemnation, the churches tend to equate revolutionary violence with institutional and oppressive violence, and in so doing fail to address the fundamental *cause* of violence in South Africa. The *Lusaka Statement* has sought to address precisely this confusion in stating that it is "the nature of the South African regime which wages war against its own inhabitants and neighbours [which] compels the [liberation] movements to use force along with other means to end oppression." It is this sentence within the statement which causes most consternation within certain groupings in the English-speaking churches.

Frank Chikane forcefully suggests that to even be able to debate violence is a luxury of which most black people have been deprived. It is a debate indulged in by those privileged few who do not experience an immediate threat to their lives. And often this is the case only because their privileged space is protected and assured by the violence of the prevailing system. For the black masses the space for such debate does not exist. The state of civil war which engulfs the townships has violated that space completely. For them the priority is the elimination of the fundamental causes of violence, whether by counterviolence or the most effective non-violent means.[26]

The *Kairos Document*'s critique of the church's moralistic rejection of all violence is not directed against its espoused commitment to non-violence. It is levelled rather against its failure to tackle the causes of violence, and against state violence, which is defined as the most "ruthless and repressive" form of violence. Revolutionary violence is, in turn, seen as a "last desperate attempt of the people to defend themselves." In a word, moralistic condemnation of revolutionary violence is seen as providing a rationalization for offering little more than token and moderate opposition to state violence. The challenge presented to the churches in the *Kairos Document* concerns the obligation to provide effective opposition to the existing order. If the churches reject violence as a theologically legitimate response to the violence of oppression, the onus is on them to provide a viable alternative form of opposition. The option which they cannot adopt, given their theological pronouncements against apartheid, is that of submission to and acceptance of the prevailing order. The *Kairos* theologians are suggesting that their cautious opposition to this order is, in effect, little more than this.

The English-speaking churches have never in their history affirmed a pacifist position; their traditional sanctuaries are adorned with the battle colors of regiments who have fought and died for "God, queen and country." Clergy and laity in these churches have fought in two world wars, and chaplains continue to minister in the South African army, air force and navy.

Honest reflection tells us that at no point have these churches with planned consistency explored the options of positive non-violent action as an alternative to armed struggle, nor have they committed themselves to such a plan of action. It is this that raises serious questions as to whether the churches are in a position to pass moral judgment on those who resort to an armed struggle for ends which they perceive to be just. When it is taken into account that these same churches have also refused to endorse the World Council of Churches' (WCC) Program to Combat Racism by providing humanitarian aid to liberation movements fighting against the apartheid regime; refused in most cases to support unequivocally the call for disinvestment; and even refused to pray for the end to unjust rule, their reluctance to share in meaningful opposition to the state becomes obvious.

If the church supports violence in any situation on any basis other than a last resort it necessarily denies its finest theological heritage, and in numerous situations it has done precisely this. It is, however, this same heritage which judges violence less harshly than it does indifference, because indifference can never be the expression of love.

Legitimate Government. The dilemma of the English-speaking churches is nowhere to be seen more clearly than with regard to the *Kairos* debate on the nature of legitimate government. Despite having declared apartheid a sin and its theological justification a heresy, these churches refuse to regard the government responsible for this sinful state as theologically illegitimate. The more recent *Lusaka Statement* has similarly raised the matter of the illegitimacy of the South African regime. The debate strikes at the heart of the moderate stance of the English-speaking churches. It requires the churches to move beyond a position of critical neutrality in the conflict between oppressors and the oppressed. It challenges the churches to take a stand diametrically opposed to the popular white myth, enshrined in the constitution, which teaches that South Africa is a country living "in humble submission to Almighty God." Rulers responsible for this constitution are rejected as the anti-Christ, as illegitimate and tyrannical. Critics of the document claim that this is a false absolutism. There is wrong on both sides we are told! The farthest the churches have been prepared to go on the question of illegitimate government is to recognize the right of individuals to protest individual unjust laws, and to pose the question concerning the moral legitimacy of the South African regime. This position is most clearly seen in the following resolution of the 1987 Conference of the Methodist Church.

Legitimacy of the Government: The Conference in implementing its pronouncements on Apartheid as a Heresy, calls into question the moral legitimacy of the South African regime as a basis for questioning the *de jure* legitimacy of that regime; therefore, recommends that its members question their moral obligation to obey unjust laws such as: The Population Registration Act; The Group Areas Act; The Land Acts; The Separate Amenities Acts; The Education Acts.[27]

The challenge facing the churches in this regard is documented throughout this book: Is there the will, and do the churches have the spiritual and moral resources to translate these words into a viable program of action? Differently stated, can they emerge from captivity to the existing structure in order to transform it?

It is here that the liberal tradition of the English-speaking churches, which historically finds common cause with conservative forces in the country, in business, the media and politics is fundamentally challenged. This liberal-conservative alliance has recurred on many occasions in history and in various parts of the world when an established era, or what some with pride called "Christian civilization," has been confronted with a crisis threatening its existence. When the very identity of all that its benefactors hold dear is at stake, liberals and conservatives find common cause in calling society back to consistency with its own ideals. To use different language, the different factions within the ruling class form a common bond against their usurpers. The inevitable problem facing those who want to salvage the old order is that the oppressed majority are invariably not demanding a society that reflects the existing ideals, but a radically different kind of society. The situation in South Africa is no exception. It is not reformed apartheid, renewed free-market capitalism or a "South African way of life" that is being sought, but the total rejection of the existing order so that a new society may be born.

From missionary times, during industrialization, and through the trauma of their response to the Bantu Education Act of 1953, the English-speaking churches have only with great difficulty responded positively to the demands of the masses in their struggle. The liberal-conservative alliance of the present manifests similar elitist tendencies by seeking to inform the broad alliance of oppressed people what is required for their own good. This is clearly seen in the response by the Methodist Church to the *Kairos Document* in which various (unspecified) alternative "courses of action" are "explored."[28] On this issue, at least, the Methodist Church continues to seek an alternative to making a choice between the conflicting sides—remaining captive to those forces which have shaped its identity from missionary times. Believing that there are values within the existing order worth salvaging, it has failed to understand the need to sacrifice all in order to obtain the pearl of great price. *Kairos* theologians argue that this "pearl of great price" has something to do with the affirmation of values which are violated and threatened by the existing order.

The liberal critics of the *Kairos Document* perceive the present order differently from its authors, who wrote from the heat of the struggle in Soweto. Herein lies the point of conflict. The existing authority in South Africa has been very "good" to whites, and it has ensured that the church occupies a privileged place in society. This reality has made it difficult for institutional churches to question the legitimacy of this order. By acknowledging state support and accepting its favor they afford it legitimacy. The colonial heritage of the church in South Africa is one which has compelled it to establish a viable working relationship with the state in order that it may be free to apply its energy to preaching the gospel. Paul fell into a similar trap. He affirmed Roman citizenship as a basis for preaching the gospel (2 Cor. 11:23; Phil. 1:16-17), but according to tradition both he and Peter were martyred by the Roman state. It is only when Christians experience the full onslaught of police brutality and military might, as has happened in Soweto and other black townships in South Africa, that they are compelled to question the legitimacy of the existing regime.

It is here that the English-speaking churches are locked in compromise. The heterogeneous membership of these churches comprises both privileged and persecuted Christians. As the *Kairos Document* puts it: "Both oppressor and oppressed claim loyalty to the same church. They are both baptized in the same baptism and participate together in the breaking of the same bread, the same body and blood of Christ." In this situation the myth of unity is maintained through compromise between the different demands of the different social groups within these churches.

The Methodist axiom of a "church one and undivided" has become a powerful symbol in that church. It has enabled this church to maintain a semblance of church unity against the strongest demands from the state as well as from some of its own members for separation. In so doing, however, it has also provided powerful incentives for the different groups within the church to compromise on their strongest convictions for the sake of unity.

The challenge facing this church, and the other English-speaking churches, is the challenge that has moderated the witness of these churches throughout their history: How to minister to different constituent groups with integrity while maintaining the unity of the church.

Whites, and those blacks prepared to conform to the established social order, experience a post-Constantinian church, accepted by and accepting of the state; those who actively contradict this tradition constitute a persecuted church akin to the early church. The respective class locations of the different constituent groups make it difficult for them to be the church in any other manner.

Throughout history it has been the persecuted church which has rediscovered theological resources long forgotten by the church. The persecuted church within the church in South Africa has rediscovered that part of the Christian tradition which recognizes that the ruling authority is not necessarily appointed by God, and that the blatant misuse of Romans 13 by totalitarian regimes to elicit blind obedience and absolute servility toward the state is a form of collaborationist theology. This rediscovery has, in turn, enabled the persecuted church to proclaim that any ruler whose political policy causes him or her in principle to become the "enemy of the common good" is a tyrant to be removed from office. This proclamation is part of the Christian tradition, born out of and repeatedly affirmed in periods of persecution. Such rulers, this theology teaches, are the enemies of God because they are the enemies of the people; thus it is the theological obligation of the church to work for their removal. The signatories to the *Kairos Document* argue that their analyses show that the apartheid regime *is* hostile to the common good and that, as such, it is tyrannical.

The English-speaking churches, obliged to minister to groups of people whose faith experiences and lived knowledge of the existing order are so vastly different, are socially unable to grasp this theological nettle. It is this inability that ensures that the official response of these churches to the state will be moderate and ultimately fall within the parameters of a privatized state religion prescribed by the Eloff Commission. At the same time, as indicated, the ideological and theological divisions within these churches can only intensify.

THE CHURCH MODERATE AND DIVIDED

The different institutional churches in South Africa have much more in common than might be at first suspected. Monolithic Afrikaner nationalism, driven by religious fervor, shows signs of diversification and mutation. A dominant form of secular, pragmatic politics is emerging in its place with religion being relegated more and more to the realm of private living. The pragmatic religion of the English-speaking churches which has traditionally criticized the appropriation of religion for Afrikaner nationalist ends has, in turn, resolutely refused to side, in theology or praxis, with the poor and oppressed. Influenced by the nature of their constituency, they have preferred not to take sides. A consequence is two churches, different in historic praxes and contemporary lifestyle, but similar in socio-political function.

The doctrinaire position of the NGK and the liberal pragmatism of the English-speaking churches are, of course, reflections of the wider South African culture. To the Afrikaner is ascribed the ideological structuring of apartheid. In the chapter which follows it will be shown that the English-speaking churches have been part of the entrenchment of segregation and racial discrimination in this country.

Adopting an attitude of superiority concerning race relations in South Africa, the South African English have come to regard themselves as more open-minded, generous and conciliatory than their Afrikaner counterparts. Yet both past and present history shows that when hearth and home is threatened the idealistic, doctrinaire Afrikaner and the pragmatic, liberal English-speaker in South Africa are little different.

Often praised for their resistance to apartheid, the English-speaking churches are nonetheless caught within its all-encompassing tentacles. Unable to provide an unequivocal rejection of the present regime, they are being placed under the spotlight of criticism in a manner which only their Afrikaner counterparts had hitherto experienced. At the same time, it has also been argued that the NGK has modified its theological support for apartheid, while continuing to provide the necessary legitimation for the state. As the South African crisis intensifies, the ideological differences between these churches are likely to become less obvious. Further, the oppressed majority within the English-speaking churches is likely to be placed under increasing pressure to rebel against the historic and moderate character of these churches. The question facing these churches is one that has disturbed sociologists as much as theologians of the church: How can an institution trapped in its own history break out of the iron cage which encompasses it?

PART TWO

A
SOCIO-THEOLOGICAL
RESPONSE

Chapter Seven

A Sociological Excursus: Religion as Domination and Rebellion

The need for socio-economic change in South Africa is a matter of simple decency. For those who suffer most it is a non-negotiable imperative. The question is: *Can* the church break out of its history of moderation and compromise and become a source of qualitative change that favors the demands of the poor and the oppressed?

This question involves more than an analysis of the intentions, consequences and corporate will of institutional churches in South Africa. It concerns the nature (epistemological identity) of religion as a social process or cultural identity through which people respond to and deal with the exigencies of their existence. This *particular* study on religion as manifested within the English-speaking churches is assessed in this chapter against a brief and necessarily limited *general* theoretical excursus into the sociological study of religion.

This excursus does not seek to provide comprehensive abstract solutions to complex historical problems, but rather to serve as a starting point for an enquiry as to whether, from a perspective of social theory, religion is realistically capable of being a source of social change. Or is religion necessarily a consolidating system which blunts the will to resist, making tolerable what is intolerable? Put differently, is the religion of the English-speaking churches ultimately a source of domination or social rebellion? The quick answer is perhaps that it is not necessarily either, but history does show that these churches have been trapped within the dominant structures of racial and economic oppression. Important for our purposes is whether they can be other than what they have been, and if so, how?

The burden of all that has been argued so far is that any theological autonomy which the different churches may have manifested as a basis from which to change society has been made relative by their socio-economic and political contexts. Herein is located their pain and promise. These are the bases of the churches' captivity as instruments of social domination, but also the possible sources of their becoming agents of social change. The churches' dominant character is formed by an inheritance shaped and formed by a dominant culture of colonialism and apartheid. At the same time, their character is deeply disturbed by a residual theology of resistance, suppressed by and in contradiction to their social location. This theology is neither silenced nor destroyed by the dominant character of the churches. It is one which haunts them as a relentless and disruptive memory.

Challenged by a society in resistance and revolution, individuals and groups within the churches look to their own resources (the Bible and their theological tradition) to locate and forge weapons with which to participate in the process of social change. Indeed, in many instances, these are quite simply the only cultural resources at their disposal. Despite this, the people of Africa and elsewhere (proselytized by colonial and missionary endeavors) have too often been required to divest themselves of their religious ideals in favor of one or another brand of Marxist-Leninist atheism as a basis for sharing in social revolution. This has often militated against the full participation of the masses in many a process of qualitative social change on this continent and elsewhere in the Third World.

Is there a religious alternative? Can religion, as discerned within the history of the English-speaking churches, provide a possible alternative basis from which to participate critically and creatively in qualitative social and economic change in South Africa?

MARX AND WEBER

Two apparently contradictory sociological models of religion are considered here as a basis for responding to these questions.

The first rejects religion as a compensatory factor for a society that has become corrupt and oppressive; Karl Marx perceives religion as the opiate of the people. The second concerns religion as a possible (yet certainly not inevitable) source of renewal; Max Weber perceives religion as a possible imaginative and creative option beyond the iron cage of history.

Religion as Social Domination

Marx's eleventh thesis on Feuerbach identifies the revolutionary center of Marxian social theory: "The philosophers have only *interpreted* the world, in various ways; the point is to change it."[1]

Marx argued that religion is a secondary social phenomenon and a product of the socio-economic circumstances of a given society. "The foundation of irreligious criticism," said Marx, "is this: man makes religion; religion does not make man."[2] Or, as he stated elsewhere, it is not "consciousness that determines life, but life that determines consciousness."[3]

Religious perceptions were for Marx essentially the projections of society, simply a manifestation of the ideals and values of existing socio-economic interests. Yet because no society is homogeneous and egalitarian, with identical values and aspirations ("The history of all hitherto existing society is the history of class struggles"—*The Communist Manifesto*), the inevitable question is, *whose* interests are portrayed in a society's ideas? Marx's answer is convincing:

The ideas of the ruling class are in every epoch the ruling ideas: i.e. the class which is the ruling material force of society is at the same time its ruling intellectual force. The class which has the means of material production at its disposal, has control at the same time over the means of mental production, so that thereby, generally speaking, the ideas of those who lack the means of mental production are subject to it. The ruling ideas are nothing more than the ideal expression of the dominant material relationships grasped as ideas.[4]

These ideas are never left unchallenged by the oppressed classes, but given the material and structural resources of the ruling class which controls the media, it is *its* ideas which are dominant. In the same way it is *its* religion which is the dominant religion of a given society.

It is important to understand, however, that Marx's critique of religion was not an end in itself, and those who seek to make it a focal point of his philosophy fail to appreciate the significance of his social criticism. Marx did not have a specifically religious axe to grind. He is quoted by a reporter in 1871 as affirming his own atheism, but stressed that this was a personal persuasion and that he could not speak for the International on such matters. Evidence seems to suggest that there were Christians in the first International, and many among those who fought and died in the Paris Commune were Christians.[5]

For Marx, the criticism of religion was an instance of a more extensive form of social criticism, which cannot be fully addressed within the confines of this study. "The criticism of religion is," he said, "the presupposition of all criticism."[6] Religion was, he argued, part of the superstructural legitimation of the existing socio-economic order: "Man has found in the fantastic reality of heaven, where he sought a supernatural being, only his own reflection."[7] For Marx, the theistic God and heaven of the Judeo-Christian tradition were the projections of squandered possibilities of what humankind could achieve in this world into another realm.

Marx readily conceded that "Religious suffering [of the oppressed] is at the same time an expression of real suffering and a protest against real suffering. Religion is the sigh of the oppressed creature, the heart of the heartless world, and the soul of the soulless conditions." Yet because religion ultimately directs the energies of the oppressed away from the causes of their oppression to an illusionary escape from it, "religion is the opium of the people." Marx in fact never lost a fascination with early Christians who, he argued, "lost their chance of the kingdom of heaven on earth because they rejected and neglected engagement in overt political action."[8]

Marx was not a church historian. He was not interested in what theologians might like to refer to as the essential character of the church, but rather its dominant contemporary forms. ("Let us not search for the secret of the Jews in their religion, but for the secret of their religion in the living Jews," he once said.[9]) His analysis of contemporary forms of religion, primarily in nineteenth-century Prussia and elsewhere in Europe, convinced him that it had been appropriated by the ruling classes to dominate the poor and legitimate the power of the ruling class.

Commenting on the use of Marxian criticism of religion in Christian theology, Alistair Kee emphasizes the importance of distinguishing "between the central place which critical thinking about religion played in the development of his [Marx's] work generally and the minor and peripheral place which criticizing religion occupied in his life."[10] By bracketing Marx's atheism and understanding of the inherent nature of religion per se, we can learn from his social critique of the manner in which the dominant religion of a given society becomes the carrier of the dominant ideas of that society. Every particular society produces its own brand of religion, and the need exists to critically assess every manifestation of religion to determine whose values and interests are being served.

> Ideas (including religious ideas) do not evolve on their own account, they do so as elements of the consciousness of men living in society. . . .Whilst in ordinary life every shopkeeper is very well able to distinguish between what somebody professes to be and what he really is, our historians have not yet won even this trivial insight."[11]

Otto Maduro speaks of the limits of our capacity to know reality. Every social group consciously and unconsciously carries its own interests in its political ideas and ideals. Autocritical "epistemological vigilance" is therefore an important tool for uncovering the "concealing and distorting" values hidden therein—whether religious or otherwise.[12]

For Marx, society was not oppressive *because* of religion. He saw religion as part of the ideological superstructure of society used by the ruling class to legitimate the oppressive order. He does not suggest that exposing the ideological bias of religion will produce true consciousness; this is for him a clearing exercise so that the real problems of society can be dealt with. Hence the paradox: "The criticism of religion was important to Marx, not as a criticism of religion, religions or religious institutions, but because it provided the model by which he could unmask the false consciousness surrounding the secular institutions such as the state, money, labor and private property."[13]

Briefly stated, Marx was not sufficiently interested in religion to offer a thorough analysis of it. His concern as a social scientist was rather the use made of it by those who controlled the material, mental and religious means of production in society. Recognizing that Marxian social analysis has made an important contribution to the social sciences, Latin American liberation theologians and others have used his social analysis (as opposed to his atheistic philosophy or metaphysics) to explain economic, social and political problems as well as the role of the church in their respective societies.

When used as a lens through which to view the history of the English-speaking churches, it is difficult not to allow that class influences have permeated and in many instances used religion (consciously and otherwise) to maintain and promote the interests of the dominant classes in South Africa. This is a process that began with colonial and missionary expansionism, intensified with the discovery of gold and continued to manifest itself in the churches' response to the Bantu Education Act, their response to the armed struggle and their theological ambivalence regarding the *Kairos Document*. In other words, social interest has been allowed to shape and form the character of the gospel. This ought to be a matter of deep concern to all theologians. To the extent that Marxian analysis serves the church in discerning this malady, the advantages of theological use being made of this aspect of Marxism are clear.

Equally important is whether Marxian analysis can contribute to an understanding of religion as a source of liberation. Alternatively stated, can religion be liberated from its captivity to the interests of the dominant classes of society without losing its historic theological identity as the church? There is, of course, historical and contemporary evidence of religion fueling the fires of revolution in much the same way that it has legitimated domination. Marx himself never cited such instances. The question is, however, whether his theory necessarily excludes the possibility of a revolutionary social base giving rise to a revolutionary religious ideology.

Theologians are compelled to take this question a step further: Are ideology and religion no more than a reflection of the social base, or can they attain a relative autonomy which impinges on the social base, transforming it rather than merely reflecting it? The debate amongst Marxists in this regard has gone far beyond Marx himself. Few sociologists would deny that the social context and, more specifically, the relations of production *are* fundamental in shaping religious and other ideas, but not all would allow that these are a straight consequence of the class position of a particular social group. Some neo-Marxists have drawn on the more dialectical dimensions of Marx's thought to identify the relative autonomy of ideology as a factor which impinges on social reality.

Antonio Gramsci, for example, sees ideology as a continuous and relatively autonomous battlefield within which people struggle for a social consciousness which locates them within either the "power bloc" of the rulers (the bourgeoisie) or the working class.[14] This is a struggle, however, that always takes place within and in direct relation to continuing material or political struggles. And, he would presumably grant, to the extent that Christianity constitutes the raw cultural material of a given society, it too constitutes an ideological battlefield within which its symbols can be (and *are*) appropriated by either the oppressor or the oppressed or both. More than that, Gramsci would allow that the uncovering of liberating dimensions within these symbols can contribute to the liberation of the existing social or material order. Differently put, while recognizing that the social and material base shapes ideology, ideology impinges on and shapes the social and material base.

For theists, God is necessarily other than and not reducible to the product of human thought and imagination, while experience shows that all theology is time- and socially-bound. Nicholas Lash's question is whether "belief in the reality of such a God [is] compatible with the conviction that all that occurs, in nature and history, is explicable, in so far as it is explicable at all, without direct reference to the reality or agency of God." His tentative answer is as thought-provoking as his question: "If it is, then there would seem to be at least a *prima facie* case for supposing that 'religious materialism' is not necessarily a contradiction in terms."[15] This is not the place to reopen recurring theological debates concerning such matters—debates that have manifested themselves in a variety of forms from deism through Bonhoeffer's secular talk of God to more recent forms of "non-theistic," "secular" and process theology. These debates concern complex questions related to the manner in which God acts in history. Does God intervene to disrupt the normal process of history? Alternatively, does God elect rather to work through the historical process? It could be argued that while Marx was an atheist his interpretation of history does not necessarily exclude the possibility of the Judeo-Christian God as an instrument of interpretation. Lash argues that to limit divine activity to the processes of dialectic materialism excludes human initiative in history, thereby leading to ethical quietism. To "limit God" on the other hand to suprahistorical intervention surely constitutes the essence of quietism. However God might choose to act in history, and there is no common theological mind on such matters, traditional theology recognizes divine initiative to involve human participation in the miracle of creative and redemptive renewal.

The Christian understanding of human determinism and freedom is no less confusing than Marx's attempt to understand humanity as victim and agent of history. At their creative best both allow for a creative dialectic, but there are deterministic strands within both Christian theology and Marx's thought that deny the possibility of human freedom. Historical analysis seems to suggest that no individual or group of people are ever totally free—they are determined by their place in society. At any particular time or place there are a finite number of political, religious, legal or philosophical responses open to people. But within these limitations persons and groups are free to make certain choices and decisions. Indeed Christians and Marxists agree that where such choices (however difficult) are shunned, humanity loses its unique character.

Given the common problems faced by Marxists and Christians, Marxian analysis serves in some instances to remind Christians of their historic calling by confronting them with the reality of the social function of their particular religion. Alternatively, it enables Christians to deal with the contradictions that exist between their declared doctrinal intentions and the actual consequences of their praxis.

First, it teaches Christians to take the reality of society seriously.

A society divided between rich and poor, haves and have-nots, oppressed and oppressors is a society with differing ideological and therefore different religious values and ideals. This means that Christians need critically to enquire whose interests different religious affirmations are serving. Disturbed by a dangerous memory of a God who is, to quote Karl Barth, "against the lofty and on behalf of the lowly; against those who already enjoy rights and privilege and on behalf of those who are denied and deprived of them,"[16] the mission of the church is to be unequivocally on the side of the oppressed. To ensure that this is *in fact* where the church finds its identity, it is required constantly to reassess its character and social location.

Second, Marxian analysis reminds Christians that theology is dependent on religious experience. It is experience that determines theology, not theology that determines experience, and because society is divided religious experiences are different. This means that theology is never neutral. It reflects the social location, values and interests of those who are responsible for it. Until recently those responsible for the articulation of theological ideals as well as those responsible for the religious means of production have been almost exclusively members of the dominant class—professional theologians, seminary-educated priests and religious functionaries whose interest it was to maintain the privileged location of the church within ruling-class structures. More recently this kind of theology has been challenged by a theology done from the perspective of the poor.[17]

Some doing this theology have been the "organic intellectuals" speaking on behalf of the oppressed. Charged with a responsibility to learn how oppressed people understand their popular faith, they have theologized against their own self-interest. But a measure of ideological suspicion has persisted concerning their efforts. This, suggests Segundo, has given rise to a kind of theology which recognizes that conversion to the perspective of the poor demands a renunciation of many of the critical and academic resources of the intellectual in order to become an instrument of the poor.[18] Gutiérrez's *The Power of the Poor in History* is, for example, a different kind of book from his earlier and more dialectical *Theology of Liberation*. Looking at the resources of the church of the poor, he identifies the evangelical riches of the poor as a resource for the

entire church. In a similar way Sobrino writes of "the poor evange-
lizing the church," recognizing that the community of the poor is
the object of God's special concern and love. Divested of all other
sources and faced with no other options the poor alone know what
it is to trust God completely. "Poverty, powerlessness, and persecution," suggests Sobrino, "constitute the real and material conditions for a church in keeping with the will of God."[19]

This is a theology that not only reflects the situation of the poor
and the oppressed, but a theology that arises out of the experience
of the poor and the oppressed. It is a theology providing creative
new insights into the basic teachings of the Bible and the traditional
teaching of the church. It is not a theology "idealizing, much less
sacralizing the poor," insists Sobrino.[20] Or, to quote Míguez
Bonino, "the poor are not morally or spiritually superior to others,
but they see reality from a different angle or location—and therefore differently."[21] This perspective is theologically important for
the simple reason that if the church is to be a church *for* the poor it
is to learn from and be evangelized by the church *of* the poor. This
is discussed further as a "theological imperative" in the next chapter.

Third, Marxism analysis reminds Christians that it is important
not merely to understand the world, but to change it. Trapped
within the dominant culture of the West, First World theologians
have followed the rationalism of the Enlightenment in seeking to
understand the world. In so doing they have capitulated to the
Hegelian axiom that "what is real is rational and what is rational is
real." In explaining (and understanding) the world, Hegel's philosophy had the effect, suggests Kee, "of showing that what is is what
should be." And to the extent to which traditional theologians, at
times through the most convoluted theodicies, have sought to
understand (and explain) a world turned upside down by sin, they
have assisted Hegel to explain and justify the contradictions of life.
But "according to Marx man is not puzzled by the world, but
oppressed in it."[22]

The heart of the Christian gospel is action-oriented with the
essential goal of turning this world the right way up. It concerns the
liberating work of God in Jesus Christ, whose mission is encapsu-
lated in the passage of scripture which Jesus chose to read in the
synagogue at Nazareth as basis for his ministry. It is to preach good

news to the poor, to proclaim liberty to captives, recovery of sight to the blind, to set free the oppressed and to announce that the time has come when the Lord will save his people (Luke 4:19). This is a message that transcends the false belief-praxis dichotomy which bedevils such large sections of modern religiosity. It concerns the wholeness of life. New Testament Christianity is not limited to *feeling* the presence of God. Nor is it limited to *believing* certain things. Jesus said: "Not every one who says to me, 'Lord, Lord,' shall enter the Kingdom of heaven, but he who *does* the will of my Father who is in heaven." This faith involves a certain way of living. Never quietistic, it involves participation in building the kingdom of God on earth.

Doctrinaire Marxists have turned Marx's phrase "religion is the opiate of the people" into a dogma which suggests that religion is merely a mechanism for the exploitation of one class by another. This affirmation is undoubtedly of historic value to the extent that religion has in many instances in South Africa and elsewhere served as a theoretical prop for political domination. The only point made here is that it is not necessarily a source of domination. It is neither in itself an opiate nor a miraculous remedy. The preceding chapters of this book have referred to dominant and alternative traditions within the history of the church.

A more interesting question concerns the possibility of the "alternative church" being a source of renewal. To pursue this question we turn to an alternative model of religion in society.

Religion as Social Renewal

If religion is a social activity shaped and molded by its socioeconomic and political base, never able to acquire more than a relative form of autonomy, the question is whether it can ever become a significant source of social renewal. Christians, of course, believe that the mystery of God operative in human life is such that it constantly makes religious renewal a social possibility. It is a salutary exercise, however, for Christians to bracket such statements of faith and simply to enquire what theoretical sociological evidence there is to support an argument in favor of creative, innovative religion.

The great sociological witness to religion as an independent variable and a source of social renewal is Max Weber, the German theorist who wrote during the latter part of the last and into the first decades of the present century. Weber's theory of religion as a source of social change provides a certain corrective to the Marxian understanding of social evolution. It must not be seen, however, as an exaggerated reversal of Marxism. Weber was not an absolute idealist who denied that economic factors are major historical levers for social change, nor did he suggest that a particular idea is *the* cause of social reality. He recognized that there are times when religion or a particular religious idea serves the upper classes as an ideology of legitimation and the lower classes as a form of otherworldly consolation. Yet, to quote Gregory Baum, "in studying the same religion over a longer period of time," Weber realized that "the relation of religion and class turns out to be very varied; it does not lend itself to easy generalizations. In history, religion has been both legitimating and innovative."[23] Weber's primary interest was the study of religion as a source of social change rather than serving to reinforce the existing order in society. It is this that locates his model of religion in an interesting juxtaposition to that of Marx— within which resides the latent possibility of a religion which is not merely the opiate of the people.

Weber's theory of religion constitutes a cry of hope in a world of sterile bureaucratic control and technological routine which excludes the possibility of what is innovative and creatively different. Modernity is for Weber the iron cage of history from which there is possibly no escape. The only potential escape, if there is an escape at all, is by drawing on the reservoir of what he regarded as "emotional life forces," the visionary dimensions of life located on the edges of society where imagination and response have a better chance of escaping the bureaucratic manipulation and routine of the dominant center.[24] Weber was essentially a social pessimist. Unlike Marx, he did not believe that society could renew itself from within its own resources. Revolution was indeed the "expropriation of the expropriator," but this, he argued, did not address the "inescapable universal bureaucratization" which hung over society like the Sword of Damocles. Weber was never totally convinced that the new could be fundamentally different from the old. Rejecting the possibility of a successful egalitarian revolution, there was for him no obvious way out of the iron cage of history.[25]

To fail to understand Weber's sense of social determinism is to fail to understand the pathos and urgency of his sense of hope, giving rise to the possibility of religious protest. It is protestation amid despair. In social despair he never quite lost hope in those "irrational" sources which lay beyond the domination of the monster of bureaucracy and rationalization.

Social bondage for Weber is all-encompassing. He saw structures created by humans—a culture, an ideology, a political system or an ecclesial structure—as so powerful that instead of them being the servants of their creators, the creators became their captives. This is related to what Rubem Alves refers to as the "arrogance of power," a notion which suggests that contemporary society is doomed to destruction not because of its weakness but because of its power. So powerful and all-embracing are modern structures, he argues, that virtually everything we do and all the innovations we make are shaped, directed and determined by these structures. We are trapped. Our presuppositions, our thoughts and our ideals are governed and organized by the society of which we are a part. Within such structures, education, knowledge, science and politics become rationalizations of the existing order. All critique is internal critique, which ultimately refines and improves the functioning of the very system which needs to be restructured. We become victims of our own achievements.

> The greatest of all creations of science is thus none of its isolated miracles. No one of them can account for the radically new quality of our human experience of this age. Science changed history when, by means of rationalization, it made it possible for power to fulfill its ultimate dream: the transformation of the whole world into Organization. Indeed, Organization is nothing more than the rationalization of power.[26]

The organizational process embraces not only particular social institutions, whether ecclesial, educational or political, but becomes the operative ideal within these institutions. It is a mechanism capable of appropriating alien, contradictory and dysfunctional behavior into an all-absorbing, all-controlling functional whole. It is this near immutable social structure which Weber

characterizes as an iron cage. It excludes genuine creativity, pro-
motes complacency and allows the victims of organized society to
believe that their skills are such that they can cope with any eventu-
ality or crisis. Ironically it is human technological and bureaucratic
power that controls society, militating against the emergence of
heroic and imaginative ideas to cope with the kind of organic crisis
that threatens to destroy humankind. To the extent that organization and bureaucracy succeed, humankind is locked into the down-
ward spiral of crisis.

Significant for Weber is the kind of person this society creates.
People subscribe to social notions of what is realistic, unwilling and
unable to venture beyond the confines of dominant society. Conformity to the existing order is regarded as society's highest goal.
The creative or unusual act is dismissed as necessarily absurd,
insane, irresponsible, heretical, subversive and anarchical.[27]

Weber's conforming person is well illustrated by comparing the
vision of tyranny as depicted in George Orwell's *Nineteen Eighty-
Four* with that of Aldous Huxley's *Brave New World*. Orwell
warned against externally imposed oppression, the presence of Big
Brother and the Ministry of Truth. Huxley identified the internali-
zation of oppression. The Orwellian victim is forced to conform;
the Huxleyan victim is convinced of the need to do so. Huxley
warned that people would come to enjoy their oppression, be
infatuated by their "achievements," convinced by the official ver-
sion of truth, and benefit from social conformity. Orwell feared a
society that banned books; Huxley feared a society within which
people no longer saw the need to read such books. Orwell feared
the concealment of truth; Huxley feared the loss of truth in a sea of
irrelevance.[28] Modernity for Weber is a state of being trapped in
mediocrity and conformity under the illusion of grandeur, while
haunted by the anticipation of social oppression, personal mean-
inglessness and philosophical/religious nihilism. It is being trapped
in a state of not being able to dream new dreams or project goals
beyond the perimeters of one's closed, organized perception of
reality. It is a mechanistic ideology whereby we are educated for
reality, ensuring that what is is also what is possible.

Weber's sociology is in rebellion against this order—demanding
that there be a way beyond the iron cage. If there is "a way out" for
him, it is found in religion, but not that of the dominant ecclesial

organization and bureaucracy. Such religion is controlled and conforming religion. Lacking in imagination and devoid of a historical mission beyond legitimating the existing order, it is itself trapped within the iron cage, stripped of the heroic creativity that is being sought. The religion which Weber affirms is a manifestation of "life forces." Religion is, for him, born in the charismata or the charisms of life, what Christians regard as grace. Weber's language acquires what theologians would identify as an evangelical ring when he speaks of this spontaneous, heroic, prophetic religion— free from bureaucratic manipulation and in contradiction to the conformity of dominant society. His description of the social prophet, in turn, reminds one of biblical and other prophetic traditions. The prophet is one who does not merely speak out but embodies protest against the existing order. Yet, in so doing, the prophet portrays the essential but forgotten values of a people. As in the Hindu popular consciousness Mahatma Gandhi was seen to portray the collective consciousness of the masses, so the Weberian prophet is received and understood by the marginalized people of a society in a manner that the high priests of the bureaucracy cannot understand. The prophet is dysfunctional and asocial in terms of society's dominant values, given at times to emotionalism and prophetic movements bordering on what society regards as pathological.[29]

Because the prophet is the manifestation of the often obscured but deepest aspirations of society, it is important to identify the location of such charisms. They are not obvious within the power centers of dominant society, but are latent within the contradictions which reside in even the most solid structures of the existing order—there to be exploited. Such aspirations and values are most potent on the edges of the centers of power and among the marginalized of society. Here is the social location of social contradiction, the realm of visions that are different, and the heart of a protest movement against the dominant social order. It is a contradiction that manifests itself, for Weber, in the sphere of visionary and creative ideas and praxis—in art, music, poetry, literature, religion and related cultural options. For Weber, it is these spheres of vision and protest which the dominant order seeks to eliminate that constitute a possible means of getting beyond the iron cage. His realism tells him, however, that the dominant order regulated by bureaucracy and routine has the inevitable tendency to control and regulate such visions and protest. This is for Weber the fundamental problem with institutional religion and organized society. It envelops and ultimately suffocates all possibility of what is new, different and liberating. This renders Weber skeptical of renewal emerging from within the center of existing structures.

If religion at its creative best is a source of liberating vision, the question is how to exploit this potential, bringing it to bear on existing institutions which have been rendered moribund by their own internal organization. We have learned from Marx that the strong and the powerful (the ruling class) control the dominant social ideas of any age, including the religious ideas. History teaches us that this class has never voluntarily surrendered power or its control of such ideas. Compelled by a sense of complacency, its members' hearts and minds are no longer restless. The present order provides the rich with much pleasure and security; they are trapped within the limitations of the existing order; they can no longer see new visions. How hard it is, suggests the Bible, for a rich person to enter the kingdom of God. Having no cause to "hunger and thirst" for what is essentially different, their dreams are limited and contained by the dominant order. It is the poor and the oppressed who dream new dreams and see new visions. Friedrich Nietzsche once asked:

> O my brothers, who represents the greatest danger for all of man's future? Is it not the good and the just? Inasmuch as they feel in their hearts, "We know what is good and just, and we have it too; woe unto those who still seek here!"[30]

Weber's creative, change-generating religion cannot be a religion of the powerful and the strong. Such religion, given its location within dominant society, is rationalized and bureaucratized to reflect the values and interests of the ruling class. It is the religion of the poor which gives expression to the dreams and aspirations of the poor and the afflicted. People intoxicated with the order that exists do not see visions. Vision is born of pain. As Buber says, "All suffering under a social order that is senseless prepares the soul for vision."[31]

The question with which we concluded the last chapter has been partially answered by making use of sociological theory of religion. We asked: How can an institution trapped in its own history break out of the iron cage which encompasses it? Is there a spiritual, cultural, liturgical, communal and/or ethical source within the Christian religion, or a transcendent lever—what traditional theology regards as an attribute of God which locates the divine independent of the world—which can enable the church to transcend its captivity?

Weber suggests that this dimension cannot be found by more of the kind of religion that is already dominant, but possibly by the celebration of the religion of the poor. At this point the apparently contradictory Marxian and Weberian models of religion find common ground. Different social contexts do produce different religious experiences and different theological formulae. Given the social, economic, organizational and intellectual domination of the dominant classes, *their* religious ideas and formulations become the dominant ideas of the church. Suppressed and overshadowed by this tradition, but neither destroyed nor defeated, the religious experiences of the poor and oppressed located on the margins of such domination are ultimately the hope of renewal for both the church and society. Indeed, it *is* the poor who must evangelize the church.

THE SOCIAL FUNCTION OF RELIGION

Is religion essentially a brake or an accelerator on social change? A brief consideration of the two extremes of the sociological spectrum on religions suggest it can be either. "Religion as opiate" and "religion as the source of social renewal" are not mutually exclusive explanations. "They may well refer to diverse layers and trends in religion, each with different characteristics and different social effects."[32] As such, religion can be both alienating and life-giving. Baum suggests that it is possible to read the Bible as a textbook on the pathology of religion—giving rise to hypocrisy, idolatry, group-egotism and collective blindness. On the other hand it can also be read as a textbook on the therapeutic nature of religion—overcoming the maladies of society by being a source of social and political renewal.[33]

The sociological excursus undertaken in this chapter has essentially confirmed what had already been theologically discerned within the history of the church: the inevitability of a dominant theology which reflects the values of the dominant classes, and the possibility of an alternative theology reflective of the marginalized and dominated classes of history. It has further identified the poor as the only possible source of institutional renewal. Given the impossibility of separating theology from its social base, and recognizing that ecclesial structures which are shared with the dominant classes are also dominated by these classes, it follows that ideas and programs of action representative of the poor are invariably found in the margins and on the edges of church structures. In many instances it is in the church on the margins of the institutional churches and outside of these structures—in the church of the streets—that the hope of Christian renewal is found. It is here that a different kind of piety is found, the liberating spirituality of the poor.

Chapter Eight

A Theological Imperative: A Liberating Ecclesiology

Within the first decades of the common era St. Paul warned Christians not to conform to the standards of this world (Rom. 12:2). Theirs, he insisted, was to know Christ in the power of his resurrection, through sharing in his suffering and by becoming like him in his death (Phil. 3:10). The church was to be a church in resistance. It was called to be different. Its membership was to be drawn from those who suffer and are put to death by those who rule.

Shaped by a dominant culture and sustained by an all-embracing ecclesial system (a Weberian-type bureaucracy) more powerful than their most articulate prophets, the institutional churches in South Africa appear trapped within their own history. Historical and contemporary analysis suggests, however, that adjacent to the social location of the dominant church is another church—marginalized and oppressed, whose knowledge of Christ *is* through sharing in his suffering and in conformity to his death.

The theological imperative is to know that the resurrected Lord offers the entire church together with all of creation the opportunity for renewal. Like St. Paul, individuals and groups within and outside of the institutional churches have throughout history been forced out of their captivity to the past to become the source of spiritual and social renewal well beyond the confines of the churches (Acts 9:1-19). On most occasions, however, the power of the bureaucracy (Weber) and the influence of the dominant ideas (Marx) within the church have been such that individuals and groups who have carried within them the seeds of possible institutional renewal have more often than not been subsumed back into the restraining organization (Alves) of the church. This constitutes the urgency behind the questions: Can the churches themselves be renewed in order to become a source of renewal in society? If so, from a theological perspective, what is the most likely *social* location of the *spiritual* renewal of the church?

To deny that the institutional churches have conformed to the dominant structures of their social contexts would be hypocritical. It would also be a denial of the most basic evangelical truth which requires every particular manifestation of the church to be subjected to the purging grace and judgment of the gospel. To refuse, on the other hand, to accept that Christ can renew his church is to deny the essence of the gospel. Often buffeted and continually subjected to the pressures and challenges of contending political and other ideologies, the institutional churches have sought to preserve their dominant identity, together with the privileges this affords, within the existing order. Yet disturbed by a residual gospel which contradicts their social location, some within these churches (and at times the churches themselves) have reached out to what they know by God's grace they can and ought to become—despite the cost and loss of social privilege.

In this final chapter the *theological* identity of the alternative church is explored and its resources for social renewal are identified. It is a church which exists within the institutional churches, but one which is marginalized by the dominant tradition of these churches. As such it rarely shapes the identity of the institutional churches. It is predominantly a community of Christ's followers located on the margins and outside of the dominant ecclesial and social structures; it is without institutional form. Inspired by a spirituality which emerges out of oppression and resistance, making no distinction between what some call the spiritual and secular, it is without what the state regards as a bona fide religious identity.

It is an alternative church to the extent that it seeks its theological center outside of itself. Turning away from what Gutiérrez has called ecclesio-centrism, it recognizes its essential identity to be among those who are marginalized by society—primarily the poor and oppressed.[1] It is a church which identifies the importance and centrality of Matthew 25:31-46 as a basis for self-understanding. It is a church for whom the poor are not merely recipients of the gospel, but heralds of the gospel and agents of change, capable of delivering the institutional churches from their captivity. In the poor and the "least important," suggests Matthew, the risen Christ is most powerfully present. It is a church for which "the Spirit is present in the poor *ex opere operato*."[2] It is a church that rediscovers a dimension of New Testament theology long neglected. The alternative church is a church not merely for the poor or with the poor but *of* the poor. As such it is a church within which a christological center is found *in* the poor. It is also a church whose members are largely drawn from among the poor and the marginalized.

The essential power of this church is found not in riches, vestments or hierarchical structures, but in the latent and actual resources of those identified in Matthew—the hungry, the thirsty, the stranger, the naked, the sick and those who are in prison. It is a church seeking to rediscover a gospel identity, reactivating the dangerous memory of its revolutionary beginnings. It is a church within the church and a church beyond the church which carries within it resources which are capable of transforming the dominant structures not only of the church but also of society.

Matthew 25:31-46 locates Christ where the institutional churches have not traditionally sought a spiritual center—a center on the edges of the dominant order. From this christological relocation a liberating ecclesiology follows: Where Christ is, there the church as the body of Christ is required to be. It is a relocation which unequivocally locates the church on the side of the poor, making its message of salvation concrete in terms of the agenda of the poor, offering liberation and redemption from personal and structural forces of domination and sinfulness which destroy their life and identity. Because these forces involve both spiritual and structural warfare and conflict, any attempt to distinguish between faith and justice, spiritual and secular, or for that matter between religion and politics collapses into an organic whole within which the one side of the equation *is* the other.

The alternative church is different from the one trapped in apartheid. Yet it can neither be ignored nor dismissed by the dominant church. It recovers the less dominant and alternative themes of suffering and powerlessness as well as those aspects of struggle, conversion, radical transformation and serious social revolution which are part of the Christian tradition.

TOWARD A LIBERATING ECCLESIOLOGY

Matthew 25:31-46 suggests that the primary and most concrete mediation between the transcendent God and human nature is the poor and repressed. The great and mysterious God of the Hebrew scriptures is revealed as being present in the Christ who emptied himself of all his glory and took on himself the form of a servant (Phil. 2:6-11).

The alternative church, the church of the poor, is a church "outside the gate" (Heb. 13:13); its members are those excluded from the dominant society, including thieves, prostitutes, criminals, outcasts and rebels. It was there that Christ was crucified. But the institutional center of the churches now is found elsewhere—at the center of society, among the powerful and those whose social location in life is essentially responsible for others being driven to the edges of existence.

The church of Matthew 25:31-46 is a church of the oppressed and repressed, the marginalized and those rejected as unworthy of high office and without influence in the highest courts of the dominant churches. A theological consideration of this church is undertaken here. Yet because the church is theologically defined as "the body of Christ" and individual Christians as "God's temple," ecclesiology is necessarily to be understood in relation to the triune God who is made known in Jesus Christ. In other words, the church is required to be a part of the dynamic and outreaching love of God, traditionally witnessed to as Father, Son and Holy Spirit.

The church's traditional doctrine of the Trinity refers to the one, indivisible, homogeneous, divine substance constituted as three individual divine persons. This Hellenistic formula constitutes a powerful witness to the unity of God made known in the history of the Jews, the life of Jesus and the creative presence of the Spirit. What is important to remember is that this formula, however interpreted in the great trinitarian debates of the East and the West, was an attempt to understand and systematize the dynamic self-revelation of God as recorded in scripture. Our understanding of this self-revelation, insists Moltmann, is not only an attempt to comprehend our experience of God but also God's experience with us. "At the moments of God's profoundest revelation," he argues, "there is always suffering: the cry of the captives in Egypt; Jesus' death cry on the cross; the sighing of the whole enslaved creation for liberty."[3] It is this, Moltmann claims, which shatters the apathetic divine categories of divine Greek philosophy, replacing them with the suffering of the passionate God.

The better the church understands and participates in God's encounter with creation, the more deeply is the mystery of God's passion revealed to the church. Because the church is called to share in God's encounter with creation and to be the body of Christ in the world, ecclesiology cannot be understood apart from the doctrine of God, which for Christians is a trinitarian doctrine.

The Mystery of God

Central to traditional theology is the belief that God is known only to the extent of God's self-revelation to humankind. It is a revelation of a God who is manifest through the great events of the Exodus, the exile, the suffering people of God, prophets rejected by their people, priests alienated from their communities and the suffering of ordinary women and men whose stories were not always regarded as significant enough to be included in the Bible. Above all, it is a revelation of that God whom the rejected and crucified Jesus understood as the revelation of one who is *Father*.

As such, it is a revelation, suggests Sobrino, within which "access to the ever greater and transcendent God comes through contact with the God who is 'lesser,' hidden in the little ones, crucified on the cross of Jesus and on the countless crosses of the oppressed of our day."[4]

The stories of God's revelation in the Bible are stories which in many instances are so far removed from the dominant religious ideas of our time that they only make sense provided we can block out all our pre-conceived ideas of who or what God is before we read them.[5] The dominant church, bolstered by its great learning and made confident by its many successes since its grand alliance with the dominant social forces in the West, finds it near impossible to succeed in this hermeneutical exercise. It may well be that only those excluded from this dominant alliance or on its extreme edges, the poor and the oppressed, can understand the stories of God's revelation and so learn little by little who God is and where God is to be found. Perhaps it is only people who experience in their own lives the suffering of the people of God in the Bible who can really understand the Bible. Indeed few will deny that the rediscovery of theology in the Third World and the reinterpretation of biblical texts from within situations of oppression in South Africa are hermeneutically liberating and devastatingly authentic. Dissatisfied with the God of the dominant churches, like Abraham who rejected the religion of his surroundings to the point of being compelled to break with the local gods, it may well be that the church is required to do what it has never succeeded in doing effectively, that is, to listen to and learn from those very people whom it believes it is called to serve. For this to happen the church is required not only to be in solidarity with the poor in the sense of making the struggle of the poor the struggle of the church, but to be enlightened by the poor and to allow itself to be taught and evangelized by them.[6]

Gustavo Gutiérrez has described this experience in a striking manner:

> In recent years it has seemed more and more clear to many Christians that, if the church wishes to be faithful to the God of Jesus Christ, it must become aware of itself from underneath, from among the poor of this world, the exploited classes, despised ethnic groups, the marginalized cultures. It must descend into the hell of this world, into communion with the misery, injustice, struggles, and hopes of the wretched of the earth—for "of such is the kingdom of heaven." At bottom it is a matter of living, as church, what the majority of its own members live every day. To be born, to be reborn, as church, from below, from among them, today

means to die, in a concrete history of oppression and complicity in oppression.

In this ecclesiological approach, which takes up one of the central themes of the Bible, Christ is seen as the Poor One, identified with the oppressed and plundered of the earth.[7]

Christian ascetics have throughout history affirmed the significance of poverty as a theological category, voluntarily withdrawing from the center of the dominant society to identify with those who cling to its margins. They have sought to draw spiritually closer to God in their quest for perfection or sanctification while serving and becoming part of the struggle for existence which characterizes the life of the poor. Such sacrifices have remained peripheral to the central mission of the church.

The church *of* the poor is formed and characterized primarily not by those who voluntarily identify with the poor (as important as this may be) but by those who are trapped within their poverty. Knowing that their own liberation is tied up with the radical transformation of society, their most *personal* quest for life is part of a *communal* struggle for survival, rendering all distinctions between a personal and social gospel void. And yet the church is called to be one, knowing neither class nor social distinction. This raises the pertinent question whether the rich and powerful, who have never known the material deprivation and alienation of the historical poor, can ever become part of this church. More pertinent: Are they in a position to comprehend the mystery of God? It is a question to which we must return.

The Mission of Jesus

The mystery of God's self-revelation in one emptied of all glory, taking the form of a servant, continues, according to Matthew 25:31-46, in the poor of succeeding generations who have servitude and deprivation imposed on them. In the person and life of Jesus, this God who is manifest in the poor calls and commands people with the words, "Follow me" (Mark 2:14). In the words of Bonhoeffer, "The gracious call of Jesus now becomes a stern command."[8]

To be confronted with the mystery of God within the poor involves an inevitable participation in the mission of God among the poor. It involves *following* Jesus as "the way, the truth and the life." Because *this* way is the way of the God of Jewish history, Jesus is the "Son of Israel" and the "Son of God," one with the Father as the Father is one with the Son (John 19:21). In the trinitarian language of the Nicene Creed the *Son* is "the only begotten Son of God, begotten of his Father before all worlds, God of God, Light of Light, very God of very God, begotten not made, being of one substance with the Father."

It is, however, with the historical encounter between God and humankind in Jesus Christ that New Testament Christology begins—not with metaphysical speculation but with obedient living, recognizing that our understanding of Jesus as the ultimate norm within whom God is made known begins in actual obedience to the call to follow him. To again quote Bonhoeffer, "Only he who believes is obedient, and only he who is obedient believes."[9] This means that the actual following of Jesus is the only authentic basis for Christology. And this *can* be the only authentic basis for ecclesiology. Called to be the presence of Christ in successive generations, the ministry of the church must be in continuity with the life and mission of Jesus.

The command that the church be in continuity with the ministry of Jesus to the poor and the oppressed is, *ipso facto*, a judgment on the wealth and affluence of the institutional church. It requires such a church to undergo a fundamental conversion, recovering its social origins. Paul reminded the Corinthian church of these origins:

Now remember what you were, my brothers, when God called you. From the human point of view few of you were wise or powerful or of high social standing. God purposely chose what the world considers nonsense in order to shame the powerful. He chose what the world looks down on and despises and thinks is nothing, in order to destroy what the world thinks is important (1 Cor. 1:26-28).

There is nothing romantic about being poor, and among the most important tasks facing the church is the elimination of poverty.

Further, there is no biblical evidence to suggest that the social composition of the contemporary church should necessarily be precisely as it was in the early church. The normative character of Christianity is the person and ministry of Jesus as recorded within the New Testament. This record leaves us in no doubt whatsoever that Jesus' primary concern was for the weak and marginalized members of society: Widows, orphans, the sick, little children, the oppressed, sinners and those sinned against. The most simple effort at political analysis, in turn, shows that a liberating ministry to this constituency of people requires the church to take sides for the weak against the strong, for the marginalized and powerless against the dominant center and the powerful, for the oppressed against the oppressor, in society as well as in the church.

The primary recipients of the gospel were the poor and marginalized, presumably because they had an inherent ability to understand the message of Jesus better than anyone else. This has profound and far-reaching implications for the church. The New Testament tells us that the sign of the arrival of the kingdom is that the poor have the gospel preached to them. Today, suggests De Santa Ana, this situation has changed. The poor have come of age, and it is they who preach the gospel to the church.[10] To the extent that it is heard, the kingdom of God is that much nearer.

The Power of the Spirit

The mission of God to humankind in the ministry of Jesus is ultimately a message of power and hope, a holistic message of liberation from both internal egocentric and external structural forms of sinful oppression.

The gospel of Jesus Christ contains many ethical imperatives for personal and communal living. It is not, however, a moralistic directory providing a blueprint for all socio-economic and political maladies or programs of reform. It is essentially a source of spiritual empowerment which convinces all people (and primarily the marginalized and weak members of society) of their God-given worth in a world that subordinates human worth to ideological and material goals. Providing a vision of God's purpose for creation, it draws people into the struggle for the realization of a world within which there is good news for the poor, liberty for the captives, recovery of sight for the blind and freedom for the oppressed, because the year of the Lord has arrived (Luke 4:18-19). According to the New Testament, to the extent that this ministry is fulfilled in the church the power of God's Holy Spirit is manifest within the church. In the words of the Nicene Creed, the *Holy Spirit* is "the Lord and Giver of life, who proceedeth from the Father and the Son, who with the Father and the Son is glorified, who spake by the prophets. . . ."

A standard criticism of theology which addresses political concerns is that it neglects the spirituality of the gospel. Indeed this is a failure of some theologies, political and other. However, most Third World theologies, and certainly Latin American liberation theology, are an inherent part of a dramatic rediscovery of the spiritual resources of the Christian tradition. The Medellín Conference returned repeatedly to the spiritual resources of liberation, Gutiérrez identified the importance of the "spirituality of liberation" in his earliest book and many other liberation theologians continue to plumb the depths of spirituality in their quest for social, economic and political liberation. Perhaps more important is that in doing so they have recovered for the entire church the neglected spiritual resources of liberation. The dominant church has not been required to suffer, and therefore not been compelled to grow spiritually. Reference has been made earlier to the great prayers of the Judeo-Christian tradition being born out of social, political and private conflict and engagement in life (chapter 5). It requires suffering for the church to understand this tradition. Not having been compelled to seek for spiritual resources with which to cope with the traumas of political conflict, the illuminating power of the spirituality of the church in its many different forms has been lost on the dominant church. What were once the cries of the oppressed to their God, the spiritual agonies of the saints, the liberation songs of an Exodus people, and the liturgical resources of those in pursuit of God's kingdom on earth as it is in heaven, have too often become the mere formal trappings of religious complacency. In such a situation it requires the witness of those who are shorn of all that gives false security—social status, merit, achievement and education—to wrench the church from its slumbers. With nothing to rely on except that grace of God which shows a preferential option for the poor, it is the marginal ones who remind the church of the liberating resources of its collective memory.

The message of Matthew 25:31-46 is that Christ is present incognito among the poor. "If to evangelise means to make it possible to meet Jesus Christ, then the poor are the people among whom Christ is present in unknown ways. They are the evangelists who bear Christ, *Christophoros!*"[11] Fundamentally alienated from the existing socio-economic and political order, having nothing to lose except oppression, the oppressed have acquired a restless freedom that makes them heralds of a source of spiritual power which offers life amid death and liberation from captivity.

A church trapped in the dominant structures of oppression, controlled by an entrenched bureaucracy, conditioned by a history of compromise and impoverished by an inability to break out of the iron cage of history can only at its own peril afford to ignore the voice of the marginal ones. Again, *not* because they are morally or spiritually superior but, to quote Míguez Bonino, because "they see reality from a different angle or location, and therefore differently."[12] This ability to escape the self-perpetuating and conforming iron cage of bureaucratic control is (in terms of our sociological excursus) the significance of the marginal people of society. Theologically this community of people carries within it a potency of divine presence to which the church is obliged to listen and respond. To the extent that it fails to do so, it fails to be a church of the poor and to this extent it fails to be a church in continuity with the New Testament.

The church of Matthew 25:31-46 is both a recipient of the Spirit of God which resides within the poor and a channel or means of God's redeeming grace extended to humankind. To the extent that it participates within the work of God among the poor, it is itself empowered by the Spirit, and so empowered and renewed it can do no other than again give itself in service to the poor. This, in addition to all else, is part of the sanctifying work of the Holy Spirit.

The Worship of the Church

This process of sharing in the renewal of the Spirit has direct implications for the worship of the church. Within the Eastern Orthodox tradition we encounter the notion of a "liturgy *after* the liturgy," the idea being that the edification and renewal of the congregation within worship is carried into everyday life. This, in turn, gives rise to what has been referred to as the "liturgy *before* the liturgy," in which the experiences of everyday life provide essential material to be taken up in worship.[13] In this sense, for the Orthodox church, worship and praxis constitute an inherent unity. "Two inseparable movements take place in the action of the liturgy, which in fact constitutes the rhythm of mission: the gathering and the sending forth."[14] The curtain which isolates worship from the harsh realities of the secular world is rent, the holy of holies is exposed to the world and the world itself becomes the dwelling place of God. The harsh realities of life are incorporated into worship, and worship becomes that place where God and the world are integrated in the minds and actions of the Christian community. This provides theological legitimation of the axiom, "Life *is* worship and worship *is* life." For all the differences between the Reformed and Orthodox worship, the centrality of worship within the former is no less obvious than it is in the latter. For the Westminster Catechism "the chief end of man is to glorify God and enjoy him forever." It is in worship that Protestants, no less than any other Christian communion, believe that the encounter between God and humankind is celebrated in its highest form.

It is with regard to worship that our theological imperative and sociological excursus again meet. Religion in its artistic and creative forms, for Weber, is part of the reservoir of the "emotional life forces" on which to draw in protest against the manipulative forces of institutional oppression. For Robert Bellah "the sacred is not simply a property of external objects" or as theologians would say, the transcendent God, "any more than it is purely a subjective feeling."[15] It is for the person of faith the most intimate relationship between subject and object, within which the worshipper (as subject) is addressed by the object of his or her worship. In this sense the initiative is with the object—whether icon, totem or sacred text. Theologically it is God as focus or object of worship who is always the subject. The worshipping community responds to God's initiative. Certainly the Christian tradition shows evidence of this response involving passive or mystical absorption, but essentially it involves thoughtful participation. As such, worship involves what Bellah calls a "poetic or prophetic" perception of life within which a community breaks out of the profane world of everyday common sense in anticipation of what is radically different.

Not all forms of worship attain these heights. At best we encounter in worship what the poet Wallace Stevens calls "a reality that forces itself upon our consciousness and refuses to be managed and mastered."[16]

Worship whose function it is to facilitate this experience, however, can become a barrier against the experience. Traditional rituals can so restrict the experience of the sacred that the creative break with the ordinary and the possibility of attaining to what is different is unlikely to occur. Vision is lost in prescription, dreams are tamed by reality and the will to action is paralyzed by conformity to the dominant order.

Worship ought to exercise a mediatory function in facilitating the possibility of reaching out to what is new—and more specifically to God's kingdom. Theologically speaking, worship enables the worshipping community to anticipate the fulfillment of the promise of a new heaven and a new earth. For this to happen the symbols of worship must fulfill a twofold purpose, pointing forward to new possibilities of existence, but also firmly grounded in and related to the past and present experience of those who worship. Differently stated, worship must emerge from the social context of those who worship and be a carrier of creative alternative options for society.

Worship as an encounter with God and a visionary anticipation of an age of justice and peace which is to come are essential ingredients of an ecclesiology which offers renewal in church and society. They are important parts of a liberating culture. Yet ultimately it is those who escape the restraining and limiting bureaucracy of the institutional churches that dream the new dreams and see the most dynamic visions. The prophet Joel defined the location of the forces of renewal in relation to the limits of life: *old* men dream dreams, he said, and *young* men see visions. He also defined the location in terms of social status: God's spirit will even descend on those who occupy the margins of the dominant order; even on servants and women! (Joel 2:28-29).

In brief, the gift of vision and new beginnings is the gift of the marginalized people to the church. It is a gift grounded in a spirituality which does not answer all the questions of the cognitive

theological tradition of the West. In many instances it is a spirituality which is a sign of God's presence rather than an explanation of
it, giving expression to a culture which regards human imagination
and creative participation to be as important a part of human
response as the articulation of rationalistic definitions. It is a
spirituality in response to a divine transcendence that is inextricably
linked with holiness and social justice. In Gregory Baum's words, it
bears witness to the majesty of God "which makes [us] tremble not
only because God wholly transcends human proportions, but because God judges the sinful world, and God's holiness is attractive
not only because it promises consolation but because it promises to
turn right-side up a world that has been placed upside down by
sin."[17]

The mystery of God revealed in the poor and the mission of Jesus
to the poor constitutes the power of the Spirit. Theologically
authentic worship is a response to this trinitarian initiative. More
than that, it is the basis for a creative sharing in it. Worship and
Christian witness which *are* part of this process present a unique
challenge to a church trapped in apartheid. This liberating ecclesiology already exists within the South African context, adjacent to
the dominant ecclesiology of the institutional English-speaking
churches. Located on the margins of the dominant churches and
"outside the gate" of dominant ecclesiology, this church within the
church and church beyond the church offers a form of life to the
institutional churches which can only be defined in terms of death
to the old self and rebirth from among the poor.

A CHURCH DISCORDANT AND DIVIDED

In preceding chapters an awareness has been established of a
church both within and outside of the dominant structures of the
English-speaking churches, an alternative church, a church in resistance and one in quest of deliverance from the iron cage of
history. In light of the above quest for a liberating ecclesiology, we
seek to further characterize this church in contrast to the dominant
church.

Matthew 25:31-46 leaves one in no doubt where Christ is to be
found in the South African context and consequentially where the
church of Christ is required to be—within the resettlement camps,

in prison cells, among the deprived and depressed non-citizens who cling to the edges of sprawling cities, those found in refugee camps and in police mortuaries.

The theological implications of such a statement are immense. They require the church as part of its primary task, which is to worship God, unequivocally to identify itself with the oppressed because *that* is where God is primarily to be found. Solidarity with the oppressed is no longer one among the many consequences of worshipping God. It is part of the Christian's primary task, which is to worship God and share in the liberating and self-giving love of God for humankind. To know this is to understand the bias of the prophet Isaiah who renounced the worship and holy days of the rulers and dominant classes of Israel whose hands were bloodied by the oppression of the poor. Better than such worship, he said, is to "see that justice is done," that "help [is given] those who are oppressed," that society gives "orphans their right," and "defends widows" (Isa. 1:10-20). To fast correctly, says Isaiah, is to "remove the chains of oppression and the yoke of injustice, and let the oppressed go free" (Isa. 58:6). Similarly, the essence of worship for Micah is "to do what is just, to show constant love, and to live in fellowship with God" (Mic. 6:8). Amos despised the worship of Amaziah, the priest of Bethel (Amos 7:10-17), and in the New Testament Jesus ridiculed the worship and religiosity of the scribes and the Pharisees (Matt. 23:13f).

Sunday worship has been described as the holiest hour of the week for a Christian. The only fair response to this affirmation is to say that it depends on the kind of worship. A disturbing implication of the paragraph immediately above is that a narrow line exists between the sacred and the demonic. The conflict concerning worship which has raged since the time of the Hebrew prophets in the eighth century BCE continues today. We have all met people who insist that they live with political conflict all week and refuse to have more of it in Sunday worship. The worship service, we are told, is a place to which one withdraws from daily tensions in order to be refreshed and spiritually renewed. The ready response to such worship is as familiar. If worship is not related to the issues of conflict which shape the lives of people, it is an opiate of escape rather than a spiritual resource for life.

Two services of worship made this conflict concrete for me in a penetrating and revelatory manner, indicating that what happens in worship is largely a reflection of the context within which it happens.

A Church "Steadfast in Dignity"

To have stood outside of a "successful" and well-attended white English-speaking church in Cape Town on a particular Sunday morning was a disturbing experience. The people who worshipped at that church were kindly and caring folk. They exchanged greetings as they made their way into the place of worship and spoke of the beauty of the crisp morning weather. It occurred to me that this was a scene that was probably more or less a mirror image of affluent congregations in many cities around the world. The difference was that this was a Sunday morning in October 1985 during what was euphemistically called a "period of unrest." In the distance the black smoke of burning tires hung over the Cape flats, which had been turned into a battle zone. Further in the distance were the troubled black townships of Guguletu, Langa and Nyanga. Then came Crossroads and further out the initial phases of the Khayelitsha complex.

The service of worship took its customary form. No reference was made to the events of the week with the exception of a sentence or two of intercessary prayer for peace in our troubled times. "I attend this church because the services always have a certain dignity about them in a world that has lost its dignity," said a parishioner.

The texts already mentioned from Isaiah and Micah and some words of Jesus came to mind. It was difficult not to be angry when recalling that this was a congregation within a church pledged to be "one and undivided." Angry because nice people were trapped, friendly people whom one would meet again during the week at the local shops. How *could* that congregation portray the agony of people whose children had been shot that past week, whose homes were destroyed or who had themselves been terrorized? It was perhaps asking the impossible. Some individuals in that congregation were involved in social and political work elsewhere, but their church remained a place for serene meditation. There was little connection between their liturgy of worship and any sense of liturgy before or after their worship. And what connection there was found itself largely unrelated to the burning tires, charred bodies and suffering not far away. It was a disturbing situation within which to ask what the social function of religion really is. Who was right, Marx or Weber? The question is simplistic, of course, and the situation within which it is asked too parochial. But that question has continued to disturb at least one person since that Sunday morning.

If one's theology insists that God was at that time more readily to be found where tires burned and beneath the black plastic shelters of Crossroads than beneath the starched white cloth on the communion table, one is compelled to cry and reach out for a different kind of church. If God is primarily among the poor rather than neutrally roving between rich and poor, oppressor and oppressed, powerful and powerless, the church is required to align itself unequivocally with the poor and oppressed. Jesus ministered to the rich and the poor, the rulers and the ruled, those who collaborated with the occupying Roman forces and the armed zealots. But he showed a preferential option for the oppressed, recognizing their inherent worth as children of God and—according to Matthew 25:31-46—among them the risen Christ is to be found. This theological reality requires the church to favor the cause of the oppressed. Yet in so doing it knows that the liberation of the oppressed is an essential part of the liberation of oppressors from the will to dominate, economic and material greed, fear, anxiety, uncertainty about the future, the escalation of violence, and captivity to a host of ideologies ranging from racial superiority to cultural chauvinism and militarism. It is also the beginning of the liberation of the church from social irrelevance and spiritual captivity.

A Church in "Uneasy Confusion"

The "unrest" had intensified since I found myself standing outside an affluent church two months earlier. Thousands of people had been detained and several hundred had been either injured or killed by police gunfire. The Advent season was characterized by a call for a "black Christmas" of resistance. A regular Wednesday evening service to which people came to remember those in prison and detention had just ended.

This service was held in a Methodist church on the edge of the

city bordering on what used to be called District Six. Across the
road is the Caledon Square police station, scene of many a police
interrogation. The scars of the violence of Group Areas legislation
which cleared this area of its "colored" occupants more than a
decade earlier could still be seen. Some derelict buildings had
survived, the first of which had been renovated to provide town-
houses for white civil servants and police personnel. Some new
buildings were beginning to appear and the Cape Technikon was
under construction. But most of the land was barren, windswept
and uninhabited. The plaque on the outside wall of this church told
a part of the story:

> All who pass by remember with shame the many thousands
> of people who lived for generations in District Six and other
> parts of this city and were forced by law to leave their homes
> because of the colour of their skins. Father forgive us.

The service that night had lasted for over two hours. The walls of
the sanctuary were covered with newsprint on which was written
the names of people detained. A few names were crossed out,
names of those who had been released, some of whom were in the
service that night. Political posters decorated the walls. The focal
point of the sanctuary was still the heavy wooden cross of Christ,
but on display that night were a large rubber bullet and a tear gas
canister—symbols of repression much as the cross was a symbol of
Roman repression in an earlier era. Freedom songs were sung and
so were some traditional hymns. Someone read from the Bible;
someone else chose to read from the Quran; another brought
greetings from ANC leaders in exile. In brief, the traditional symbols of Christianity merged with those of a battle being fought in
the streets of Cape Town. Political slogans were chanted and
liturgical prayers were recited. The national anthem, *Nkosi Sikelel'*
iAfrika, was sung and the benediction followed an exegetical sermon preached by the resident minister, based on a verse from the
Sermon on the Mount.

A sympathetic and a supportive visitor from Chicago who had
come "to show solidarity" posed the revelatory question: "I am
feeling a little uneasy," he said. "My heart tells me that what
happened here tonight was Christian worship, but something keeps

reminding me that these services have been condemned by several people, including some church leaders, as a place of revelry for political radicals. Is this religion or politics? Right now I am confused."

Again the question came to mind: Who was right, Marx or Weber? History is cluttered with examples of revolutionary religion, but can religion truly break the iron cage of history? Can religion produce a qualitatively different kind of society? Is the kingdom of God a real possibility? Or had the brave words of Christians that night been merely more political grist for the mill of an oppressed people in rebellion? Has the gospel a distinctive contribution to make to a crisis which tightens its grip on a nation and holds the institutional church together with all institutions of dominance in its iron trap?

The dominant church has a certain dignity about it. Its apparent steadfastness and seeming ability to endure the vicissitudes of succeeding ages is an appealing characteristic which produces an illusion of eternity. The alternative church, in terms of traditional values, raises questions of uneasiness and confusion among even its most fervent admirers. But then what is truly *alternative* tends by definition to leave people with few past experiences on which to draw to enable them to cope or understand. It constitutes an Abrahamic journey into the unknown, where mistakes will be made but promises can also be fulfilled. The gospel teaches that heaven and earth will become new, and the demand of marginalized people is that something qualitatively new be realized.

A pertinent question is whether what is "creatively new" can penetrate the more traditional institutional structures of the church, drawing on the material, political and theological resources of the dominant church? There are churches, each with their own buildings, resources and social standing in every dorp and every black township throughout the country! More important is whether the alternative church *can* inject life, commitment to radical change and the power of the marginal people of God, among whom the risen Christ is found, into that church. Or is Weber right, and the problem that the existing organization of these institutions is so powerful that any sources of renewal are simply enveloped and subsumed? Can the power and potential for renewal that resides within an oppressed and marginalized people overcome this? Is it powerful enough? And if this is the primary locus of the risen Christ, is Christ powerful enough? Our sociological excursus allows for renewal, but more important is that the gospel imperative demands it.

WORSHIP AS CULTURAL CHANGE

We need an Archimedean lever with which to lift the dominant church out of its parochial captivity and conformity, facilitating its exposure to the renewing resources and energy of the alternative church. Worship, as a regular assembly point for church members and the major character-forming event of the Christian church, is potentially one such lever. It is here that the self-understanding of Christians in their quest for theological meaning and purpose is shaped and formed. The symbols of the Christian faith (the cross, resurrection, discipleship, grace, forgiveness, repentance, prayer and many others) are here unpacked, interpreted and explained on a regular basis, enabling Christians to understand the events of their daily lives in relation to the central teaching of the church. As such, worship is intended to be a means of grace, an event within which the gracious power of God's spirit is related to the needs of the community. In Latin America basic Christian communities have become a focal point for this integration of grace and communal activity, and in many places in South Africa Bible-study groups, house churches and communal worship services fulfill a similar function. The regular Sunday service of worship, however, continues to be the major event within which the Christian character of the majority of church members is formed. As such it is the major culture-forming event of the dominant Christian church.

Whatever else Christians may believe about God, they believe that God is what is most real, most significant and the ultimate form of reality. If worship does not relate God to the events of daily life it can only be concluded that such events are not of great or ultimate significance. If, on the other hand, the symbols of faith and by implication God *are* related to issues of daily living these issues necessarily acquire a theological significance. Political, social and personal issues begin to be wrestled with in terms of the resources of the Christian tradition. Questions which relate to social egalitarianism or the redistribution of land resources become more than a political issue. For the Christian they constitute a locus within which to encounter God.

On a personal level, the question whether restitution ought to be made to a particular person as a basis for reconciliation becomes more than a matter of individual social, psychological or material cost. It becomes an issue in relation to which to experience the presence of God. To reintegrate religion into life, enabling it to become a means of discovering God's will in relation to a concrete issue of life and an anticipation of God's purpose for the human community, destroys any attempt to uphold a distinction between the sacred and the secular. Life itself comes to be seen as the realm within which God lives, moves and has being. This, in turn, means that our vigorous participation in life with all its threats of death and promises of life is a participation in the being of God. To return to the trinitarian consideration dealt with earlier, it involves participating in God's dynamic love and becoming a means of God's gracious love extending to humankind.

When the perception of the God whom we worship is shaped by a theological interpretation of Matthew 25:31-46 as outlined in the first part of this chapter, it becomes clear that the experience of existence to which God's grace is to be primarily related in worship is that of the poor and the oppressed. This rejects that worship, however dignified and proper, which is unrelated to the smoke of burning tires within eyeshot of churches across South Africa. If worship is indeed the place where Christians encounter God, it is important that this God be the God revealed in Jesus Christ as the God of the oppressed and the poor. A cynic once suggested that while it is a basic Christian belief that humankind is made in the image of God, Christians have ever since sought to create God in their own image. This was the essential failing of nineteenth-century theology, a malady better understood by Feuerbach and Marx than by most theologians.

The dominant church, we have argued in this study of the English-speaking churches, has allowed itself to be shaped and molded into the shape and character of the dominant society. The more disturbing question is whether this church has not, like the church of so many succeeding generations, also created for itself a God in this dominant image? Of course the poor and oppressed are not immune from doing the same, and quick has come the retort of dominant theologians suggesting that black and liberation theologians are simply duplicating the theological error of their oppressors. What is beyond doubt, however, is that the God revealed in Jesus Christ was without qualification or reserve a God found among the poor and oppressed, and a God who chose the side of the poor and oppressed in their conflict with the rich and the powerful. It is this that calls into serious *theological* question the "balanced ministry" of English-speaking churches to both sides of the political divide in South Africa—and its concern to allow itself to be shaped by the demands of both blacks and whites.

The church's primary duty to worship God is a central theme within traditional theology, and reference has already been made to the threat of state interference in worship (in 1957 and 1987) as the raw nerve of ecclesial sensitivity. The alternative church needs to learn from these experiences in its evangelical mission to transform and revitalize the dominant church. If the dominant church is to be renewed at all, this perhaps can only be accomplished by appealing to its own understanding of worship. It is here that any paradigm shift from a church of protest to a church of resistance needs to begin.

Simply stated, for the dominant church to become a significant force for social change, it needs to be convinced that social engagement is as basic to its essential identity and primary responsibility as worship itself. For this to happen it needs to rediscover the importance of the eighth-century BCE prophetic critique of worship already referred to, and the significance of Matthew 25:31-46 for ecclesiology. This broader understanding of worship which resists any attempt to separate what happens within the sanctuary of worship from the social context of the poor and the oppressed has revitalized the alternative church. This is a gift of renewal which the alternative church offers to the dominant churches.

It is a gift which can only threaten a church that has hitherto protested without being drawn into the melee of resistance. The cost of this transition is high, and many will refuse to pay the cost of this kind of discipleship. Because the appeal is for the church to take seriously its *own* tradition which affirms the centrality of worship, one can only hope that the appeal will at least be understood. And because the appeal is for the church to return to the prophetic tradition and the essential teaching of Jesus, it will hopefully be taken seriously.

Robertson Smith has argued that for a religious transformation to succeed, it must appeal to the religious beliefs which a particular people cherish most.

> No positive religion that has moved men has been able to start with a tabula rasa to express itself as if religion was beginning for the first time; in form if not in substance, the new system must be in contact all along the line with the older ideas and practices which it finds in its possession. A new scheme of faith can find a hearing only by appealing to religious instincts and susceptibilities that already exist in its audience, and it cannot reach these without taking account of the traditional forms in which religious feeling is embodied, and without speaking a language which men accustomed to these forms can understand.[18]

Differently stated, the only way to motivate Christians who form part of the dominant tradition of the church to share in the renewal of the church and indeed of society is to enable them to discover the implications of their own values. In so doing they will uncover the revolutionary potential of that part of their own tradition which has been forgotten or suppressed. To return to a concept repeatedly referred to in the preceding pages of this book, it has to do with the reawakening of the dangerous memory which has haunted and disturbed the church throughout its history. It is a memory of that Jesus who identified himself with sinners, publicans, prostitutes and rebels—marginalized people. It is a memory of one crucified "outside the gate." It is a celebration of a Christ whose presence continues to be made known in those whom Matthew 25:31-46 defines as the least important people of society.

The affirmation of these theological values can simply remain at the level of theory or moral idealism if they do not emerge from a community which is itself grounded among the marginal people and is itself located outside the gate. Emmanuel Mounier identifies the kind of risk and liability involved:

> Too many idealists, pacifists, beautiful souls and noble hearts have made of the spiritual a place of refuge for the various kinds of rheumatisms which life confers. At the first sign of

pain, one submerges himself in the ideal, and together with the great spirits of all ages and religions emptied in advance of their flesh and flame reduced to the status of moral phantasms, constructs a holy triple alliance of sweetness against mission as a man.[19]

A theology of the poor and oppressed which does not emerge from the actual engagement in the struggles of the poor and oppressed can be no less a form of opium or escape from the harsh realities of existence than some form of otherworldly religion. And there is a sense in which the former can demonstrate less integrity than the latter. A church which charitably ministers *to* the poor or that speaks *for* the poor is not a church *of* the poor. And a theology which merely speaks about the church of the poor, or takes refuge in a notion of an ideal church of the poor without being part of this church is ultimately not vastly different from a theology which makes no pretense to be promoting the cause of the poor and oppressed. It is also more sinister.

The fundamental criticism which alternative theology levels at the dominant church is not that it fails to criticize the structures of the dominant order (this the English-speaking churches have done admirably, if only in terms of their understanding of the problems involved) but that by being part of these structures itself, it both perpetuates and legitimates them. What makes a church of the poor different is that it not only articulates but makes concrete and begins to institutionalize the new cultural visions in actual history-making groups. It becomes part of an emerging social and political alternative to the existing order.

In so doing, the church of the poor gives concrete expression to the biblical concept of truth which is always more than *gnosis*. It concerns a *way* of living which relates the ordering of society in accordance with the declared will of God. To quote Míguez Bonino: "There is no truth outside or beyond the concrete historical events in which men are involved as agents."[20] It concerns "doing the truth" or, as Karl Barth put it, "belief in the ultimate significance of the historical process."[21]

The challenge of the alternative church is a challenge which each successive age of the church is obliged to face. The New Testament teaches that few are prepared or able to meet the challenge. It is a challenge that has Jesus informing the rich young man "how hard it will be for rich people to enter the Kingdom of God" (Mark 10:17-27). It is a word which the church dominant in power and riches needs to hear. It is also the issue with which each individual Christian is compelled to wrestle.

THE OFFENSE OF THE GOSPEL

The offense of the gospel in its many facets is central to the New Testament message. St. Paul accepted that to some the gospel was nonsense and to others foolishness (1 Cor. 1:18-25). Today as ever the very notion of the church of the poor being a source of renewal for the institutional church simply does not make a great deal of sense in terms of middle-class values.

When certain of the "hard sayings" of Jesus are considered, some ask whether they constitute good news at all. "Happy are you poor; the Kingdom of God is yours! . . . But how terrible for you who are rich now; you have had your easy life! (Luke 6:20, 24). To the rich young man Jesus said "sell all you have and give the money to the poor" (Mark 10:21), and elsewhere he taught that no compromise between God and money was possible (Matt. 6:24). His disciples were astounded by what he said and asked "who then can be saved?" (Mark 10:26), while the Pharisees simply laughed at him (Luke 16:14). The poor clearly understood the message of Jesus to be good news, but one can understand why the rich "went away sad" (Mark 10:22).

Many an ingenious interpretation of these sayings has enabled the rich and favored of the dominant church to circumvent the challenge of this message. Indeed already within the New Testament one evangelist explained that is was the "spiritually poor" to whom the kingdom of God belongs (Matt. 5:3). St. Paul was able to identify a number of prominent people in different parts of Asia among the leaders of the churches he established, and James clearly saw the need to rebuke the Christian community for having deviated from its humble beginnings (James 5:1-6). Robert H. Smith suggests that sections of the early church showed signs of affluence and ample means, implying that from the beginning the church began to deviate from the poverty of Jesus.[22] Be this as it may, it is simply not possible to deny that Jesus' own ministry was anything but good news to the rich and the powerful. In fact, it was they who plotted to have him crucified.

Not many people, despite their avowals to the contrary, are absolute biblical literalists at the level of translating every scriptural injunction into direct practice. We need not agonize too long as to whether by God's grace a camel can go through the eye of a needle. If, however, we affirm the New Testament as the normative basis of our faith, it *is* necessary to make the "hard" as well as the "easy" sayings of Jesus a formative part of our lives and of the ministry of the church. Briefly stated this seems to suggest that in addition to all else required, Christians are to accept that the gospel can only become good news to the rich when they cease to be rich! Yet simply by virtue of having once been rich, together with all the privileges of education, social graces and political influences, one can never know poverty in the sense that those trapped within the structures of poverty know it. Those who voluntarily take poverty on themselves always have the opportunity of climbing out of their poverty in a way not possible for those whose poverty is of a hereditary kind. It is this which prompts the question posed earlier in this chapter—will the rich ever be able to understand the mystery of God and the pertinence of the gospel? Is middle-class mentality such that it cannot fully understand the gospel? Or are all things possible with God?

The primary concern of the Christian is not, however, to engage in further variations of the debate on who can be saved. Many quietistic tendencies have been read into the Reformers' doctrine of salvation, and certainly Luther's crass dismissal of the Epistle of James as an "epistle of straw" portrays a serious deviation from the religion of Jesus. The strength of the evangelical emphasis on salvation as a free gift of God is, however, that it frees the Christian from a preoccupation with his or her own salvation to participate in society in a selfless and uninhibited manner. And the challenge of the sayings of Jesus concerning what has come to be described as a "preferential option for the poor" is lost if allowed to degenerate into a sterile debate on who can or cannot be saved. Albert Nolan's observation is correct:

> The option for the poor is not a choice about the *recipients* of the gospel message, *to whom* we must preach the gospel; it is

a matter of *what gospel* we preach to anyone at all. It is concerned with the *content* of the gospel message itself. The gospel may be good news for the poor and bad news for the rich but it is a message for both the poor and the rich.[23]

Part of the significance of Matthew 25:31-46 for the institutional church consists in the fact that it is addressed to people who are themselves neither hungry, thirsty, homeless strangers, naked, sick or imprisoned. The question is, however, whether one who does not know the same kind of daily suffering as the poor can do more than offer charity and relief to those who do suffer. If one does not know the reality of daily humiliation, the repeated shattering of one's dreams, police harassment, frustration, fear and defeat, one cannot fully identify with the oppressed or understand their mistrust of those who may seek to take their sufferings on themselves. An awareness of this predicament which merely finds refuge in guilt and remorse also misses the challenge of the option for the poor. Recognizing then the limitations which proscribe those who are not poor from the actual suffering and anger of the poor and oppressed, the burning question concerns the practical manner in which the non-poor can identify with and become part of the church of the poor. The answer has something to do with risking security, comfort and reputation within the dominant society and, in terms of accepted values, working against self-interest. In so doing, in a limited way one shares in an experience of oppression and begins in a restricted sense to understand both the frustration of the poor—and what the prophets have referred to as the anger of God.

The challenges which face the church and individual Christians committed to an option for the poor are numerous and varied.[24] For some these include the *kenosis* experience of divesting themselves of wealth and separating themselves from the dominant society. This is done knowing that the imitation of the poor in their deprivation, in isolation from other exigencies of the liberation struggle, does not liberate the poor from their captivity. It may, however, remove some of the barriers which separate one from the poor. It says something about the integrity of the church's or a person's option for the poor. For others it involves a pastoral "preference" or even "exclusivity" for the poor against the rich.

For others it includes a prophetic denunciation of the rich and the powerful.

As important as these options are, for the option for the poor to involve the liberation of the poor and the oppressed it *must* include taking sides in the structural conflict between the oppressor and the oppressed. It is this confrontation with the structural dimensions of the sin of oppression, involving the taking of sides on political, economic and social issues, that contradicts the narrow spiritual focus that characterizes the dominant church in South Africa today. What has already been said in the earlier chapters of this study indicates the concern of the English-speaking churches to alleviate the harsh effects of the existing structures of oppression. This pastoral concern has further, in some instances, resulted in prophetic protest concerning existing forms of oppression. It has not, however, regarded the existence of these forms of oppression to be in direct confrontation with its primary responsibility to worship God, except when the formal services of worship are under attack.

To suggest to an affluent white congregation that the toleration of oppressive laws and structures is a negation of worship would probably result either in the kind of laughter the Pharisees indulged in or a congregational walkout. Yet this, in essence, is what Isaiah, Micah and Jesus had to say about some acts of worship with which they were familiar. If worship is the major character-forming event of the Christian community, the issues of the day with which Christians are expected to wrestle need to be brought into the place where Christians relate the sacred symbols of their tradition to the events of their daily lives.

If this integration does not take place within worship, there is little chance that it will happen outside of worship. Rafael Avila suggests that if in worship we limit ourselves to perpetuating the tradition of church as it has been taught to us we are irresponsible. We are merely preservers of the past. Our unique calling as Christians is a different one. "We are principally creative agents," he argues, "of living tradition." For this reason "we believe ourselves obliged to risk a discontinuity with the past" in making our worship relevant to the present. He quotes from the Vatican II *Constitution on the Sacred Liturgy*:

For the liturgy is made up of *unchangeable elements* divinely instituted, and *elements subject to change*. The latter not only may but ought to be changed.[25]

This ultimately is the key to renewal: In making the past relevant to the present we preserve it for the future. If the oppressed in South Africa cannot see the significance of the historic church in their present crisis, it will have no significance for their future. This is the challenge that faces the dominant church. Its hope of renewal is found among the poor and the oppressed.

Worship, as the major cultural expression of the alternative church located within the margins of society, constitutes an integrating exercise of the sacred and secular, religious and political, personal and communal. It is this gift which the alternative church offers the dominant church—so often isolated and removed from the center stage of the crisis-bearing events of this time. It is a gift which could mean the end of the church's fragile unity and the end of its already waning social standing and influence in dominant society.

THE PROMISE OF LIFE

The paradox of the gospel is this: It tells us that life is worth more than food, and the body worth more than clothes (Matt. 6:25). We are to be concerned above all else with the kingdom of God (Matt. 6:33) and must be prepared to sacrifice a hand, a foot or even an eye in order to enter the kingdom of God (Mark 9:43-47). Indeed we must be prepared to accept the cross (or repression) which will be thrust on us and even to die in obedience to Jesus (Mark 8:35). Yet in so doing we will be provided with all we need (Matt. 6:33) and discover that in being prepared to sacrifice our life we will gain it (Mark 8:35). More than that, in so doing the quality of life that will be ours is "life in all its fullness" (John 10:10). The source of this life is the incarnate Word of God made known in Jesus (John 1:4) and encountered today in the oppressed poor who are without food or adequate water, displaced, homeless, without sufficient clothes, sick or in prison (Matt. 25:31-46).

This is a gospel which is predisposed toward those marginalized by the dominant society. They have little to lose except their poverty, and have been persuaded by successive generations of oppression that life is a hair's breadth away from death. This equips the poor and oppressed to understand the challenge of the poor man of Nazareth who calls them to lose even that which they have in quest of a qualitatively different life—if not for themselves then for successive generations. It is a life not measured by that which moth and rust can destroy and others take from us (Matt. 6:20) or by material greed (Luke 12:15), but by a "righteousness" (Matt. 6:33, *RSV*) or a form of material existence described in Matthew (chapters 5 and 6).

Middle-class mentality finds it nearly impossible to understand this paradox. It is this paradox that persuades Bonhoeffer that the only option for the dominant church is naked obedience to the gospel. "We must boldly assert," he writes, "that the first step of obedience must be taken before faith can be possible." Hence the axiom quoted earlier, "Only he who believes is obedient, and only he who is obedient believes."[26] But how difficult it is for those who are accustomed to giving orders and teaching others to be obedient to the gospel to learn from the poor who are inclined in a special manner to understand the gospel.

This is the challenge that faces the church at this moment in history.

> It is serious, very serious. For very many Christians in South Africa this is the KAIROS, the moment of grace and opportunity, the favourable time in which God issues a challenge to decisive action. It is a dangerous time because, if this opportunity is missed, and allowed to pass by, the loss for the Church, for the gospel and for all the people of South Africa will be immeasurable. Jesus wept over Jerusalem. He wept over the tragedy of the destruction of the city and the massacre of the people that was imminent, "and all because you did not recognise your opportunity [KAIROS] when God offered it" (Luke 19:44).[27]

Postscript

Newspapers have printed pictures of clergy marching in front of political banners. Television programs have projected church leaders as spokespersons for the political "left." The Eloff Commission of Inquiry into the SACC has accused this council of "preaching revolution" and a gospel "concerned with political, social and economic issues." Some ask whether the church is emerging from the captivity of the ruling class to become a revolutionary force for change.

It is a question which must be considered in relation to the socio-theological analysis of the preceding chapters. There it has been argued that the institutional churches have formed an integral part of the dominant socio-economic order, and as this order has changed the churches have adapted themselves to the new circumstances. It has also been argued that in spite of a dominant theology legitimating the church's political propensity toward the status quo, there is a contradictory theological identity evident in the history of the church. This is an identity that can be traced back to the life of Jesus. As a dangerous memory it disturbs the complacency of the church, serving to remind it of the extent to which it has deviated from its earliest calling. This residual memory keeps alive the possibility of the churches being activated, under certain circumstances, to share in the emergent social revolution in South Africa, affording them the opportunity to contribute to the shape and character of the new order.

While seeking to provide moral guidance to the state, the churches have without exception refused to reject the theological legitimacy of the dominant order. The history of this acquiescence is there to be seen, extending from British capitalist-colonial interests in the nineteenth century to the dominant racial-economic structures of contemporary forms of apartheid. Theological and

221

social forces have driven the churches into conformity, and church leaders have explained the submission of the churches to the demands of the state by arguing that social acceptance and prominence of the institutional church provides the most viable basis from which to minister to the victims of oppression.

Throughout history, however, individuals and marginalized social groups within the church have regarded it as their theological obligation, and that of the churches, to question the legitimacy of an oppressive state and resist its laws. In so doing they have been prepared to risk their own lives, and call into question the theological identity of the churches to which they belong.

The history of the English-speaking churches shows that despite their institutional location on the side of the dominant order, they have been disturbed and at times shaped by this alternative theology of resistance. Unable to be protagonists for radical change they have on occasions found themselves cautious supporters of the oppressed people's struggle for political liberation.

Instances of the church's cautious and moderate resistance to the state at different points of history have been identified in the foregoing pages of this study. These include, in more recent times, the affirmation of the theological justification of apartheid as a heresy, a willingness by sections of the church to support a call for prayers for an end to unjust rule, a sense of compulsion to consider seriously issues of economic sanctions, the need to debate the armed struggle, and an obligation to give careful consideration to the *Kairos Document*. These are issues that have in many instances threatened to destroy the tenuous unity of the English-speaking churches. They have not always been responded to as thoughtfully as many would have hoped, and in some instances the responses have merely manifested the entrenched conservatism of large sections of church leadership. A careful analysis of these responses, however, does suggest that the churches have in recent times felt some compulsion not to reject completely the ecclesially threatening and politically deviant initiatives of dissident individuals and groups within their ranks. The *Lusaka Statement*, for example, has produced less acrimony in the English-speaking churches than the more moderate decision of the WCC to provide funding for humanitarian purposes to the liberation movements in southern Africa a decade earlier. While economic sanctions are not supported by any of the English-speaking churches except the United Congregational Church of Southern Africa, neither has any of these churches rejected such initiatives completely. The Methodist Church of Southern Africa, in the face of substantial pressure from its black membership, reversed a decision of its president to reject the *Theological Rationale* in support of the June 16 call to prayer for the end to unjust rule; and despite the obvious problems in sections of the church with the *Kairos Document*, this church was forced to revise its initial overtly hostile response to the document. All this suggests a less submissive stance by the English-speaking churches to the state than has been the case in earlier decades.

Does this mean that the essential character of the English-speaking churches is in the process of changing, however reluctant and careful the process? The response of these churches continues to be cautious and moderate. They continue to be divided by the same forces and influences that have traditionally divided them. This suggests that the churches are essentially social respondents to the dominant order, while being theologically compelled to cope with a disturbing residual theology of resistance.

To conclude: (1) History is ahead of the church, and as the socio-political nature of the country changes, the church finds itself drawn into and conforming to the changing context. (2) As the political struggle intensifies, the preoccupation of the churches with their own agenda (often in isolation from wider socio-economic and political affairs of the time) comes to be seen as increasingly parochial, anachronistic and irrelevant to the needs of their own members. In this situation some Christians, and especially those who suffer most from the existing order, are rediscovering the residual political significance of the Christian gospel. And as the reality of the emerging new society confronts the institutional churches, they begin to realize, like so many other institutions, that it is in *their* interest to change. It seems, however, that the impulse to do so is primarily from outside "secular" forces which activate the churches' internal theological resources. (3) A vacuum of protest has been created by restrictive and oppressive state action against progressive leaders and political groupings. Compelled by a residual memory of resistance, the churches have been constrained to allow some within their ranks to fill that vacuum. To varying degrees such individuals enjoy a measure of support from the churches, but the institutions themselves remain trapped within and shaped by the dominant social structures of the country. The oppressed of society are the marginalized and even the oppressed of the church, and it is they who hear and respond to the residual gospel of liberation in a manner in which the dominant church, however empathetic, can never respond. As the crisis intensifies the oppressed find themselves in conflict not only with the state but also with the churches to which they belong—accounting for the emergence of black caucuses and progressive pressure groups within the different English-speaking churches.

To fail to allow for a latent non-suppressible theology of resistance within the churches is to fail to do justice to the history of resistance within both state and church. It is also to reduce religious thought not only to a simple by-product of the prevailing socio-economic order, but to make it the exclusive possession of the ruling class. It is to deprive the oppressed of a liberating religious faith.

The question facing Christians is not whether the church is likely to be at the vanguard of social change in South Africa. History suggests that this is not likely. The question is rather whether the liberating resources of the Christian tradition, suppressed by generations of acquiescence to changing cultural, political and economic forms of domination, can be rediscovered with sufficient dynamic to enable Christians to share creatively in the process of change. It may well be that the revolutionary role of the church depends less on the conscious intentions of religious groups than it does on the objective social conditions in which the message of the church is proclaimed. The message of the exodus, the story of the cross, and the victory of the risen Christ over the forces of evil are potent symbols in their own right, but proclaimed by the oppressed in a situation of crisis they can become such that the gates of hell cannot prevail against them.

This theology of the oppressed disturbs all but the most insensitive of Christians. It motivates troublesome priests and inspires oppressed Christians in their engagement in the South African political struggle. It is also a tradition which is recognized and appealed to by progressive secular groups who perceive the church to be an ally in their struggle.

What must not be lost sight of is that there is also a variety of social forces and privileges which prevent the institutional churches from grasping hold of this possibility. The marginalized church of the poor and oppressed offers the institutional churches perhaps the only possibility of discovering what it means to be a liberating church. But the cost may well be too high. Past history weighs on all individuals and social institutions, and the church is no exception (Rom. 7:24). Theologically, however, we are constrained to say that churches too can be reborn even when they are grown old (John 3:4).

Perhaps the major sign of hope within the institutional churches is the emergence of a new kind of leadership, representative of the aspirations of the oppressed majority. It is a leadership that is willing and able to act ecumenically and corporately in opposing the state. Preeminent among such leaders are Allan Boesak, Moderator of the NG Sendingkerk; Frank Chikane, General Secretary of the SACC; and Desmond Tutu, Anglican Archbishop of Cape Town. The oppressed masses within the churches instinctively understand their message, recognizing it to be an essential part of the residual gospel of liberation—often neglected and suppressed in the dominant message of the dominant churches. A consequence is an unprecedented move to incorporate the churches into the liberation struggle of the oppressed. Such action will not go unchallenged by the forces of oppression and this constitutes the battle for the soul of the church.

Notes

INTRODUCTION

1. K. Marx and F. Engels, *Selected Works: The Eighteenth Brumaire of Louis Bonaparte* (Moscow: Progress Press, 1968), p. 95.

2. J.-B. Metz, *Faith in History and Society: Towards a Practical Fundamental Theology* (London: Burns and Oates, 1980), pp. 88f.

3. Barbara Tuchman, *The March of Folly: From Troy to Vietnam* (London: Abacus, 1985), pp. 2–4.

CHAPTER 1

1. E. G. Knapp-Fisher, *The Churchman's Heritage* (London: Black, 1952).

2. Stephen Neill, *A History of Christian Missions* (Harmondsworth: Penguin Books, 1973), p. 61.

3. Edmund Bishop, *The Genius of the Roman Rite* (London: Robinson, 1902), p. 5. For an essay on the social identity of the Anglican Church see T. D. Verryn, "Not Angels, But Anglicans," in *Denominationalism: Its Sources and Implications*, ed. W. S. Vorster (Pretoria: University of South Africa, 1982), pp. 39–61.

4. Peter Hinchliff, *The Church in South Africa* (London: SPCK, 1968), p.71; J. W. de Gruchy, *The Church Struggle in South Africa* (Grand Rapids: Eerdmans, 1979), p. 17.

5. Alan Paton, *Apartheid and the Archbishop* (Cape Town: David Philip, 1973), p. 286.

6. Charles Villa-Vicencio, "An All-Pervading Heresy" in *Apartheid Is a Heresy*, ed. J. W. de Gruchy and C. Villa-Vicencio (Cape Town: David Philip; Grand Rapids: Eerdmans, 1983), p. 66.

7. Quoted in André Hugo, "Christelik-Nasionaal in Suid-Africa," *Pro Veritate* (May 1968).

8. Dietrich Bonhoeffer, *No Rusty Swords* (New York: Harper and Row, 1965), p. 309.

9. Reinhold Niebuhr, *Moral Man and Immoral Society* (New York: Charles Scribner's Sons, 1932), p. 87.

10. A. Dreyer, *Die Kaapse Kerk en die Groot Trek* (Cape Town: NG Kerk, 1929).

11. de Gruchy, *The Church Struggle in South Africa*, pp. 18–21.

12. C. F. A. Borchardt, "Die Afrikaner Kerke en die Rebellie" in *Teologie en Vernuwing*, ed. I. Eybers, A. Konig and C. Borchardt (Pretoria: University of South Africa, 1975), pp. 85–116.

13. T. Dunbar Moodie, *The Rise of Afrikanerdom* (Berkeley: University of California Press, 1975), pp. 215–33.

14. For a consideration of this development see R. T. J. Lombard, *Die Nederduitse Gereformeerde Kerke en Rassepolitiek* (Pretoria: NG Kerkboekhandel, 1981); A. J. Botha, *Die Evolusie van 'n Volksteologie* (Bellville: UWC Publishers, 1984). The heresy debate is recorded in de Gruchy and Villa-Vicencio, *Apartheid Is a Heresy.*

15. D. J. Bosch, "Nothing but a Heresy" in de Gruchy and Villa-Vicencio, *Apartheid Is a Heresy*, pp. 24–38.

16. Hermann Giliomee, Inaugural Lecture, delivered on 11 June 1986, "The History in Politics," New Series No. 126, p. 9., published by University of Cape Town.

17. *Transactions of the Missionary Society* (London, 1804), 1:480. Quoted in Giliomee, p. 10.

18. de Gruchy, *The Church Struggle in South Africa*, pp. 7–8. Also Chris Loff, "The History of a Heresy" in de Gruchy and Villa-Vicencio, *Apartheid Is a Heresy*, pp. 10–23.

19. B. Spoelstra, "Denominationalism with Reference to the Three Afrikaans Churches" in Vorster, *Denominationalism: Its Sources and Implications*, p. 21.

20. B. Spoelstra, *"Die Doppers" in Suid Afrika, 1760–1899* (Cape Town: Nasionale Boekhandel, 1963), p. 61.

21. For an outline of "traditional" apartheid theology see Charles Villa-Vicencio, "South Africa's Theologised Nationalism," *The Ecumenical Review*, vol. 29, no. 4 (October 1977).

22. G. D. Cloete and D. J. Smit, eds., *A Moment of Truth: The Confession of the Dutch Reformed Mission Church 1982* (Grand Rapids: Eerdmans, 1984).

23. *Ecunews* (February 1982).

24. Quoted in Glenda Kruss, "Religion, Class and Culture—Indigenous Churches in South Africa, with Special Reference to Zionist-Apostolics" (M.A. thesis, University of Cape Town, 1985), p. 68.

25. T. D. Verryn, *A History of the Order of Ethiopia* (Cleveland: Central Mission Press, 1972), pp. 17–32.

26. Verryn, p. 5.

27. Verryn, pp. 61f.

28. Itumeleng Mosala, "African Independent Churches: A Study in Socio-Theological Protest" in *Resistance and Hope*, ed. C. Villa-Vicencio and J. W. de Gruchy, (Grand Rapids: Eerdmans. Cape Town: David Philip, 1985), p. 110.

29. *African Independent Churches: Speaking For Ourselves* (Braamfontein: Institute of Contextual Theology, 1985).

30. For these and other declarations see, de Gruchy and Villa-Vicencio, *Apartheid Is a Heresy*, pp. 145–48.

31. Andrew Prior, ed., *Catholics in Apartheid Society* (Cape Town: David Philip, 1982), p. x.

32. Hinchliff, p. 10. Also de Gruchy, *The Church Struggle in South Africa*, p. 2.

33. The text of this Confession is printed in de Gruchy and Villa-Vicencio, *Apartheid Is a Heresy*, pp. 160–61.

34. *Ecunews*, vol. 7 (September/October 1984), p. 28.

CHAPTER 2

1. Monica Wilson, "Missionaries: Conquerors or Servants of God?" *South African Outlook* (March 1966; reprinted January 1983), pp. 13–16.

2. Selope Thema, "Thinking Black: The African Today," *Advance* (April 1929). Quoted in James Cochrane, *Servants of Power: The Role of English-speaking Churches 1903–1930* (Johannesburg: Ravan Press, 1987), p. 4.

3. James Wells, *Stewart of Lovedale* (London: 1908), p. 216.

4. J. Philip, *Researches in South Africa* (London: Duncan Books, 1828), vol. I, ix–x; vol. II, 227.

5. Greg Cuthbertson quoting Gladwin and Saidin, *Slaves of the White Myth* in "The English-Speaking Churches, Colonialism and War" in *Theology and Violence: The South African Debate*, ed. C. Villa-Vicencio (Johannesburg: Skotaville Press, 1987), p. 17.

6. *The Christian Express,* vol. VIII (95) (1 August 1878), pp. 1–2.

7. J. W. de Gruchy, "English-Speaking South Africans and Civil Religion," *Journal of Theology for Southern Africa*, no.19 (June 1977), p. 45.

8. P. Hetherington, *British Paternalism and Africa: 1920–1940* (London: Frank Cass, 1978), p. 112.

9. J. Bond, *They Were South Africans* (London: Oxford University Press, 1956), p. 56.

10. Quoted by Peter Hinchliff, "The English-Speaking Churches and South Africa in the 19th Century," in *English-Speaking South Africa Today: Proceedings of the National Conference, July 1974*, ed. André de Villiers (Cape Town: Oxford University Press, 1976), p. 172.

11. Monica Wilson, "Co-operation and Conflict: The Eastern Frontiers" in *The Oxford History of South Africa*, ed. Monica Wilson and Leonard Thompson (Oxford: Clarendon Press, 1969 and 1971), 1:252. Also David Welsh, "English-Speaking Whites and the Racial Problem" in de Villiers, *English-Speaking South Africa*, p. 220.

12. C. W. de Kiewiet, *The Imperial Factor in South Africa* (Cambridge: The University Press, 1937), p. 159.

13. Welsh in deVilliers, *English-Speaking South Africa*, p. 226.

14. De Kiewiet, p. 159.

15. Cochrane, p. 25.

16. Cochrane, p. 26.

17. De Kiewiet, pp. 190, 194. Also David Welsh, *The Roots of Segregation, Native Policy in Natal: 1845–1910* (Cape Town: Oxford University Press, 1971), p. 77.

18. Walter Rodney, *How Europe Underdeveloped Africa* (Washington, D.C.: Howard University Press, 1974), pp. 205–81.

19. R. H. W. Shepherd, *Lovedale South Africa: 1824–1955* (Lovedale: Lovedale Press, 1971), pp. 27–32.

20. Janet Hodgson, "Zonnebloem College and Cape Town: 1858–1870," *Studies in the History of Cape Town*, vol. 1, ed. C. Saunders (Cape Town: UCT, 1979): 1–16.

21. Frank Molteno, "The Historical Foundations of the Schooling of Black South Africans" in *Apartheid and Education: The Education of Black South Africans*, ed. P. Kallaway (Johannesburg: Ravan Press, 1986), pp. 57, 67.

22. R. Elphick, "Africans and the Christian Campaign in Southern Africa" in *The Frontier in History: North America and Southern Africa Compared*, ed. H. Lamar and L. Thompson (New Haven and London: Yale University Press, 1981), pp. 270–307.

23. Leonard Thompson, "The Subjection of African Chiefdoms, 1870–1898," *The Oxford History of South Africa*, vol. 2, p. 251.

24. B. Lincoln, "Notes Towards a Theory of Religion and Revolution," in *Religion, Rebellion, Revolution: An Interdisciplinary and Cross Cultural Collection of Essays*, ed. B. Lincoln (London: Macmillan, 1985), p. 271.

25. Samuel Broadbent, *A Narrative of the First Introduction of Christianity Amongst the Baralong Tribe of the Bechuanas, South Africa* (London: Wesleyan Mission House, 1865), p. 81.

26. Robert Moffat, *Missionary Labours and Scenes in Southern Africa* (London: John Sow, 1842), pp. 243–44.

27. P. W. Harrison, "Instructing Missionaries Misleading Natives," *South African Outlook* (November 1925).

28. Desmond Tutu, "Viability" in *Relevant Theology for Africa, The Church in South Africa*, ed. H. J. Becken (Durban: Lutheran Publishing House, 1973), p. 41.

29. Hinchliff in deVilliers, *English-Speaking South Africa*, p. 173.

30. Peter Hinchliff, *The Anglican-Speaking Church in South Africa* (London: Darton, Longman & Todd, 1963), pp. 10–11, 28–29. Also in deVilliers, *English-Speaking South Africa*, p. 174.

31. Peter Hinchliff, ed., *The Journal of John Ayliff: 1797–1862* (Cape Town: A. A. Balkema, 1971).

32. N. Majeke, *The Role of the Missionaries in Conquest* (Johannesburg: Society of Young Africa, 1952), p. 52.

33. A. Hastings, *Mission, Church and State in Southern Africa* (Pretoria: Society for the Propagation of the Faith, 1985), p. 5.

34. William Shaw, *A Defence of the Wesleyan Missionaries in Southern Africa*. Quoted in Hastings, p. 6.

35. See *Kairos Document: Challenge to the Churches*, rev. 2nd ed. (Johannesburg: Skotaville, 1986), pp. 9–11.

36. Hastings, p. 6.

37. Majeke, p. 63

38. G. N. Uzoigwe, *Britain and the Conquest of Africa* (Ann Arbor: University of Michigan Press, 1974), p. 186.

39. Uzoigwe, p. 27.

40. Hetherington, p. 10.

41. Welsh, *The Roots of Segregation*, p. 44; T. R. H. Davenport, *South Africa: A Modern History* (Johannesburg: Macmillan, 1977), p. 247.

42. Gabriel Setiloane, *The Image of God Among the Sotho-Tswana* (Rotterdam: A.A. Balkema, 1979), p. 133.

43. Hinchliff in de Villiers, *English-Speaking South Africa*, p. 176.

44. Welsh in de Villiers, *English Speaking South Africa*, p. 221.

45. J. Guy, *The Heretic: A Study of the Life of John William Colenso, 1814–1883* (Johannesburg: Ravan Press, 1983), pp. 256–75.

46. Hinchliff, *The Anglican-Speaking Church in South Africa*, pp. 82f. Also in de Villiers, *English-Speaking South Africa*, p. 176.

47. Welsh in de Villiers, *English-Speaking South Africa*, p. 221.

48. R. U. Moffat, *John Smith Moffat: Missionary—A Memoir* (London: 1921; reprint, New York: Negro Universities Press, 1969), p. 330.

49. *British Weekly* (12 April 1900), cited by Cuthbertson in Villa-Vicencio, *Theology and Violence*, p. 25.

50. Stewart Papers, BC106 (J. W. Jagger Library, University of Cape Town), cited by Cuthbertson in Villa-Vicencio, *Theology and Violence*, p. 27.

51. Hinchliff in de Villiers, *English-Speaking South Africa*, p. 177.

CHAPTER 3

1. Quoted in Francis Wilson, *Labour in the South African Gold Mines, 1911–1969* (Cambridge: Cambridge University Press, 1972).

2. Colin Bundy, *Re-making the Past: New Perspectives in South African History* (Cape Town: Dept. of Adult Education and Extra-mural Studies, 1986), p. 45.

3. See, for example, F. R. Johnstone, *Class, Race and Gold* (London: Routledge & Kegan Paul, 1976).

4. Johnstone, p. 16.

5. Thomas Pakenham, *The Boer War* (London: Weidenfeld and Nicholson, 1979), p. 554.

6. Transvaal Chamber of Mines, *Fifth Annual Report (1893)*, quoted by Francis Wilson in de Villiers, *English-Speaking South Africa*, p. 163.

7. Julius Lewin, *Politics and Law in South Africa* (London: Merlin Press, 1963), p. 98. Also D. Welsh, "English-speaking Whites and the Racial Problem" in de Villiers, *English-Speaking South Africa*, p. 226.

8. Johnstone, p. 126. Also essays by H. Bradford and B. Bozzoli in *Putting a Plough to the Ground*, ed. Beinart, Delius and Trapido (Johannesburg: Ravan Press, 1986); B. Bozzoli, *Townships, Labour and Protest* (Johannesburg: Ravan Press, 1979).

9. See W. A. de Klerk, *The Puritans in Africa* (London: Rex Collings, 1975), p. 106.

10. Dan O'Meara, *Volkskapitalisme: Class, Capital and Ideology in the Development of Afrikaner Nationalism, 1934–1948* (Cambridge: Cambridge University Press, 1983).

11. G. B. A. Gerdener, *Recent Developments in the South African Mission Fields* (Cape Town: N. G. Uitgewers, 1958), pp. 168–75.

12. See B. Rose and R. Tunmer, eds., *Documents in South African Education* (Johannesburg: Ad Donker, 1975), pp. 260–67.

13. Cochrane, p. 112.

14. Cochrane, p. 138.

15. Hinchliff, *The Anglican-Speaking Church in South Africa*, p. 216; cf. Cochrane, p. 294.

16. Methodist Church of South Africa, *Minutes of Conference (1929)*, p. 177. Quoted by Cochrane, p. 139.

17. Gerdener, p. 174.

18. Leo Kuper, *An African Bourgeoisie: Race, Class and Politics in South Africa* (New Haven: Yale University Press, 1965), p. 201.

19. Elfriede Strassberger, *Ecumenism in South Africa 1936–1960* (Johannesburg: SACC, 1974), p. 30.

20. *Church News*, vol. XX1, no. 11 (November 1955).

21. J. W. de Gruchy, *The Church Struggle in South Africa* (Grand Rapids: Eerdmans, 1979), p. 88.

22. Monica Wilson in *South African Outlook* (March 1966), p. 16.

23. See Patrick Furlong, *The Mixed Marriages Act (1949): A Theological Critique Based on the Investigation of Legislative Action and Church Responses to This Legislation* (M.A. thesis, University of Cape Town, 1984), pp. 102–5.

24. De Gruchy, *The Church Struggle in South Africa*, p. 61.

25. W. A. de Klerk, "English-Speaking South Africans Today," *South African Outlook* (December 1977).

26. See Otto Maduro, *Religion and Social Conflicts* (Maryknoll: Orbis Books, 1982), pp. 122–23.

27. Stanley Greenberg, *Race and State in Capitalist Development* (Johannesburg: Ravan Press, 1980), pp. 26–27, 385–410.

28. Greenberg, p. 406.

29. Quoted in Cochrane, p. 113.

30. Quoted in Cochrane, p. 214.

31. Heribert Adam, "The Failure of Political Liberalism," in *The Rise and Crisis of Afrikaner Power*, ed. Heribert Adam and Hermann Giliomee (Cape Town: David Philip, 1979), pp. 145–76.

32. Buti Tlhagale, "Towards a Black Theology of Labour," *Voices from the Third World*, vol. VI, no. 2 (December 1983), p. 3.

CHAPTER 4

1. Thomas Karis and Gwendolyn Carter, eds. *From Protest to Challenge: A Documentary History of African Politics in South Africa* (Stanford: Hoover Institution Press, 1977), vol. 3, ed. by Thomas Karis and Gail Gerhart, p. 29.

2. Tom Lodge, "The Parents' School Boycott: Eastern Cape and East Rand Townships, 1955," in Kallaway, *Apartheid and Education* p. 266.

3. See M. Horrell, *Bantu Education to 1968* (Johannesburg: S.A. Institute of Race Relations, 1968); *The Education of the Coloured Community in South Africa: 1652–1970* (Johannesburg: S.A. Institute of Race Relations, 1970); in Rose and Tunmer.

4. Quoted in Frank Molteno, "The Historical Foundations of the Schooling of Black South Africans," in Kallaway, *Apartheid and Education*, p. 67.

5. A speech by Dr. H. F. Verwoerd delivered in the Senate on 7 June 1954, quoted in Rose and Tunmer, p. 264.

6. Rose and Tunmer, p. 262. Italics added.

7. *South African Outlook* (November 1 and December 1, 1954).

8. Trevor Huddleston, *Naught for Your Comfort* (Johannesburg: Hardington and Donaldson; London: Collins, 1956), p. 172.

9. R. G. Clarke, *For God or Caesar? An Historical Study of Christian Resistance to Apartheid by the Church of the Province of Southern Africa, 1946–1957* (Ph. D. thesis, University of Natal, 1983), p. 536.

10. Huddleston, p. 171.

11. *South African Outlook* (1 June 1954). Italics added to the words "unhurried development."

12. Clarke, pp. 595–69.

13. *Church News*, vol. XX, no. 11 (17 November 1954).

14. *South African Outlook* (November 1 and December 1, 1954).

15. Horrell, *Bantu Education to 1968*, p. 13. See also Brigid Flanagan, "Education: Policy and Practice," in *Catholics in Apartheid Society*, ed. Andrew Prior (Cape Town: David Philip, 1982). Recent comment on the Roman Catholic schools is provided in correspondence with Brother Jude Petersen of the Catholic Institute of Education, dated 16 April 1987.

16. John S. Peart-Binns, *Ambrose Reeves* (London: Victor Gollancz, 1973), pp. 121–22.

17. An editorial entitled "The Bishop's Decision," in *The Star* (22 November 1954). Quoted by Clarke.

18. A letter to the editor published in *The Star* (25 October 1954).

19. Huddleston, pp. 172–73.

20. Huddleston, p. 171.

21. Alan Paton, *Apartheid and the Archbishop: The Life and Times of Geoffrey Clayton* (New York: Charles Scribner's, 1973), p. 235.

22. Clarke, p. 602.

23. Clarke, p. 536.

24. See Tom Lodge in Kallaway, *Apartheid and Education*; and Karis, Carter and Gerhart, vol. 3. The quotation by Dr. A. B. Xuma is from *South African Outlook* (2 May 1955).

25. *Evening Post*, (18 August 1955).

26. Huddleston, pp. 159–60.

27. Clarke, p. 600.

28. Paton, pp. 240–41.

29. C. Villa-Vicencio, *Between Christ and Caesar: Classic and Contemporary Texts on Church and State* (Grand Rapids: Eerdmans; Cape Town: David Philip, 1986), pp. 200f.

30. For a discussion on the emergence of the PCR, see Elizabeth Adler, *A Small Beginning* (Geneva: WCC, 1974).

31. A more complete discussion of the theology involved in this decision is found in C. Villa-Vicencio, "Violent Revolution and Military Disarma-

ment: The Ecumenical Debate" in Villa-Vicencio, *Theology and Violence.*

32. In a letter addressed to the Netherlands Reformed Church (2 November 1978).

33. *The Minutes of the Synod of the Diocese of Cape Town, 1979*, p. 69.

34. *Proceedings and Decisions of the Sixty-Ninth General Assembly of the Presbyterian Church of Southern Africa, 1970*, pp. 61–3.

35. *Year Book of the United Congregational Church of Southern Africa, 1972*, pp. 188–91, 204.

36. *The Minutes of the Ninety-Sixth Annual Conference of the Methodist Church of Southern Africa, 1978*, pp. 269–70. Also *The World Council of Churches and the Methodist Church of Southern Africa* (Cape Town: Methodist Publishing House, 1979).

37. De Gruchy, *The Church Struggle in South Africa*, pp. 133–34.

38. Kenneth Kaunda, *Kaunda On Violence* (London: Collins, 1980), p. 121. See also pp. 131–32 for Kaunda's response to the distinction between humanitarian and arms aid.

39. *Reports Presented to the Twenty-First Assembly of the United Congregational Church of Southern Africa, 1987*, pp. 143–146; *Proceedings of the Twenty-First Assembly of the United Congregational Church of Southern Africa, 1987*, p. 21.

40. *Divestment* is said to occur when a church, university or city authority, for example, sells shares in a foreign company because that company does business in South Africa. *Disinvestment* occurs when the foreign company closes or sells its South African operation and withdraws.

41. Mark Orkin, *Disinvestment: The Struggle and the Future* (Johannesburg: Ravan Press, 1986).

42. Letter to the Editor, *Sunday Times* (6 January 1985).

43. *United Church Observer*, Toronto (April 1987), p. 35.

44. *A Pastoral Letter from the Southern African Catholic Bishops' Conference on Economic Pressure for Justice*, 1 May 1986. Italics added.

45. Press release by Noel Bruyns, SACBC Information Officer, 12 February 1987.

46. Margaret Nash, ed., *Women—A Power for Change: SACC Conference Report* (Johannesburg: SACC, 1985), pp. 80–82.

47. *The Minutes of the Synod of the Diocese of Cape Town, 1986*, pp. 22–28.

48. *Papers of the General Assembly of the Presbyterian Church of Southern Africa, 1986*, pp. 96–100; *Proceedings and Decisions of the General Assembly of the Presbyterian Church of Southern Africa, 1986*, pp. 203–4.

49. *Proceedings of the Twentieth Assembly of the United Congregational Church of Southern Africa, 1986*, pp. 20–21.

50. *Minutes of the One Hundred and Fourth Annual Conference of the Methodist Church of Southern Africa, 1986,* pp. 326–27. Italics added.

51. Bishop, p. 5.

52. Peter Ainslie Memorial Lecture (Grahamstown: Rhodes University, 1968).

CHAPTER 5

1. Karl Marx and Friedrich Engels, *Collected Works* (London: V. Lawrence and Wishart, 1975), vol. 5, pp. 36–37.

2. Alistair Kee, *Constantine Versus Christ* (London: SCM Press, 1982), p. 154.

3. J. B. Metz, *Faith in History and Society: Towards a Practical Fundamental Theology* (London: Burns and Oates, 1980), pp. 88f.

4. See, for example, Jacques Ellul, *The Politics of God and the Politics of Man* (New York: Seabury, 1973); *Autopsy of Revolution* (New York: Knopf, 1971); *The False Presence of the Kingdom* (New York: Seabury, 1970); *Hope in the Time of Abandonment* (New York: Seabury, 1973).

5. For a discussion on the historical development of church-state relations see C. Villa-Vicencio, *Between Christ and Caesar*.

6. This process is analyzed in such publications as: W. A. de Klerk, *The Puritans in Africa*; T. Dunbar Moodie, *The Rise of Afrikanerdom* (Berkeley: California University Press, 1975); *Journal of Theology for Southern Africa: South African Civil Religion,* no.19 (June 1977).

7. A. N. Pelser, ed., *Verwoerd Speaks* (Johannesburg: Perskor, 1966), p. 21.

8. For an analysis of these Commissions, see C. Villa-Vicencio, in "Theology in the Service of the State: The Steyn and Eloff Commissions" in Villa-Vicencio and de Gruchy, *Resistance and Hope*, pp. 112–125.

CHAPTER 6

1. A. Luckhoff, *Cottesloe* (Cape Town: Tafelberg, 1978). See also de Gruchy and Villa-Vicencio, *Apartheid Is a Heresy.*

2. Compare *Human Relations and the South African Scene in the Light of Scripture* (Cape Town: Dutch Reformed Church Publishers, 1976), pp. 18 and 71, and the *Kerk en Samelewing* synod report (14–25 October 1986), pp. 8 and 53–54. For references to the original sources cited in the analysis that follows see C. Villa-Vicencio, "The NGK Statement: Church and Society. Racism Not Apartheid Is a Sin," in *PCR Information*, 1986/No.23. Also published in *The Reformed Journal*, 36/11, 1986. Translations from the Afrikaans text are mine.

3. Statement issued by black delegates to the Consultation on Racism, 14 February 1980, in *Ecunews*, 27 February 1980, no. 4, 1980, p. 11.

4. "A Theological Rationale and a Call for the End to Unjust Rule," a document published for the 16 June 1985 prayer services, is included in Villa-Vicencio, *Between Christ and Caesar*. See also Allan Boesak and C. Villa-Vicencio, eds., *When Prayer Makes News* (Philadelphia: Westminster Press, 1986).

5. See documentation included in the *Journal of Theology for Southern Africa*, vol. 52 (September 1985). Also published in Boesak and Villa-Vicencio, *When Prayer Makes News*.

6. Karl Barth, *Community, State and Church: Three Essays*, ed. Will Herberg (New York: Doubleday and Co., 1960), p.136.

7. Barth, p. 178.

8. See C. Villa-Vicencio, "Some Refused to Pray: The Moral Impasse of the English-Speaking Churches" in Boesak and Villa-Vicencio, *When Prayer Makes News*, pp. 43–59.

9. *Rapport*, 9 June 1985. See also, Boesak and Villa-Vicencio, *When Prayer Makes News*, pp. 51, 65.

10. *Minutes of the One Hundred and Third Annual Conference of the Methodist Church of Southern Africa, 1985*, p. 308.

11. Ibid. pp. 62–64.

12. See *Journal of Theology for Southern Africa* vol. 52 (September 1985); and Boesak and Villa-Vicencio, *When Prayer Makes News*, for responses by the churches to the *Call to Prayer*.

13. See the discussion on the media coverage of the *Call to Prayer* in Alan Brews, "When Journalists Do Theology" in Boesak and Villa-Vicencio, *When Prayer Makes News*, pp. 60–74.

14. Ludwig Feuerbach, *The Essence of Christianity* (New York and London: Harper and Brothers, 1957), pp. 122–23. Cited in J. W. de Gruchy, "Prayer, Politics and False Piety" in Boesak and Villa-Vicencio, *When Prayer Makes News*, p. 97.

15. Karl Marx and Friedrich Engels, *Collected Works*, pp. 36–37.

16. See also Villa-Vicencio, "Some Refused to Pray," pp. 44–5.

17. Second General Conference of the Latin American Bishops, *The Church in the Present-Day Transformation of Latin America in the Light of the Council*, Volume II, *Conclusions* (Washington: National Conference of Catholic Bishops, 1979), pp. 32, 55–56.

18. See "Southern Africa Today," *Journal of Theology for Southern Africa*, no. 45 (December 1983), p. 77.

19. De Gruchy, "Prayer, Politics and False Piety," p. 99.

20. For responses to the *Kairos Document* see publications by the Institute of Contextual Theology. Also editions of the *Journal of Theology*

for Southern Africa, following the September 1985 publication of the *Kairos Document.*

21. *Minutes of the One Hundred and Fourth Annual Conference of the Methodist Church of Southern Africa, 1986,* pp. 85–86. "A Response to the Kairos Document from the Methodist Church of Southern Africa" was submitted to the Methodist Conference by its Doctrine Committee and referred to the Methodist people "to assist the process of reflection."

22. A submission by the Doctrine Committee of the Methodist Church of Southern Africa to that church's 1987 Conference.

23. *Proceedings and Decisions of the General Assembly of the Presbyterian Church of Southern Africa, 1986,* p. 6.

24. *Proceedings of the Twentieth Assembly of the United Congregational Church of Southern Africa, 1986,* p. 42.

25. I am particularly indebted to my colleague, Itumeleng Mosala, for this word study.

26. Frank Chikane, "Where the Debate Ends," in Villa-Vicencio, *Theology and Violence.*

27. See *Daily Record* of the 1987 Conference of the Methodist Church of Southern Africa, p. 94. To be included as question 29.6.15 in *Minutes of the One Hundred and Fifth Annual Conference of the Methodist Church of Southern Africa, 1987.*

28. Submission of the Doctrine Committee of the Methodist Church of Southern Africa to that church's 1987 Conference.

CHAPTER 7

1. Karl Marx, *Early Works* (New York: Penguin Books, 1975), p. 423.

2. Karl Marx, "Towards a Critique of Hegel's Philosophy of Right" in *Karl Marx: Selected Works,* ed. David McLellan (Oxford: Oxford University Press, 1977), p. 63.

3. Karl Marx, "German Ideology" in *Selected Works,* p. 176.

4. José Miranda, *Marx Against the Marxists* (Maryknoll, New York: Orbis Books, 1980), p. 280.

5. Karl Marx, "Contribution to the Critique of Hegel's Philosophy of Right" in *Selected Works,* p. 63.

6. Ibid., p. 63. Quoted from text in *Marx and Engels on Religion,* ed. R. Niebuhr (New York: Schocken Books, 1964), p. 41.

7. Ibid., p. 64.

8. Karl Marx, *The First International and After: Political Writings 111* (New York: Vintage Books, 1974), p. 324. See also Miranda, pp. 277–78.

9. Karl Marx, "The Jewish Question" in *Selected Works,* p. 47. See also

Boris Nicolaievsky and Otto Maenchen-Helfen, *Karl Marx: Man and Fighter* (London: Penguin Books, 1976), p. 6.

10. Alistair Kee, *Domination or Liberation: The Place of Religion in Social Conflict* (London: SCM Press, 1986), p. 62.

11. A. Giddens, *Capitalism and Modern Social Theory: An Analysis of the Writings of Marx, Durkheim and Weber* (Cambridge: Cambridge University Press, 1971), p. 42.

12. Maduro, *Religion and Social Conflicts*, p. 27.

13. Kee, p. 64.

14. See C. Mouffe, *Gramsci and Marxist Theory* (London: Routledge and Kegan Paul, 1979), p. 226; Giddens, p. 43.

15. Nicholas Lash, *A Matter of Hope: A Theologian's Reflections on the Thought of Karl Marx* (Notre Dame: University of Notre Dame Press, 1981), p. 136.

16. Karl Barth, *Church Dogmatics* (Edinburgh: T. and T. Clark, 1957), p. 386.

17. For a discussion on conflict within the religious means of production see Maduro, pp. 89–91.

18. J. L. Segundo, "The Shift Within Latin American Theology," *Journal of Theology of Southern Africa*, no. 52 (September 1985).

19. Jon Sobrino, *The True Church and the Poor* (London: SCM, 1984), p. 121.

20. Sobrino, p. 95.

21. J. Míguez Bonino, *Toward a Christian Political Ethics* (Philadelphia: Fortress Press, 1983), p. 17.

22. Kee, p. 68.

23. Gregory Baum, *Religion and Alienation: A Theological Reading of Sociology* (New York: Paulist Press, 1975), p. 165.

24. Arthur Mitzman, *The Iron Cage: An Historical Interpretation of Max Weber* (New York: Knopf Books, 1970), p. 5; Julian Freund, *The Sociology of Max Weber* (London: Allen Lane), p. 26.

25. Mitzman, pp. 181–92.

26. Rubem Alves, *Tomorrow's Child* (London: SCM Press, 1972), p. 15.

27. Alves, pp. 25f, 66f.

28. See Neil Postman, "Amusing Ourselves to Death." Address to 36th Frankfurt Book Fair, October 3–8, 1984.

29. References to the prophet are found scattered in Weber's *Sociology of Religion* and elsewhere. See also Talcott Parson's "Introduction" in Max Weber, *The Sociology of Religion*.

30. Friedrich Nietzsche, *Thus Spake Zarathustra*, quoted in Alves, p. 109.

31. Martin Buber, *Paths in Utopia*, quoted by Alves, p. 111.

32. Baum, p. 85.

33. Baum, pp. 62–84.

CHAPTER 8

1. Gustavo Gutiérrez, "The Poor in the Church" in *Towards a Church of the Poor*, ed. Julio De Santa Ana (Maryknoll: Orbis Books, 1981), p. 122.

2. Sobrino, p. 95.

3. Jürgen Moltmann, *The Trinity and the Kingdom of God* (London: SCM, 1981), pp. 4, 16, 21f. Also pp. 61f.

4. Sobrino, p. 56.

5. See Cornelis Van Peursen, *Him Again!* (Richmond: John Knox Press, 1969).

6. Sobrino, p. 121; De Santa Ana, p. 164.

7. Gustavo Gutiérrez, *The Power of the Poor in History* (London: SCM, 1983), p. 211.

8. Dietrich Bonhoeffer, *The Cost of Discipleship* (London: SCM, 1962), p. 57.

9. Ibid., p. 54.

10. De Santa Ana, p. 126.

11. De Santa Ana, p. 164.

12. Míguez Bonino, p. 43.

13. De Santa Ana, p. 168.

14. I. Bria, ed., *Martyria/Mission* (Geneva: WCC, 1980), p. 9. See also Villa-Vicencio, *Between Christ and Caesar*, pp. 178–84.

15. Robert Bellah, "The Dynamics of Worship" in *Beyond Belief* (New York: Harper and Row, 1970), p. 210.

16. Wallace Stevens, *Opus Posthumous* (New York: Alfred A. Knopf, 1954), p. 238. Quoted in Bellah, "Transcendence in Contemporary Piety" in *Beyond Belief*, p. 197.

17. Gregory Baum, "Peter Berger's Unfinished Symphony" in *Sociology and Human Destiny*, ed. Gregory Baum (New York: Seabury Press, 1980), p. 119

18. Robertson Smith, *The Religion of the Semites* (Oxford: Oxford University Press, 1927), p. 83.

19. Quoted in Fleet, "Bellah's Sociology" *The Ecumenist*, Vol. 18, no. 2 (January/February, 1980).

20. José Míguez Bonino, *Doing Theology in a Revolutionary Situation* (Philadelphia: Fortress Press, 1975), p. 88.

21. Míguez Bonino, *Toward a Christian Political Ethics*, pp. 44–45.

22. Robert H. Smith, "Were the Early Christians Middle Class? A Sociological Analysis of the New Testament" in *The Bible and Liberation: Political and Social Hermeneutics*, ed. N. Gottwald (Maryknoll: Orbis Books, 1983), pp. 441–57.

23. Albert Nolan, "The Option for the Poor in South Africa" in Villa-Vicencio and de Gruchy, *Resistance and Hope*, p. 190.

24. Nolan, pp. 189–98.

25. Rafael Avila, *Worship and Politics* (Maryknoll: Orbis Books, 1981), p. 4.

26. Bonhoeffer, pp. 57, 54.

27. *The Kairos Document: Challenge to the Church*, 2nd ed. (Johannesburg: Skotaville, 1986), p. 1.

Index